Social Indicators Research Series

Volume 1

General Editor:

ALEX C. MICHALOS

University of Northern British Columbia,
Prince George, Canada

Editors:

ED DIENER

University of Illinois, Champaign, U.S.A.

WOLFGANG GLATZER

J.W. Goethe University, Frankfurt am Main, Germany

TORBJORN MOUM

University of Oslo, Norway

JOACHIM VOGEL

Central Bureau of Statistics, Stockholm, Sweden

RUUT VEENHOVEN

Erasmus University, Rotterdam, The Netherlands

QUALITY OF LIFE IN SOUTH AFRICA

Edited by

VALERIE MØLLER

University of Natal, South Africa

Reprinted from Social Indicators Research 41(1–3), 1997

KLUWER ACADEMIC PUBLISHERS
DORDRECHT / BOSTON / LONDON

Library of Congress Cataloging-in-Publication Data

ISBN 0-7923-4797-8

Published by Kluwer Academic Publishers,
P.O. Box 17, 3300 AA Dordrecht, The Netherlands.

Sold and distributed in the U.S.A. and Canada
by Kluwer Academic Publishers,
101 Philip Drive, Norwell, MA 02061, U.S.A.

In all other countries, sold and distributed
by Kluwer Academic Publishers,
P.O. Box 322, 3300 AH Dordrecht, The Netherlands.

Printed on acid-free paper

Printed in the Netherlands.

TABLE OF CONTENTS

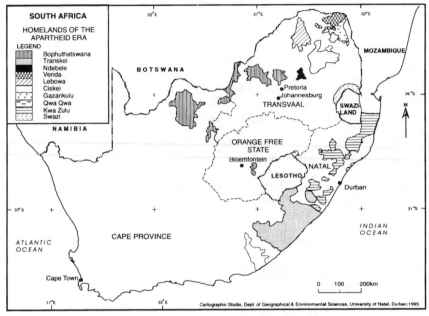

Map 1. South Africa under apartheid

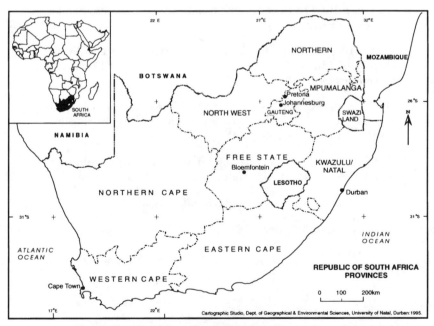

Map 2. South Africa after 1993: the nine new provinces

Editorial

VALERIE MØLLER

SOUTH AFRICA'S EMERGENT "SOCIAL INDICATORS MOVEMENT"

South Africa's transition to democracy in the 1990s has evoked a statistical awakening reminiscent of the "social indicators movement" of the 1970s. This special issue on South African quality of life seeks to capture this new fascination with social indicators and the manner in which social researchers, policy makers and the general public are approaching the task of social reporting in the post-apartheid era. As some contributors to this special issue on quality of life in South Africa note, an adjunct of apartheid has been the absence of comprehensive and credible social indicators to assist with policy formation. Fresh interest in capturing South African quality of life in statistics in the post-apartheid era has helped to fill the gap. Former mistrust of official statistics has been replaced with a – perhaps exaggerated – faith in the power of social indicators to guide and monitor the changes occurring in the new democracy.

The current value attached to social indicators as tools to chart progress in achieving the societal ideal envisaged by the new government may be short-lived. South Africa may have to learn painfully – as did the early pioneers of the social indicators movement in the developed nations (see Andrews et al., 1989: p. 404), that it takes time for social change to manifest itself in social accounts. It is possible that in the near future disillusionment may replace the current enthusiasm expressed by South Africans with their vital statistics. Meanwhile, it is a healthy sign that South Africans are learning to appreciate not only the power but also the pitfalls of placing too much faith in numbers. Serious efforts are underway to produce social indicators to promote an open society which takes stock of its development potential and shortcomings.

Social Indicators Research **41**: 1–14, 1997.
© 1997 *Kluwer Academic Publishers. Printed in the Netherlands.*

Some of the major concerns of the emergent South African social indicators movement are the *comprehensiveness, quality, and comparability* of data.

Under apartheid, official statistics were fragmented and excluded the nominally independent states created by the last government. Another anomaly was that many of the most widely used statistics in the public domain, such as poverty datum lines, were produced by independent research organisations in the private sector and at universities. Lacking was the official national social survey which is the "backbone" of the social indicators movement (Vogel, 1994). The task of conducting multipurpose national surveys to monitor changing social patterns was left mainly to the commercial sector. For example, the privately sponsored Institute of Race Relations undertook the formidable task each year of compiling an update of statistics on social change from a myriad of sources to build a comprehensive picture of society.

As a result of past omissions, South Africa's social statistics have tended to be piecemeal and lacked continuity which has rendered data comparison over time difficult. This situation may not necessarily improve in future due to zealous attempts to make continuous refinements to data collection methods. Adjustment of political boundaries, better records of events, and revised sampling procedures to reflect new political boundaries may make comparisons of current and older data collections tricky. If analysts are not prepared to make the appropriate adjustments, comparisons with the past may be abandoned altogether and 1994 might become the baseline for trend studies in future.

Social reports are descriptive documents which tend to avoid normative evaluations and conclusions. Nevertheless, despite efforts to maintain neutrality, social indicators and the reports on these indicators tend to be judgmental. The normative aspect, may be subtle or implicit, as in the selection and ordering of data, disaggregations, the organisation of materials and the blending of different types of data (Vogel, 1994: p. 246). South African quality of life researchers appear to be aware that social indicators cannot be entirely neutral. Indeed, South African compilers of social indicators seem to be intent on influencing policy through social indicators and tend not to shy away from making political statements in their reports. For example, the preoccupation with inequality and poverty in South African social reports has strong political overtones.

Social commentary is also implicit in the manner in which data is compiled and presented. The post-apartheid era has created its new fashions in data presentation. Unlike the fragmented black and white statistics of the apartheid era, the carefully designed samples of the transition era are capable of producing comprehensive statistics for the country as a whole and capturing South African quality of life in a single figure. At the same time the many dimensions of inequality still call for finer breakdowns of the data to show up regional and sectoral disparities. Breakdowns of statistics by gender and province have gained in popularity. Gender equality is a policy goal entrenched in the new constitution. Provincial breakdowns serve as planning tools for the nine new provinces which compete for their share of scarce national resources.

It will become obvious to the readers of this issue that social reporting for South Africa is still very much in its infancy; basic social indicators appear to be in a state of flux. This is evident where national and international indicators for South Africa do not tally; where contributors to this volume debate the accuracy of important social indicators such as unemployment; and where they cite different estimates of income inequality.[1] Nevertheless, in spite of the quirks in the evidence, the broad brush picture of South African quality of life painted in all the papers is not dissimilar.

MILESTONES

This report on quality of life in South Africa may be regarded as a milestone in the society's new social indicators movement. The idea for a special issue on the topic was born when the editor of *Social Indicators Research*, Professor Alex Michalos, visited South Africa in February 1996 and presented workshops on thirty years of social indicators research in different parts of the country. The workshops were attended by members of the small but growing group of South African researchers from many different disciplines who are engaged in what we have called the new South African social indicators movement. Responding to the enthusiasm of his audiences, Professor Michalos invited South Africans to assemble a collection of papers on South African quality of life in the post-apartheid era.

The authors whose contributions appear in this issue, represent a wide range of disciplines in the social sciences including economics, sociology, psychology, political science and development planning, as well as different ideological perspectives. In common they have a belief in the power of social indicators to tell a cogent story of South Africa and its future. This does not mean that their faith in the value of social indicators is blind. A common thread running through the contributions to this issue is a healthy distrust of uneven measurements and critical appraisal of data quality and comparability. This issue of *Social Indicators Research* devoted to South African quality of life may be seen as a serious attempt of South African researchers to take stock of the first products of the emergent social indicators movement.

To our knowledge this collection may be the first to present the work of individual South African social indicators researchers to an international audience.[2] In the early 1980s, Schlemmer and Møller, working out of the Centre for Social and Development Studies at the University of Natal, launched what was to become a longitudinal study of South African quality of life conceived in the tradition of Andrews and Withey's (1976) research on subjective well-being. To date, papers on results from the Quality of Life Research Project (Møller and Schlemmer, 1983, 1989; Møller, in press) have been the only reports on South African quality of life to appear in *Social Indicators Research*.

In turn, this report builds on important milestones in data collection for South Africa's new social indicator movement (Møller, 1995). The Project for Statistics on Living Standards and Development, variously referred to as the World Bank / Saldru study or simply the "poverty study" by colleagues writing in this issue, was launched with broad consultation and participation on the eve of the country's first open general elections in April 1994. This poverty project was influential in shaping the Central Statistical Service's revised October Household Survey, which aims to track future changes in social and living conditions (see CSS 1995, 1996).

A recurrent theme in this issue is the lack of reliable and up to date population figures. At the time of writing in early 1997 the country is awaiting the first results of its post-apartheid population census conducted in October 1996, which represents a further milestone in South Africa's social indicators movement. Census '96, which was launched as a nation building exercise, clearly reflects the fresh enthusiasm for social indicators for South Africa. In the run up to the 1994 universal franchise elections, South Africans had been promised "a better future." Census '96 promised to provide the necessary information to plan for this better future for all the people. In October 1996, an appeal went out to South Africans to "play your part in the miracle" of the "great counting of the people" just as they had participated in the earlier events which gave birth to democracy: the general elections of April 1994 and the local government elections of November 1995.

Several of the articles in this issue make reference to the election slogan of "a better life for all" and the new government's Reconstruction and Development Programme (RDP), aimed to improve the quality of life of all South Africans. The directive to line functions in government departments to collect "key performance indicators" to track progress with service delivery has spurred data collection activities at all levels of government. Appropriately, one contribution to this issue has the RDP as its special focus.

The entrepreneurial spirit gripping the country at the moment is also evident in the new social indicators movement. The authors of two papers in this issue present composite indices tailor-made for South African use. Klasen introduces an index designed to identify pockets of poverty and inequality in South Africa; Gill and Hall have constructed an index to guide decision-making in the allocation of development resources.

South Africans are gradually turning to subjective data and opinion polls to better understand the mood of the country and the direction in which it is heading. It is telling that the 1993 Saldru study and its sequel, the 1995 October Household Survey, referred to above, included a subjective measure of household satisfaction with living conditions. Given this editor's interest in subjective well-being, this special issue includes reports on both *objective and subjective* indicators of quality of life. In an interesting departure from conventional use of subjective well-being as an *outcome* measure of quality of life, two teams of researchers reporting in this issue use indicators of subjective well-being as *predictor* variables. Beukes and van der Colff assess community potential for development on the basis of their subjective measures and Mattes and Christie link subjective well-being to popular support for democracy.

OVERVIEW OF THIS ISUUE

The report is divided in five sections. The *first section* introduces readers to the challenges facing post-apartheid South Africa in terms of population characteristics and the backlog in development. The papers in this section present the first products of South Africa's emergent "social indicators movement." Inequality in the distribution of the country's wealth and opportunities is a dominant theme in the papers in this section and the ones to follow. The *second section* singles out two interrelated problems of the transition period which have their roots in the last days of the apartheid period: the two contributions discuss statistics on crime and violence and the incidence of post-traumatic stress disorders resulting from experience of violent events. A *third section* reports on social surveys as tools for monitoring progress in achieving goals of democracy and development in the transition period. The two papers in this section present results of opinion surveys. The first paper reports on perceived benefits of the country's ambitious Reconstruction and Development Programme; the second paper reviews perceptions of well-being and trust in the new government. The *fourth section* includes two case study applications of social indicators. The case study of Bloemfontein, a medium-sized city, explores the use of social indicators for assessing the empowerment of township residents. The case study of Gauteng reports on an index for prioritising development needs in a metropolitan area. Finally, the *fifth section* brings readers full circle and returns to the expectations that ordinary South Africans have for the future. Optimism and hope for the future is the topic discussed in the last paper of this issue.
A more detailed description of select contents of the papers follows.
    By way of background *Lawrence Schlemmer and Valerie Møller* give a brief introduction to South Africa's social history and the country's socio-economic makeup which is mirrored in its social accounts. Their overview includes international comparisons and

recent trend data for South Africa. The latter show a still very deeply divided society with large backlogs in development and evidence of deprivation and social fragmentation. Drawing mainly on survey evidence, the paper discusses the less tangible signs of tears in the social fabric and the expectations which South Africans hold for the future. Schlemmer and Møller conclude that a current reading of South Africa's social indicators should temper some of the optimism about the country's future. A major challenge ahead will be to avoid new forms of "apartheid" between the economically privileged and the marginal "have nots" on the periphery.

Stephan Klasen summarises the main findings on poverty and inequality which emerged from the Saldru survey conducted in late 1993 for the Project for Statistics on Living Standards and Development. This project produced the most widely used database on poverty in the 1990s.[3] Klasen discusses South African poverty from an international perspective and gives a profile of South Africa's poor. He also attempts a comparison of income- and non-income based measures to identify deprived categories. Using the international poverty measure of share of population having less than US $1 a day, South Africa's poverty rate stands at about 25% which is considerably higher than many comparable middle-income countries but is less than other sub-Saharan countries. The poverty report shows that income inequality is a major feature of South African quality of life. The poorest 40% of households, equivalent to 53% of the population, account for less than 10% of total consumption; the top 10% of households, with only 5.8% of the population, account for over 40% of consumption. Of significance for the theme of this special issue is that the poverty study confirms the link between subjective and economic well-being. Klasen reports that all poor are predominantly dissatisfied with their living conditions, while rich people are mainly satisfied. Klasen speculates that the dissatisfaction of the poor might be the result of poor living conditions or the low rank which the poor occupy in a highly unequal society.

Ros Hirschowitz and Mark Orkin pick up the theme of inequality in South Africa when discussing results of the 1994 October Household Survey, the latest available at the time of writing in October 1996. The survey aims to supply selected social indicators against which to measure change in growth over time as and when new government policies are implemented. Hirschowitz and Orkin argue that although South Africa is a middle-income country, it is not the underdevelopment of the country as a whole that characterises it, but rather the skewed and uneven distribution of access to resources that enables people to live productive lives. They conclude that inequality and the resultant relative deprivation are important factors to take into account in future planning for South Africa. From their viewpoint, tackling development means addressing past inequality. They recommend an integrated approach to development which sees poverty alleviation, employment creation, the supply of infrastructure and human resource development as part of the same process.

Julian May and Andy Norton report on findings emerging from the South African Participatory Poverty Assessment (SA-PPA), which was undertaken in 1995 and 1996 to provide a fuller understanding of poverty from the perspective of the poor themselves. Designed as a qualitative study to follow on the quantitative Saldru poverty study of 1993, the SA-PPA drew on 15 linked studies and 25 research sites countrywide. Local people in the communities under study were engaged as analysts with outsiders typically acting as facilitators for the research process. The article gives the definitions of poverty drawn up by the poor themselves and describes personal experiences of the poverty traps which prevent South Africans from escaping poverty. Wealth-ranking exercises in local communities classified 50% of the population as poor, a result which compares closely to the 53% poor identified in the Saldru study. The Saldru study found that poverty correlated with household dissatisfaction. Similarly, May and Norton report that happiness was employed as a yardstick for measuring poverty in the follow-up study. The poorest households in one community under study were described as "unhappy" while the households in the most secure income category were seen as "happiest" of all. In conclusion, May and Norton recommend that the unique insights into the personal experience of poverty should not be overlooked when formulating policy to assist the poor to improve their quality of life. Their analysis points to the concepts of sufficiency, access to goods and services, and vulnerability as particularly useful ones for analysing poverty. Vulnerability stresses that poverty is not only about being poor but is also about the risk of becoming poor or poorer if circumstances should change.

In their paper on the mental health of South Africans, *Hirschowitz and Orkin* describe some of the scars which years of political violence have left on ordinary South Africans. A nationwide survey on health status and health care found that approximately five million or 23% of the adult population had been exposed to violent events (i.e. as victims or perpetrators of violent attacks or as witness to one's home being torched). Just under 4 in 5, and more urban than rural persons who had experienced a violent event, showed symptoms of post-traumatic stress disorder (PTSD). The authors note that even though people may attempt to rebuild their lives, to cope at work and socially, the scars left by negative experiences through the development of PTSD are a reality. Hirschowitz and Orkin conclude that the undeclared war fought against the people of South Africa during the apartheid era has taken its toll. In their view, healing the nation will involve revealing the full extent of political violence committed during the apartheid era and setting in place the professional counselling services and community support structures to deal with the effects of violence.

Antoinette Louw examines crime trends during the transition period and public perceptions of crime. She reports that fear of crime is on the increase in the 1990s and overshadows other problems expressed by South Africans from all walks of life. A popular viewpoint is that the current "crime wave" is the recent product of policies or peculiarities of the new government. Louw observes that the apartheid order generated crime rather than controlling it. Although crime statistics are subject to changing police recording patterns, it is certain that levels of crime increased steadily during the 1980s with a dramatic rise in crime occurring in 1990. One of the most worrying features of the current crime scene in South Africa is the propensity for violence. The country's murder rate of 45 (international average is 5.5 per 100 000 population) makes it one of the most murderous countries in the world. However, the murder rate has declined in recent years. Louw discusses how the broader sociopolitical and economic changes in South Africa have impacted on the nature of crime since the onset of the political transition. She attributes the increase in murders in 1990 to rising political violence in the pre-election period and the drop in the murder rate in 1994 to the decline in political violence following the first open general elections. The prognosis for South Africa, Louw concludes, is that crime levels will get worse before there are signs of improvement. While development may reduce crime in the longer term, it currently creates more opportunities for crime and promotes the social inequalities which encourage crime.

Clive Corder outlines the spirit and objectives of South Africa's Reconstruction and Development Programme (RDP) and presents a range of measures of success including popular assessments of its benefits in the first eighteen months of its operation. Drawing on the results of three cross-sectional social surveys conducted between December 1994 and December 1995, Corder reports that overall awareness of the RDP increased since its launch in mid-1994. By the end of 1995 over four in five urban adults were aware of the RDP. Unusual were the relatively higher levels of awareness among black South Africans given their lower level of media consumption. The RDP was perceived to have had a beneficial effect in a number of areas including installation of electricity and access to water. One in five urban blacks stated they had already benefited from the RDP and just under one in two expected future benefits, mainly in the form of jobs and job training, housing and education. Following a discussion of the possible implications of failure of the RDP to deliver, Corder argues that the RDP could become the victim of its own success in communicating so effectively to a deprived populace promises of a better life to come. The RDP may have raised expectations which may be difficult to meet even in the longer term.

The case study of quality of life conducted by *Elwil Beukes and Anna van der Colff* in the black townships of Bloemfontein takes human development as the point of departure. Beukes and van der Colff use conventional measures of life quality, satisfaction with life as a whole and domain satisfactions, to assess the potential for human development. Their research also compared objective living conditions with subjective assessments. The tensions which exist between self-assessed adequacy of resources that people have at their disposal and the perceived usefulness of these resources for improving quality of life are considered to be "windows of opportunity" by Beukes and van der Colff. The majority of respondents felt that their lives had improved since the April 1994 elections and expected to be satisfied with life as a whole in five years time. This optimism is taken as an indicator of human development potential: willingness to tackle development challenges and to deal with issues in a resourceful and self-reliant manner. Moreover, township residents also appeared to be willing to make major inputs into the improvement of their life chances. The authors conclude that their study makes a case for using quality of life assessments to indicate positive and creative tensions between current and desired future conditions. The future task for policy makers will be to realise this expressed potential for self-reliance.

The paper by *Peter Gill and Peter Hall* gives insight into some of the practical and ethical dilemmas which South Africa's development planners currently face. The authors argue that social indicators can play a useful role in informing development decisions under conditions of transparency, scarce resources, and development gaps between areas "so large that it is difficult to know where to begin." To assist with the problem of identifying which areas need housing and services more urgently than others, Gill and Hall have developed an index in a computerised system called the Development Indicators Monitoring System (DIMS). The authors discuss the research philosophy underlying the development of the index and its construction and then demonstrate an application designed to assist planners in deciding how to allocate funds for the provision of housing and services in Gauteng province. The example shows that the choice of priority areas is sensitive to index construction and will depend, for example, on the planners' definition of acceptable standards of service delivery and whether absolute or relative needs are considered more important. The authors conclude that development prioritisation will always remain an essentially political decision-making process which calls for the appropriate use of the available tools such as the one developed by Gill and Hall.

Robert Mattes and Jennifer Christie argue that citizens' perceptions of well-being matter politically. In their paper they present data from two nationwide surveys of attitudes and values to explore the political consequences of perceived quality of life. Noting that the material improvements to quality of life and redressing inequality have become the centrepiece of the new government's political agenda, Mattes and Christie consider the intriguing possibility that citizens' evaluations of quality of life could play an important role in shaping evaluations of government and democracy. They ask whether people link their own immediate circumstances (referred to as *personal* and household quality of life) to these evaluations or whether people focus on broader social conditions (*collective* quality of life). Their survey results indicate that *collective* but not *personal* quality of life is strongly related to support for government leaders and the democratic system. Mattes and Christie conclude that South Africans have not as yet learned to distinguish between the incumbents of government and the system of democratic government. Voters appear to be holding both government and the democratic system accountable to collective developments. At a time when trust in government and satisfaction with democracy are low, this presents a challenge to the development of a democratic political culture in South Africa.

In the mid-1970s, a private social research company, Markinor, had the foresight to track socio-political indicators in anticipation of the dramatic changes which were to take place over the next twenty years. This wealth of trend data, which is more strictly comparable over time than other indicators reviewed in the special issue, adds depth to South Africa's emergent social indicator movement.

In her paper on monitoring optimism in South Africa, *Mari Harris* of Markinor traces the changing mood of the country drawing on data from repeat surveys conducted by her research company over the past three decades. The Markinor data documents the mindset of South Africans and shows that South Africans have adjusted their perspectives in line with the changes which have swept the country. The article discusses indicators of optimism, happiness, personal economic well-being, social harmony and trust – all essential elements in an emerging democracy according to Harris. Results show that the mood was more buoyant and confident after the April 1994 elections than two years later, but blacks have remained more optimistic than whites over the period. In her conclusions, Harris stresses the important contribution which opinion polls can make to nation building by communicating the needs and aspirations of different segments of society.

THE FUTURE OF SOCIAL INDICATORS FOR SOUTH AFRICA

A concluding comment may be apposite. The papers in this issue cannot claim to be exhaustive of all the dimensions of the social condition, but they do give a fairly comprehensive picture of South African quality of life trends in the mid-1990s. The story told by the social indicators reviewed here is clear. An enormous task lies ahead if South Africa is to transform itself into the ideal society. It will not be easy to bring the good life to all citizens as envisaged by the government in waiting on the eve of the April 1994 elections. As Schlemmer and Møller point out in their introduction, South Africa's negotiated settlement and its transition to democracy had a fairy-tale quality. Dismantling apartheid might have been the easiest part; sustaining a fragile democracy and achieving a better life for all may be more difficult. Most of the contributors to this issue would agree that it is too early to predict the future; the evidence presented so far only gives scattered clues to the outcome. South Africa's social indicator movement must sustain its momentum to write the sequel to this issue which tells the unfolding tale of South African quality of life in the next millennium.

ACKNOWLEDGEMENTS

The workshops on social indicators held in Durban, Cape Town, and Pretoria in 1996 which brought South African researchers together to discuss the idea of a report on quality of life and the coordination of the project were made possible by a generous research grant from the Human Sciences Research Council to the Quality of Life Research Unit, University of Natal, Durban. The support of the Human Sciences Research Council is gratefully acknowledged.

NOTES

[1] The Gini coefficient is currently widely cited as an indicator of the vast wealth differentials in South African society. A number of contributors to this issue refer to a value of the Gini coefficient which indicates that it is the most unequal society in its income category. However, more recent updates and wider comparisons place South Africa in a slightly less extreme position.

[2] In 1995, South Africa prepared an official report, the "National Social Development Report" for presentation at the World Summit on Social Development

held in Copenhagen, Denmark and sent an official delegation to Beijing, China, to present a country report on the status of women to the United Nations Fourth World Conference on Women.
[3] The study was conducted by the World Bank and the Southern Africa Labour and Development Research Unit (Saldru) in the Department of Economics at the University of Cape Town (see Saldru, 1994; Ministry in the Office of the President, 1995).

REFERENCES

Andrews, F. M., M. Bulmer, A. L. Ferris, J. Gershuny, W. Glatzer, H.-H. Noll, J. E. Innes, D. F. Johnston, D. Macrae Jr, J. Vogel, and M. Ward: 1989, 'Whatever happened to social indicators? A symposium', Journal of Public Policy 9(4), pp. 399–450.

Andrews, F. M. and S. B. Withey: 1976, Social Indicators of Well-Being (Plenum Press, New York).

Central Statistical Service (CSS): 1995, October Household Survey 1994. Statistical Release P0317. Pretoria, South Africa.

Central Statistical Service (CSS): 1996, October Household Survey 1995. Statistical Release P0317. Pretoria, South Africa.

Ministry in the Office of the President: Reconstruction and Development Programme: 1995, Key Indicators of Poverty (South African Communication Services, Pretoria).

Møller, V.: 1995, 'Indicators for Africa: The October Household Survey', Indicator South Africa 12(3), pp. 86–90.

Møller, V.: 1997, 'South African quality of life: post-apartheid trends', Social Indicators Research (in press).

Møller, V. and L. Schlemmer: 1983, 'Quality of life in South Africa: Towards an instrument for the assessment of quality of life and basic needs', Social Indicators Research 12, pp. 225–279.

Møller, V. and L. Schlemmer: 1989, 'South African quality of life: A research note', Social Indicators Research 21, pp. 279–291.

South Africa Labour and Development Research Unit (Saldru): 1994, South Africans rich and poor: Baseline household statistics. School of Economics, University of Cape Town, Rondebosch, South Africa.

Vogel, J.: 1994, 'Social indicators and social reporting', Statistical Journal of the United Nations 11, pp. 241–260.

Quality of Life Research Unit
Centre for Social and Development Studies
University of Natal
Durban 4041
South Africa
E-mail: moller@mtb.und.ac.za

LAWRENCE SCHLEMMER and VALERIE MØLLER

THE SHAPE OF SOUTH AFRICAN SOCIETY AND ITS CHALLENGES

ABSTRACT. South Africa's negotiated settlement and its transition to democracy reads like a modern fairy tale. A brief review of South Africa's social indicators serves to temper some of optimism about the country's future. The indicators reflect the society's quality of life which has been shaped by its turbulent history. Political "caste formation", changing political alliances, the reforms intended to forestall the demise of apartheid, and the race for global competitiveness have left indelible marks on the society's social indicators. A comparison of living conditions in South Africa with those of roughly comparable economies indicates that the country lags behind in securing overall and widespread socio-economic upgrading of the population at large. A review of a cross-section of South African indicators and their trends over time shows that South Africa is still a very deeply divided society with a very large backlog in socio-economic development. There is evidence of breakdown in the society's social cohesion. Popular expectations of future quality of life indicate that the euphoria following on the first democratic elections has been replaced by a sense of realism among all sectors of the population. It is concluded that quality of life as reflected in South Africa's social indicators may get worse before it improves. The challenge will be to avoid new forms of economic "apartheid" which would depress the quality of life of marginal sectors of the population at the expense of the economically privileged.

KEY WORDS: South Africa, social indicators, social history, quality of life

1. BACKGROUND TO SOUTH AFRICA'S SOCIAL INDICATORS: DIVISION, CONFLICT, CONVERGENCE AND THE SEARCH FOR NATIONHOOD

Social indicators analyses in the South African context face the interesting challenge of having to encompass one of the more complex societies in the world. As most readers know, the society is divided by very considerable socio-economic inequality, by ethnicity, race and by a distinction between a well-established industrialised and commercialised economy on the one hand and a marginal economy based on subsistence production in traditional rural areas on the other. South Africa is also a relatively large country with quite considerable geographic and climatic variation.

Social Indicators Research **41**: 15–50, 1997.

As with any other society, the social and economic features of modern South Africa are the product of its history, which in South Africa's case has been remarkably turbulent. In fact, South Africa has only been a unified country for a very brief period. Until 1910 it was a region which comprised British colonies and independent Boer republics, both established after decades of war against Bantu-speaking tribes. In the 19th century, South Africa was a multinational region, with a number of traditional "monarchies" tucked in amongst more modern and dominant Afrikaans and British administrations.

The unification of South Africa came as the result of British imperial diamond and gold mining interests precipitating the Anglo-Boer war. This war, the most expensive armed conflict which had been fought in world history up to that time, produced a new consolidated state, the Union of South Africa, and with it a brief forty years of uneasy reconciliation between the interests of British colonialism, cosmopolitan capitalism and Afrikaans settler-colonial nationalism. In this period the various African national units, some of whom had attempted to resist European domination before and during the process of unification, were treated as little more than part of the environment – social appendages and a source of cheap labour. This phase ended with the ascendancy of Afrikaans nationalism in the late nineteen forties and the emergence of apartheid which was to lead to the "re-fragmentation" of the country into the white-controlled core society and independent or semi-autonomous reserves or "Bantustans" in the less-developed areas of subsistence economy. Soon afterwards, in the early to mid fifties, a consolidated resistance to white domination on the part of the African and other "non-white" groups began to gather momentum, leading to, inter alia, the "Defiance Campaign" of the mid to late fifties and the well-known Sharpville massacre of protesters by the white government in the early sixties. After the banning of the resistance movements a period of struggle in exile followed, echoed by the youth-based protest of the Soweto uprising in South Africa itself in the late seventies. It was only in the early eighties, however that internal adult-based resistance, in co-ordination with the exile movements, reached a pitch of intensity necessitating the declaration of successive "states of emergency" by the government and a response by the black communities in the form of the "ungovernability campaign" – local boycotts of municipal administrations and the disruption of schools and other institutions. Local black leadership was never fully united, however, and a split between the majority based "Charterists" (the African National Congress in alliance with the South African Communist Party and other Marxist-inclined formations), the smaller breakaway Pan Africanist Congress with a more "Africanist" emphasis, a "Black Consciousness movement" and the predominantly Zulu-based Inkatha movement which has followed what the African National Congress regarded as a more collaborationist strategy of institutional opposition.

The phase of Balkanisation or "separate development" and resistance to it has only recently ended, with the negotiated settlement between the white-dominated government and the major liberation movement, the African National Congress in alliance with organised labour and other progressive formations. The independent ministates have been reincorporated and a new, consolidated democracy established. Hence South Africa in a full civic and constitutional sense has only been an undivided country since the first open general election of April, 1994.

Throughout this history, however, and indeed as one of its major moving forces, a modern and over-arching economy was developing, based initially on colonial trade in commodities and then on mining and commercial agricultural capital. This economy, while centred on the Witwatersrand (today Gauteng province) and few other core areas and harbours in the so-called "common" area of South Africa, drew its inputs but particularly its labour from the entire region. Labour was obviously highly fragmented, largely unskilled, and had weak bargaining power in the economy, and a segregated and stratified labour market emerged, initially with British and immigrant Europeans at the apex and the centre of control. As Afrikaans nationalism mobilised and organised its labour and political power, white Afrikaners moved up the economic hierarchy, assisted by mergers between Afrikaans and the English-cosmopolitan capital in the mining and financial fields. At the same time white Afrikaners consolidated their position in the civil service after the election victory of the National Party in 1948. By the end of the seventies, white Afrikaners, a community which had been burdened with a "poor white" problem in the earlier years of the century, had drawn virtually level with the white Anglo-Saxon and immigrant middle class.

The convergence of socio-economic conditions among whites was accompanied by deepening poverty in the African subsistence areas, as populations and density on the land increased. At the height of apartheid, conditions in these subsistence areas were further undermined by relocations of African communities from the common area of the society into the so-called African homelands. Labour was drawn from these areas through migrant contract work in terms of which African workers could work on annual contracts in the common areas of the economy but could not bring their families with them.

By the seventies, an elaborate socio-economic gradation and differentiation had emerged in South African society. Whites were dominant in the executive and administrative classes, with very little *formal* differentiation between Afrikaans and English-speakers, although the former tended to dominate in the civil service and the latter in the private sector. Between the whites and the Africans, the Asian and coloured (people of mixed blood) minorities had a broadly intermediate status. They were formally segregated in terms of housing and, with the exception of a small, mainly Muslim Indian business class, occupied blue-collar positions in the integrated economy. Later in 1983 the intermediate status of these minorities was to be formalised by the establishment of separate chambers of parliament affording them some representation in the central government subject to the over-riding authority of the white parliament.

Below the coloured and Asian minorities was a category of Africans which had retained tenuous but highly valued formal rights to permanent residence and work in the "common areas", but which was residentially confined to scheduled African "township" areas, and which was subject to limitations on occupational mobility in terms of so-called "job reservation" regulations, insisted on by the white trade unions. This category was large, exceeding the white, coloured and Asian populations of the common area in sheer numbers, but generally its socio-economic conditions were beneath those of the "intermediate" minorities. They were predominantly the unskilled labouring classes (perhaps caste would be the more appropriate description) of the common society and economy since, for decades they were prohibited from obtaining the skilled artisan qualifications or experience which whites, coloureds and Asians could acquire.

Then outside this sphere of association with the core South African political economy were the temporary contract African workers, living in the main in single-quarter hostels, who were expected to identify with the appendage states in the subsistence areas, the homelands or the Bantustans, as they were sometimes called. The supply of labour from these subsistence areas was further facilitated by the establishment, with state assistance, of industries on the borders of the African subsistence areas. Within these states, however, a small elite emerged, formed around positions in the separate civil services and around local African businesses. Membership of these elites conferred relatively great material advantages compared with the surrounding grinding poverty in the over-crowded subsistence economies, and hence these elites generally supported the overall system of separate development. They had a relationship to the economic "centres" in the white economy roughly analogous to that of the so-called "comprador bourgeois" classes in Latin America to the centres of imperial capitalism.

This pattern is the underlying "template" of South Africa's current "social economy" and its patterns of indicators, but, since the mid eighties, it has been substantially modified by powerful forces. African labour became increasingly mobilised by an emerging labour movement broadly aligned to the liberation movements in exile. Under the United Democratic Front, also aligned with the liberation movement in exile, as already indicated, strongly mobilised protest movements challenged the administration and control of the segregated "non-white" areas. In response to these challenges, the government embarked on programmes of reform which, while intended to weaken the political justifications for resistance and protest, slowly began expanding the socio-economic opportunities for the subjugated categories of the population. Some of the major gaps in formal entitlements began to be narrowed. Needless to say, the reform strategies were very definitely too little too late to neutralise the forces which were to bring a re-integration of territory and inclusive politics in the early nineties. This liberation struggle, spearheaded by the ANC alliance, was supported by international economic sanctions and constraints on the inflow of foreign capital, and had the consequence of forcing the government to adopt a strategy of "inward industrialisation", protected by exchange controls, which meant that the South African economy lost several years of exposure to the competitive requirements of the increasingly globalised world economy.

Thus today, the *social indicators* of the society reflect its history of social and political "caste-formation", the changing alliances of politically privileged groups and the reforms which were intended to forestall the challenges to white hegemony, as well as an economy which is a late-starter in the race for global competitiveness. It is too soon for the indicators to adequately reflect the socio-economic shifts which have just recently occurred since democratisation, although some of them are signalled by certain trends.

The articles which follow in this issue will explore various patterns in detail but it is necessary in this introduction to present a cross section of indicators and their trends over time in order to depict the outlines of the social "anatomy" of the society. While the relative importance of a variety of indicators can be debated at length, we will assume that income, expenditure, other living standard measures, occupation (and unemployment), educational levels, family composition, life expectancy, housing patterns, dependence on welfare, access to amenities and services, indexes of poverty, the United Nation's Human Development Index (HDI), and crime and violence should provide a sufficiently comprehensive picture of the objective dimensions of the social economy.

These objective conditions, however, acquire their full significance as they compare with conditions in other roughly comparable economies, and also as they compare with the expectation of the population. Some attention to these relativities is necessary in forming an adequate assessment of the South African social condition.

2. SOUTH AFRICA IN COMPARATIVE PERSPECTIVE

In Schedule I we present in tabular form the available international comparisons between South Africa and averages, with selected country examples, of three sets of countries: the "upper-middle-income"

SCHEDULE I
Development indicators for select upper middle-income and sub-Saharan African economies

Type of economy Country	GNP p c rank (top rank = 133) 1996[1]	GNP p c US $ 1994[1]	GNP p c Avg. amn. growth (%) 1985–94	Gini,[1a] index	Income share,[1a] Lowest 20%	Income share,[1c] Highest 20%	HDI 1992[2]	Real GDP p c minus HDI rank 1992[2]
Upper-middle income		4 640	1.4					
Greece	106	7 700	1.3	–	–	–	0.907	21
Mexico	101	4 180	0.9	50.3	4.1	39.2	0.842	–6
Hungary	99	3 840	–1.2	27.0	4.0	22.6	0.856	0
Malaysia	96	3 480	5.6	48.4	4.6	37.9	0.872	8
Czech Republic	95	3 200	–2.1	26.6	10.5	23.5	0.822	–14
Mauritius	94	3 150	5.8	–	–	–	0.821	–28
South Africa	93	3 040	–1.3	58.4	3.3	47.3	0.705	–15
Brazil	92	2 970	–0.4	63.4	2.1	51.3	0.804	1
Lower-middle income		1 590	–1.2					
Botswana	88	2 800	6.6	–	–	–	0.763	–7
Namibia	75	1 970	3.3	–	–	–	0.611	–31
Low-income		360	–1.1					
Lesotho	49	720	0.6	56.0	2.8	43.4	0.473	17
Zimbabwe	37	500	–0.5	56.8	4.0	46.9	0.539	0
Zambia	28	350	–1.4	46.2	3.9	31.3	0.425	6
Kenya	17	250	0.0	57.5	3.4	47.7	0.481	7
Mocambique	2	90	3.8	–	–	–	–	–

SCHEDULE I
Continued

Type of economy / Country	Life expectancy at birth (years) 1994[1]	Infant mortality rate (per 1 000 live births)		Avg. annual population growth rate %		One year olds fully immunised against TB % 1990–93[2]	AIDS cases (per 100 000 people) 1993[2]
		1980	1994[1]	1980–90	1990–94[1]		
Upper-middle income	69	54	36	1.9	1.7		
Greece	78	18	8	0.5	0.6	–	1.7
Mexico	71	53	35	2.0	2.0	97	5.4
Hungary	70	23	12	-0.3	-0.3	–	0.3
Malaysia	71	30	12	2.6	2.4	99	0.1
Czech Republic	73	16	8	0.1	-0.1	–	0.2
Mauritius	70	32	17	0.9	1.3	87	0.3
South Africa	64	67	50	2.4	2.2	66	4.2
Brazil	67	74	56	2.0	1.7	98	7.3
Lower-middle income	67	66	36	1.7	1.4		
Botswana	68	63	34	3.5	3.1	50	68.5
Namibia	59	90	57	2.7	2.8	92	71.8
Low-income	56	118	86	2.7	2.5		
Lesotho	61	84	44	2.8	2.3	98	15.4
Zimbabwe	58	82	54	3.3	2.5	79	86.0
Zambia	47	90	108	3.5	3.0	88	239.3
Kenya	59	72	59	3.4	2.7	95	10.3
Mocambique	46	157	146	1.6	2.2	66	1.0

SCHEDULE I
Continued

Type of economy Country	Urban population (% of total population) 1980	Urban population (% of total population) 1994[1]	Television (per 100 000 people) 1992[2]	Percentage of total population with access to: Safe water 1993	Percentage of total population with access to: Sanitation 1993[1,b]
Upper-middle income					
Greece	58	65	20	100	–
Mexico	66	75	15	78	66
Hungary	57	64	41	100	–
Malaysia	42	53	15	78	94
Czech Republic	64	65	–	–	–
Mauritius	42	41	22	100	100
South Africa	48	50	*10*	100	*91*
Brazil	66	77	21	96	73
Lower-middle income					
Botswana	15	30	2	90	88
Namibia	23	36	2	–	36
Low-income					
Lesotho	13	22	1	46	–
Zimbabwe	22	31	3	84	58
Zambia	40	43	3	59	55
Kenya	16	27	1	–	49
Mocambique	13	33	0	22	21

Sources and Notes:
[1] World Development Report 1996, (World Bank, 1996).
[2] Human Development Report 1996, (UNDP, 1996).
[a] Figures are the latest available (1986/87–1993) on income or consumption drawn from nationally representative household surveys; the South African figures are based on 1993 per capita expenditure data.
[b] World Development Report 1996; Figures for South Africa, Botswana and Zimbabwe (safe water) supplied by the Development Bank of Southern Africa. Sanitation includes pit latrines.

economies, the "lower-middle-income" economies and the "low-income-economies" which are heavily concentrated in Africa. Informed readers will not require to be warned that these international statistics are not always of the highest quality. There are countries whose only hope of claiming some success in governance lies in the "cooking" of the figures which they furnish to international agencies, but the figures given are the only indicators available and they are undoubtedly better than nothing at all in making international comparisons. Needless to say the South African statistics are not above reproach either, as will be seen in due course, but once again have some utility.

What do the international comparisons tell us of the kind of society which South Africa is? In broad average terms it is securely placed in the upper-middle-income developing economies, although it is rather well below the average in this sector in GNP per capita terms. In recent years it has not improved its performance to keep pace with other countries in this sector although its economic performance subsequent to the figures presented, with a GNP growth rate of over 3% in 1995 and a predicted 2% or more for 1996, suggests that it is secure in this category.

This upper-middle-income status puts South Africa well ahead of the rest of sub-Saharan Africa, with only the atypical island economy of Mauritius and, at a somewhat lower level, the rather artificial mining-based economy of Botswana in South Africa's broad company. The high growth rates of these two economies in recent times, however, means that a premier economic position in sub-Saharan Africa for South Africa is by no means secure. The sheer relative size of South Africa's economy, however, gives it an importance beyond its per capita indices, South Africa's GNP is some 38% of that of the whole of sub-Saharan Africa, and it has approximately 38% of the motor vehicles in the whole of Africa and one third of the continent's paved roads. It also has the continent's largest harbours and a massive advantage over the entire continent in terms of "R & D" and technical capacity.

There are anomalies in South Africa's indices of development, and these mainly concern the relative level of human development and welfare. South Africa's Human Development Index (HDI) in 1992 was well below what its per capita GNP might have predicted, and below that of Botswana which is classified in the lower income category. Life expectancy at birth in 1994 was some five years below that of the average in the upper-middle-income countries and in fact below that of the lower-middle-income countries (64 versus 67 years). This low life expectancy is due largely to a relatively high infant mortality rate, in terms of which South Africa, with Brazil, is way behind the averages of both the upper-middle and the lower-middle-income countries. South Africa's population growth rate, although falling, is more typical of the lower-income countries than of the upper-middle-income category within which South Africa is classified.

These very telling anomalies would suggest the effects of a relatively high degree of extreme poverty in South Africa. This is not necessarily the case. In South Africa the income share of the poorest 20% of the population is not substantially lower than that of most upper-middle-income economies and it is also rather typical of that of most African countries given as examples. South Africa's "Gini" coefficient of inequality, although high and only slightly lower than that of notoriously unequal Brazil, is roughly similar to that of most other African countries and tends to be at almost the same level as many Latin American economies. In terms of the income share of the richest 10% of the population, South Africa (and Brazil) are much more unequal than the other countries in the upper-middle-income group but rather similar to those of poorer African countries.

Broadly speaking, then, South Africa lags behind its overall economic indices in terms of human development, and while this is no doubt partly due to the fact that the lower income levels of its population live in conditions which approximate to those of poorer African countries rather than to those of countries at its level of economic development, there may be additional explanations as well.

The most obvious explanation is that it reflects the consequences of apartheid, which undoubtedly aggravated the income inequality in the country, and also through social and geopolitical segregation prevented a spread and distribution of development within the population at large. However, there are specific factors which contribute to the problem which one cannot directly attribute to apartheid. The extent of the spread of literacy appears to be an important factor.

In 1990, for example, among South Africa and its closest neighbours: 22 countries in sub-equatorial Africa, the following comparisons were of interest (more recent figures for all the countries were not readily available).

South Africa in relation to the average for 22 sub-equatorial countries in Africa

	South Africa	22 Country Average
GNP per capita (US $)	2670	710
Years of schooling	3,9	2,3
Life expectancy at birth (years)	61,7	55,8
Infant mortality rate per 1000	67	94
Adult literacy (%)	70	64

Source: Africa Institute, Pretoria.

These figures suggest that South Africa is much closer to sub-equatorial Africa in terms of the last three indicators than it is in terms of income and years of schooling. There is clearly a substratum of the South African population which is deeply "third world." It might have persisted even if apartheid had not existed (as seems to be the case in some South American countries) but we would not deny that public policy in general had a great deal to do with the persistence of under-development of a part of the South African population.

Maternal literacy is commonly considered to be a critical variable in the health and welfare of children, and it seems to be clear that in this respect South Africa lags well behind its relative status in terms of GNP per capita. The figures above suggest that advances in modern education, while lifting the average level well above that of sub-equatorial Africa, was not eliminating the under-developed population sector as rapidly as many might have imagined – indeed, because of high early school drop-out rates, it might be associated with increasing social inequality in the society.

3. RECENT TRENDS IN SOCIO-ECONOMIC INDICATORS

In Schedule II some recent trend data are presented which generally reflect substantial progress in South African health and socio-economic indicators. Along with fairly rapid urbanisation (the

SCHEDULE II
Socio-economic indicators: South Africa

	Year	Black	Coloured	Indian	White	Total
Population and Health						
• Population in thousands	1987[2]	26 314	3 069	913	4 911	35 207
	1994[6]	30 944	3 473	1 039	5 192	40 648
	1995[8]	31 676	3 602	1 051	5 215	41 544
• Population living in urban areas (%)	1987[2,a,b]	40%	70%	93%	90%	
	1992[4]	59%	85%	96%	92%	
• Average annual population growth (%)	1980–85[5]	3.08	1.93	1.84	1.41	2.70
	1990–95[5]	2.68	1.91	1.39	.45	2.31
• Human Development Index (HDI)	1980[5]	0.394	0.532	0.655	0.739	0.557
	1991[5]	0.500	0.663	0.836	0.901	0.677
• Life expectancy at birth (years)	1983[1]	58	59	65	70	–
	1992[4]	63	63	67	73	64
• Infant mortality (per thousand)	1985[5]	64	42	15	9	54
	1994[5]	54	36	10	7	43
• Maternal mortality (per thousand)	1993[7]	2.6	0.4	0.2	0.1	
• AIDS (share of cases)	1994[6]	90%	4%	0%	6%	
• Use of modern contraception	1984[7]	44%	66%	69%	80%	
	1994[7]	66%	74%	77%	80%	

SCHEDULE II
Continued

	Year	Black	Coloured	Indian	White	Total
Education						
• Per capita expenditure (1994 Rands)	1985[3]	1 238[c]	2 854	4 435	8 787	
	1994[5]	1 524[a]	3 601	4 423	4 772	
		2 110[c]				
• Pupil teacher ratio	1987[2]	41[c] : 1	25 : 1	21 : 1	16 : 1	32 : 1
	1994[5]	40[a] : 1	23 : 1	22 : 1	20 : 1	
		37[c] : 1				
• No education (all ages) (%)	1980[5]	47%	30%	25%	14%	39%
	1991[5]	34%	24%	18%	11%	30%
• No education (20 years and older) (%)	1995[8]	17%	9%	5%	0.2%	13%
• Standard 10 results (% passed)	1986[2]	50%	64%	87%	92%	
	1993[7]	39%	86%	93%	95%	
	1994[6]	49%	87%	93%	97%	
• Standard 10 results (% matric exemptions)	1986[2]	13%	13%	33%	45%	
	1994[6]	13%	22%	51%	42%	
Employment						
• Unemployed[d]	1980[14]	11%	4%	4%	2%	8%
	1994[6,14]	41%	23%	17%	6%	33%
• Management composition	1992[6]	2.3%	2.5%	1.6%	93.4%	
	1994[6]	3.8%	3.0%	2.2%	90.9%	

SCHEDULE II
Continued

	Year	Black	Coloured	Indian	White	Total
Income						
• Average monthly earnings in 1995 Rand	1985[2]	1 459	2 638	1 903	5 279	
	1995[9]	1 608	1 809	3 865	6 228	
Employees	1995[9]	1 597	1 562	2 949	4 921	
Self-employed	1995[9]	1 661	3 862	9 288	13 094	
• Ratio: monthly earnings 1995/1985	1995/85	1.1:1	0.7:1	2.0:1	1.8:1	
• Average annual p c income in 1990 Rand	1980[10]	1 742	4 295	5 742	22 552	
	1987[2]	1 246	3 000	4 560	14 880	3 433
• Average annual p c income in 1990 Rand	1991[10]	1 710	3 885	6 945	21 121	
	1993[6]	2 717	6 278	12 963	32 076	7 062
• Income share	1980[10]	25%	7%	3%	65%	
	1987[3]	27%	8%	4%	62%	
	1993[6]	29%	5%	7%	59%	
• P c income as % of white income	1994[6]	13%	27%	40%	100%	
• Change in p c income 1980–91	1980–91[10]	–0.2%	–0.9%	1.7%	–0.6%	
• Change in income share 1975–1991 of						
poorest 40%	1975–91[10]	–48.0%	–18.7%	–20.4%	–30.5%	–25.0%
richest 40%	1975–91[10]	43.4%	1.4%	2.4%	24.7%	4.1%

SCHEDULE II
Continued

	Year	Black	Coloured	Indian	White	Total
Income (continued)						
• Change in mean income 1975–1991 of						
poorest 40%	1975–91[10]	-41.5%	-4.0%	2.4%	-39.8%	
richest 20%	1975–91[10]	38.2%	19.9%	30.7%	0.0%	
Poverty						
• Poor people[e] (%)	1993[6]	57%	20%	7%	2%	46%
• Poor children[e] (%)	1993[6]	64%	23%	10%	2%	54%
• Prevalence female-headed households[f] (%)	1994[7]	30%	22%	13%	15%	26%
• Malnutrition in children (%)	1993[7]	28.3%	19.1%	6.1%	4.9%	25.4%
Household income distribution						
• Percentage of households/						
Population group in income range (%)						
Annual household income (Rand):	1993[12]					
0–7 000		95%/43%	3%/14%	0%/ 6%	2%/ 4%	–/33%
7 000–20 000		86%/41%	8%/38%	2%/22%	4%/ 9%	–/35%
20 000–70 000		45%/15%	14%/46%	6%/54%	35%/49%	–/23%
Over 70 000		6%/ 1%	3%/ 3%	6%/18%	85%/39%	–/ 8%

SCHEDULE II
Continued

	Year	Black	Coloured	Indian	White	Total
Social old-age pensions						
• Maximum yearly pension payable (1990 Rand)	1985[11]	1 932	2 862	2 862	4 403	
	1993[11]	3 081	3 081	3 081	3 081	
• Pensioners claiming pensions	1980[11]	58%	83%	67%	39%	
	1993[11]	90%	85%	62%	20%	
• Pension as % of *average* wage	1980[11]	9%	16%	16%	30%	
	1993[11]	16%	16%	16%	16%	
• Pension as % of *average group* wage	1980[11]	17%	24%	18%	14%	
	1993[11]	25%	21%	15%	8%	
Access to services						
• Electricity for lighting from public supply	1994[8]	37%	84%	99%	99%	55%
	1995[9]	51%	84%	99%	99%	65%
• Telephone in dwelling	1994[8]	12%	43%	72%	87%	31%
	1995[9]	14%	38%	74%	85%	32%
• Piped water in dwelling	1994[8]	27%	76%	98%	98%	48%
	1995[9]	33%	72%	97%	97%	51%
• % with adequate water	1995[9]	54%	86%	96%	96%	67%
• Flush/chemical toilet/ventilated pit latrine in dwelling or on site	1994[8]	46%	87%	98%	100%	62%
	1995[9]	51%	81%	99%	100%	65%

SCHEDULE II
Continued

	Year	Black	Coloured	Indian	White	Total
Access to services (continued)						
• Refuse removal by local authority	**1994**[8]	37%	82%	95%	93%	53%
	1995[9]	43%	80%	94%	92%	58%
• Housing shortages: total	**1986**[4]	628–1 118	90–100	44	1–25	
(estimated thousands) urban only	**1990**[4]	1 284	43	3	1	
total	**1995**[9]	21	41	109	158	54
• Housing: average value (R '000) urban	**1995**[9]	31	45	111	157	76
rural	**1995**[9]	13	24	60	172	21

Sources and notes:
[1] Race Relations Survey 1983, (South African Institute of Race Relations, SAIRR, 1984).
[2] Race Relations Survey 1987/88, (SAIRR, 1988).
[3] Race Relations Survey 1988/89, (SAIRR, 1989).
[4] Race Relations Survey 1992/93, (SAIRR, 1993).
[5] Race Relations Survey 1994/95, (SAIRR, 1995).
[6] Race Relations Survey 1995/96, (SAIRR, 1996).
[7] National Social Development Report (RSA, 1995).
[8] October Household Survey 1994, (CSS, 1995).
[9] October Household Survey 1995, (CSS, 1996).
[10] Whiteford and McGrath, 1994: Distribution of income in South Africa.

SCHEDULE II
Continued

[11] Van den Berg 1994: Issues in South African social security.
[12] Office in the Ministry of the President, 1996: Children, poverty and disparity reduction.
[13] Public Works Green Paper.
[14] Development Bank of Southern Africa information.
[15] Mostert et al., 1997: Demography handbook.

[a] Includes former independent homelands.
[b] Includes dense settlements in peri-urban areas not primarily dependent on agriculture.
[c] Excludes former homelands.
[d] 1994 figures are for the expanded definition of unemployment, people able and willing to work. The expanded definition includes discouraged workseekers.
[e] Poverty line in 1993 is an estimated R840 per month for an urban household, R740 per month for a rural household.
[f] Mean household income for female-headed households was R1 141 per month versus R2 089 for all households.

indices of which are very approximate), there has been a drop in infant mortality and an increase in the Human Development Index which in part reflects infant mortality. A sharp increase in the use of modern contraception is reflected among the African majority which is associated with the fall in the rate of population increase.

Similarly, there has been a fall in the percentage of people with no education, indications of very recent increases for Africans in telephone ownership, electricity, refuse disposal services in urban areas, piped water in dwellings in African areas, and for Africans in particular, a sharp rise in state old age pensions and pension pay-out rates, which is of wide significance because of the dependence on old age pensions by wider family groups in poorer areas.

At the same time some indicators are not moving and these reflect a situation in which the capacity of the economy and the administration is not able to cope with the demands made on it. Pupil-teacher ratios seem to be static at a higher level among blacks; pass rates in the final school examinations for blacks have not improved above the 1986 level, due in large measure to the destabilisation of schools by unrest; per capita incomes for the extended period between 1980 and 1991 were static, although more recent increases are possible, as suggested by results for 1993; housing shortages have not declined – in fact figures not presented in the schedule for 1995 would suggest that they have doubled since 1986 in absolute terms among Africans. Most importantly, perhaps, the data in the schedule suggest that unemployment has risen very sharply for blacks; the figures are perhaps doubtful (see later) but the underlying trend is disquieting. One therefore sees evidence in these figures of very inconsistent performance of the South African political economy in securing an overall and widespread socio-economic upgrading of the population at large.

4. RACIAL INEQUALITY: TRENDS OVER TIME

Data in same schedule (Schedule II) allow some assessment of trends in racial differentials. South Africa has established notoriety because of its racial divisions and in many respects its future success as a society will be measured in terms of the narrowing of racial differentials. In some cases the rate of change in the indicators for blacks, coloured people and Asians is more rapid than that for whites simply because the whites have reached a point of "saturation" at a very high level. For example, this applies in the use of modern contraception, infant mortality, percentage of population urbanised, per capita expenditure on education, success rates in school examinations, and access to domestic services.

The data on state old age pensions is one of the clearest cases of racial equalisation. Recent policy, by standardising pensions, has sharply increased black old age pensions and kept those for whites, while leaving the "intermediate" groups roughly static. At the same time the percentages of whites and Indians claiming state pensions is falling due no doubt to an increase in independent social security in old age.

In education the figures show that in basic terms the schooling gap between blacks and whites is closing, but the fastest progress is being made by coloured and Indian pupils, with whites at or close to saturation point in terms of possession of some education. The figures for university exemption passes in the final examinations, however, suggest that a quality gap is probably narrowing more slowly. Indians have emerged as the group with the highest achievements in education. This is interesting because, relative to whites, Indian education was also under-funded in the past, which has not prevented remarkable progress in this sector. In parenthesis, this illustrates the fact that by no means all social achievement is due to state support levels – community and family support is at least as important.

Therefore, the fact that the racial differentials between blacks and whites in state support per pupil are closing rapidly should not lead to the expectation that there will be a commensurate improvement in the quality of outcomes in black education. Until such time as a strong culture of learning emerges and a respect for rules and authority in the educational system, African education is likely to lag behind that of other groups almost irrespective of state policy. As an aside, however, it seems likely that separate indictors for race will be phased out from now on and therefore the real progress or lack of it in education might never be known.

The most serious racial inequalities are found in the sphere of incomes and material circumstances. Poverty, as defined in the schedule, is a very clear majority phenomenon among blacks, while it is at a level of a quarter or less among other groups, with whites at a point of being well-nigh rid of poverty in their midst. One has to be somewhat cautious here, because what counts as poverty in South Africa would come close to relative comfort in most of the rest of Africa and even India. The measure of poverty used is the so-called Minimum Living Level, which makes provision for quite respectable levels of expenditure on things like clothing and recreation. Poverty as defined in the table, therefore is not dire deprivation. A more telling index of poverty is implied in the levels of child malnutrition: just under one-third of black families, some one-fifth of coloured families and minorities of well under 10% of Indian and white families is probably the rough extent of *sheer deprivation*, as opposed to serious material constraint, in the society. These levels of dire poverty are tragically high, however, and the racial inequalities reflected are equally substantial.

An important question is whether or not the racial differentials are narrowing. Although the racial income shares are gradually shifting away from the formerly dominant position of whites, this is due more to differences in population growth than to changes in relative affluence. The figures for the per capita income gap between whites and blacks are very confusing. The figures suggest that the gap narrowed from some thirteen to one in 1980, to some twelve to one in 1993 and then to under eight to one in 1994. The sudden shift between 1993 and 1994 is not plausible and it would suggest that the figures are not comparable. Both the 1993 and 1994 estimates are based on surveys whereas the 1980 and 1991 figures are based on census results. All one can say is that it would seem as if there has been some narrowing of the racial per capita income gap but that the extent of this narrowing is uncertain.

Average monthly earnings as presented in the schedule are probably more consistent because they are based on similar types of surveys, the latest being the Central Statistical Service's October Household Survey. Between 1985 and 1995, black earnings as reported in surveys increased by a factor of 1.1 to one, higher than the decrease among coloured of .7 to one, but lower than the increase among whites of 1.8 to one. Indians had the highest rate of increase in earnings of 2.0 to one. What these results suggest is that the earnings gap between whites and Indians, on the one hand, and blacks and coloureds on the other, has been *widening*. These estimates do not take account of taxation, however, and if one allows for this the earnings gap between whites and blacks has been *roughly static*.

In 1995 the white to black earnings ratio is 3.9 to one, compared with some 3.6 to one in 1985, both of which have to be interpreted in the light of the fact that black dependency on earners is much higher than that of whites, and allowing for this in making rough estimates of per capita income would confirm the earlier trends reported in per capita income.

It is very difficult to draw firm conclusions from such shaky data, but the *impression* gained is that while racial gaps in per capita income may have narrowed since the eighties, but particularly in the nineties, the earnings gap per average family earner has not narrowed between blacks and whites. Indians seem to be the group which has made rapid relative advances. Perhaps we may add that the earnings gap in *salary and wage earnings* has narrowed between blacks and whites, but the white and Indian earnings are driven up by very much higher earnings from entrepreneurship. Among Indians, for example, the "gap" between entrepreneurship income and salary and wage income is three to one, and much the same among whites.

One has to conclude that in terms of widespread impact, the income gaps between whites and blacks are not narrowing to an extent that the perceptions of income inequality are likely to be softened. If there is a mollifying factor it lies in the zone of income overlap between the races. The 1993 data in the schedule show that the zone of overlap is the household income range of R20 000 per annum to R70 000 per annum. In this income range, white and black South Africans are both well represented – they diverge at the margins. Nearly half of the consumers in this category, which could perhaps be described as "lower middle class" are black, although only some 16% of blacks themselves could be described as lower middle to middle class. The more comfortable "middle class" (R70 000 or more) is still dominantly white, to the extent of some 85%.

The averages discussed up to now disguise a far more dramatic trend which has been occurring in incomes within racial groups, namely growing intra-racial inequality. In all groups, between 1975 and 1991, and there is every reason to believe that the trend has

intensified, the poor have been getting poorer. This in large measure is due to the rise in unemployment. Among Africans the mean
income of the poorest 40% dropped by over 40%, by over 30%
among whites and by some one-fifth among Indians and coloureds.
The richest 10% on the other hand, has increased its share of income
among Africans by over 40%, among whites by some 25% but with
no change among coloureds and Indians.

Taking the mean incomes of the top 20%, shows that once again
Africans have become more affluent by nearly 40%, coloureds and
Indians by 20 to 30%, but that whites have remained static. These
estimates suggest that whites have only gained among the "super-
rich", whereas the gains among Indians and coloureds are in the
levels just below the top income groups. The African income distribution has "stretched" quite dramatically, both from the top 20% and
top 10% down to the lower levels of income. If feelings of progress
and envy (relative deprivation) are influenced substantially by comparisons with those closest to oneself, which is often suggested, then
these figures may represent the key to an intensification of material
and class consciousness in the society.

Unemployment is critical to the distribution of material welfare,
and so is the phenomenon of the incomplete household, in which
a single parent, usually a mother, if she has employment has to
work for lower wages than men, and bring up a family. It is this
phenomenon which is commonly taken to contribute substantially
to the "underclass" phenomenon in the inner city areas of the USA
for example. The data in the schedule show that female-headed
households are at a very high 30% among Africans, also high among
coloureds at some 22% and at round 15% among whites and Indians.
These figures understate the contrasts, however, because among the
latter groups, a substantial number of female-headed households are
those of widows and divorcees with means of support.

Unemployment is the greatest nemesis of material progress, but
regrettably, due to the fact that there is no adequate registration of
the unemployed in South Africa, the extent of unemployment is even
more uncertain than the other indicators discussed. According to the
estimates in the schedule, unemployment among blacks, coloureds
and Indians increased some fourfold between 1980 and 1994, and
threefold among whites but at a much lower level. The 1994 esti-

mates include persons willing to accept work but not actively seeking work (the ILO "extended definition") whereas the earlier figure almost certainly included only those seeking work. Nevertheless, one can safely assume that, *as recorded*, unemployment increased some *2.5 times* over the 14 year period, and that, once again as recorded, it is some 6 times higher among blacks than among whites, due largely to differences in training and employability.

Recent research by co-author Schlemmer, however, suggests that one has to be very cautious in approaching the official estimates of unemployment in South Africa. On the basis of a survey among 11 000 South Africans nation-wide in 1995, it appeared that some 34% of economically active South Africans *claimed* to be unemployed. This estimate was consistent with the growth in unemployment which would have occurred after the official estimate of 33% in late 1994. However, some 20% of the unemployed admitted to having personal earnings from ad hoc work, and 70 to 80% of the unemployed admitted to having money for *personal* expenditure on a range of items, including over 70% who admitted to having the money to spend on new clothing and entertainment. Some 66% of the unemployed spent more than R50 per month on personal clothing and the median expenditure on personal clothing was no lower than the median amounts spent by unskilled labour fully employed in the formal sector. The unemployed persons themselves claimed that this money was obtained from employed family members. When asked what the lowest income level was at which they would accept a job offered to them, the median minimum was as high as the wages typically paid to unskilled persons in the formal sector. On the basis of these and other calculations, the study concluded that there was much less material deprivation among the unemployed than was typically assumed. Furthermore, it was concluded that the real rate of unemployment was unlikely to be higher than 25%. There is a great deal of "hidden employment", mainly in the informal sector which is not measured in official statistics, and there is also a great deal of exploitation of employed family members by the unemployed waiting for market-related job opportunities (Schlemmer, 1996).

An unemployment rate of 25% is nonetheless very high, among the highest in the world, and well above the current European average of some 11% (*The Economist*, November 1996). Equally sobering is the fact that unemployment is increasing all the time. South Africa requires a growth rate of between 5 and 7% in order to absorb the new job-seekers every year, but because of the steadily increasing use of labour-saving technology in the country's attempts to become more competitive in the international export markets, growth rates of this order are fairly inconceivable, particularly since factors yet to be discussed tend to make investor confidence rather brittle in South Africa.

Given the inevitability of the unemployed depending on or exploiting employed relatives for their survival and lifestyle needs, which, as we have seen, are not insubstantial, the effects on community welfare extend well beyond the unemployed. As we have already suggested, the unemployed are a major source of deepening poverty among the very poor.

One of the most stark indicators of inequality is the racial distribution of management positions. The data in the schedule show that up to 1994 the penetration of management positions in the private sector by people other than white was fairly slight, although tending to increase sharply from small base percentages among Africans. It is very probable that there has been much more marked black job-advancement subsequent to 1994, but most of it has been in the public service and the percentages of Africans in top corporate jobs are still very low, giving rise to some quite strenuous demands from black lobby groups for the legal imposition of quotas and targets for black appointments. Legislation along these lines is currently being prepared. Legislated "affirmative action", while a very understandable demand in South Africa, carries with it the risk of reinforcing the salience of race in the society and of possibly creating a culture of entitlement which will weaken attempts to improve the efficiency of South Africa's employing institutions. If affirmative action has the effect of raising rates of emigration of skilled whites then the effect on the economy will be severe, because South Africa has an overall shortage of skills in the technical, managerial and professional fields.

5. SOME MORE GENERAL INDICATORS OF SOCIAL COHESION

Partly related to the problem of high and rising unemployment is the problem of high crime rates. The following summary is drawn from a major study sponsored by the banking group NEDCOR, in which Dr Robin Lee and co-author Schlemmer conducted the research. Serious crime increased by 38% between 1990 and 1995, a growth rate of over 6.5% per annum, or three times the population growth rate. Rape has nearly doubled over the period, and while some serious crimes have shown a tendency for the rate of increase to decline this year, rape is escalating even more rapidly.

The overall crime rate in South Africa, at some 5 650 per 100 000 of the population is well above the international average of 2 660 for countries which publish statistical records. Yet curiously, there are a number of very stable and orderly countries in which the crime rates well exceed that of South Africa's: namely USA (5 800), France (6 170), Germany (7 100), Netherlands (7 600), UK (8 990), Canada (11 440), New Zealand (13 250), and Sweden (14 190). Part of the answer to this curiosity is that these types of countries keep crime records which are probably far superior to those of less developed countries and to those of South Africa. Serious crimes are a better basis of comparison because they are less likely than crime in general to be under-reported,

South Africa's murder rate in 1994 of 45 per 100 000 people compared with the international average of 5.5 per 100 000 and was exceeded only by that of neighbouring countries like Swaziland and Lesotho and by those of Colombia and The Bahamas, with Sudan and Guatemala at roughly two thirds the level of South Africa. In terms of assault, South Africa with 840 per 100 000 was also far higher than the international average of only 142.

In the first eight months of 1995, 18% of dwellings in South Africa experienced 1.26 instances each of crime or violence in which householders were the victims. In the case of black residential areas the levels were some 45% higher, some 47% of South Africans felt that it was probable or very probable that they would be victims of crime in the coming year and 46% of South Africans considered crime to be South Africa's most serious problem.

Among businessmen, 82% of large businesses, 68% of small businesses and 45% of businesses in malls or protected centres had experienced some sort of crime, including commercial crime, over the preceding 24 months. The effects of this level of crime on business and investor confidence does not need explanation. The

NEDCOR project estimated that the cost of crime able to be calculated amounted to R31 Billion in 1995, or nearly 6% of GDP. This does not include much higher costs to the society of the consequent loss of investor confidence.

The explosion of crime has overwhelmed a police service which came to depend very largely on controls on the movement to assist it in ensuring the security of residential suburbs and business areas. The police also suffered a critical loss of popular legitimacy because of their role in the imposition of apartheid laws. Furthermore, political rhetoric and the necessary restructuring of the police force has tended to undermine the morale to the extent that some accounts suggest 35% daily absenteeism among police ranks. A consequence of this is that, of the crimes reported, only some of 16% resulted in an arrest in 1994/5. If one allows for unreported crimes, for every 1000 crimes committed, less than 8% result in a conviction. Crime pays in South Africa (see NEDCOR, 1996).

Crime is a major indicator of a breakdown in social discipline and very high levels of social aggression in South Africa, and it has cost the country very dearly in terms of business confidence. Other indicators of this breakdown in the normative cohesion of society can be given. Well under one third of households in the black townships of major metropolitan areas are paying for their municipal service charges, which is contributing to the fiscal crisis in local government. A similar picture emerges in regard to the paying of television licences, traffic fines, and in regard to tax evasion, although the latter problem may be gradually being brought under control. The theft of copper cable has caused a serious loss of revenue to telecommunications, service disruptions and the postponement of new services (*Business Day*, January 27, 1997). Recently the Director General of Health claimed that South Africa held the world record for teenage pregnancies. The rate of HIV infection among women attending pre-natal clinics in one province, KwaZulu-Natal, is approaching 20% (and at certain clinics as high as 30%) and the other provinces are fast catching up. HIV is mentioned because it is to a degree an indicator of reckless behaviour and a lack of discipline. A recent report in *The Economist*, January, 4, 1997, records South Africa's road death rate per 1000 vehicles at 1.9 compared with only 0.2 in the UK and USA. Kenya and Morocco record higher figures than South Africa but there poor roads contribute to the problems. The estimated cost to the South African economy of road accidents is 3.3% of GDP (*Business Day*, January 7, 1997). The social fabric in South Africa is fairly threadbare at the present stage.

One plausible hypothesis for the crime and breakdown of social discipline is that it is a disguised form of racial hostility – a way of getting at the white middle class as revenge for the decades of apartheid. There may be elements of this in some of the actions but the crime statistics make it very clear that most of the people robbed, raped and murdered are in fact blacks. Apartheid has to take some of the blame in other senses, however.

Apartheid made most authority in the previous system illegitimate. People in the townships who attempted to defend moderate, respectable and responsible behaviour were often depicted as "Uncle Toms" of a type by the much more attractive and heroic radical activists. Apartheid also drew so much attention to itself that many black people could have been forgiven for thinking that there was only one single dimension of legal discrimination which prevented them from enjoying the lifestyle they so envied in the white middle classes.

Furthermore, the struggle against apartheid, and the methods adopted by the erstwhile authorities in defending it, cheapened human life. At some stages in the mid to late eighties the number of deaths in political violence were higher in relation to the population than any other situation of conflict short of outright civil war.

One has to add to these dimensions the fact that any major transition from one form of authority to another in any society tends to weaken social controls and restraints on individuals. The further problem is that the large underclass, with its broken families and over-crowded homes tends to hand its children over to street-corner gangs for their socialisation. All these elements in combination are probably quite sufficient to explain the high levels of social aggression and crime in the new South Africa. Explaining the problems, however, is very much easier than the restoration of social authority.

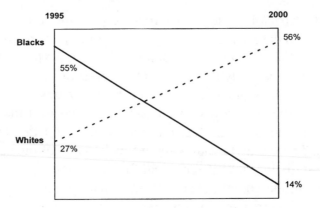

Figure 1. Present and future levels of unhappiness.

6. ATTITUDES AND EXPECTATIONS

In 1995, co-author Møller undertook a nation-wide quality of life investigation, in which levels of personal happiness were probed. A striking result emerged as regards current levels of *unhappiness* and the respondent's expectations of what they would be by the year 2000 (see Figure 1). These results show just how negatively whites view the future compared with blacks (Møller, 1995: pp. 49, 51).

Surprisingly, however, there is rather little indication of a current euphoria associated with the establishment of majority rule in 1994, as many people might have expected. The election euphoria was a brief phenomenon. Møller (1996) tracked the levels of overall "happiness" among blacks on the basis of comparable national samples in 1983, 1998, May 1994 (immediately after the election), 1995, and 1996, with the following result for "happy" and "very happy" combined:

Blacks: Levels of personal happiness over time

1983	1988	MAY 1994	1995	1996
49%	36%	85%	47%	59%

Møller points out that personal happiness indicators are usually found to be rather stable over time. The first democratic elections in South Africa, therefore must have had an exceptionally powerful effect on popular sentiments, but it seems to have been more in the nature of short lived celebratory sentiment rather than indicating any change in the framework of public sentiment among black South Africans. There was always the possibility, however, that more serious political and economic expectations could have been raised.

In December, 1994, co-author Schlemmer conducted a nation-wide survey of expectation among black people (n 1437, personal interviews, fieldwork by MarkData). The study included other groups as well but the form of questions differed so that only the results for blacks are briefly summarised). Respondents were asked what they felt the "... *most important things were that government should do for the people now that a new government is in power*". The distribution of spontaneous replies was as follows – multiple answers summed, therefore answers exceeded 100%.

Better services – all combined:	62%
Job creation:	51%
Housing provision:	47%
Improved education:	28%
Free education:	9%
Improved wage/working conditions:	15%
Improved roads in areas:	14%
Improved/free health care:	11%
Expanded welfare provision:	9%
Better old age provision:	6%
Telephones:	4%
Combat crime:	3%
More recreation facilities:	3%
Equal rights:	3%
(remainder < 3%)	

The respondents were then asked *when they expected the benefit to be provided*. The distribution of expectations was as follows:

Immediately:	35%
In one to two months:	13%
Within six months:	11%
Within in 1 year:	23%
Within 5 years or longer:	5%
Don't know:	4%

Thereafter the respondents were asked: *"If these things do not happen what will be the main cause?"* (spontaneous answers coded)

Financial constraint on government:	23%
Excessive demand/overpopulation:	28%
Such development takes time:	8%
Instability/strikes/disruptions:	5%
Nobody's fault/other answers:	5%
Government incompetence/corruption, etc.:	*17%*
Lack of concern/uncaring government:	*9%*
Don't know:	26%

Among the African National Congress supporters, the answers did not differ significantly from the percentages above. The pattern of replies above suggests that a sense of priorities is well developed in the black population, and that at the time there was a keen expectation of near immediate gratification of needs and expectations. As a matter of fact, in reply to an additional item some 45% of respondents as early as 8 months after the new government had assumed office indicated that the government performance was "not as good as expected." In February, 1994, before the first open election, de Kock et al. (1994) of the Human Sciences Research Council asked a nation-wide sample of voters how soon they expected their standards of living to improve. Among Africans, some 36% expected improvements within one year. In the results quoted above, over 80% of respondents in the December 1994 survey expected the benefits they identified to materialise within one year. It seems clear that the elections and the outcome had an effect in stimulating expectations.

Yet, other answers suggest that the perceptions are tinged with realism. There is clearly a grasp of financial constraints and of the problem of an overload of needs and demands. In fact, the results above suggest that it is only among some 26% of the black electorate that delays by the government in meeting expectations will be seen as default and failure by government. This is a large proportion of people but it is far from being the kind of majority which could destabilise the new democracy on the basis of disappointed expectations. The expectations of this category are likely to be countered or tempered by the greater realism of the majority.

By 1995, the realism may have deepened to the point that pessimism was setting in, A study by co-author Møller, compared with identical probes in 1988 and 1983 on general expectations of improvement or deterioration in the lives of respondents (fieldwork by MarkData, n 5587 (1983) n 3772 (1988) n 2142 (1995)) asked whether the lives of respondents were getting better or worse. The "nett" response, obtained by subtracting the worse from the better, yielded the following:

Life Improving (+) or Deteriorating (−)

	Black	Coloured	Indian	White	Total
1983	+14%	+46%	+37%	+47%	+30%
1988	−20%	+38%	+35%	+36%	+18%
1995	+2%	+17%	+12%	+2%	+4%

Whereas blacks were understandably very pessimistic in the 1988 survey – the darkest hour before the dawn in the liberation struggle – their collective mood improved but by 1995 there was a sufficient realism or pessimism that the perceptions of the future were more negative than they had been in the darkest days of apartheid in 1983. The pessimists who accounted for 30% of blacks did not anticipate any real changes in the lives of ordinary people by the year 2000 and feared that unemployment and the breakdown of law and order would continue to depress their quality of life (Møller, 1995).

An Institute for Democracy in South Africa (Idasa) national opinion poll on the perceived performance of the new democracy, also conducted in 1995, established, among other findings, that no more than 41% of South Africans of all races were satisfied with the new democracy. Among Africans it was understandably higher, but short of a majority at 47%. Only some 35% of Africans felt that general conditions in the country had improved. However, Idasa point out that these finding were very similar to their earlier findings in 1994, suggesting once again that the anticipated surge of wild and unrealistic populist fervour had not occurred in South Africa (Idasa, 1996).

7. CONCLUDING COMMENTS

South Africa's negotiated settlement and its transition to democracy has been almost a modern fairy tale. Nearly three years later it remains a model for the resolution of conflicts elsewhere in the world. This brief review of South Africa's social indicators should perhaps temper some of the optimism about the country's future which can really only be indulged in at a considerable distance.

It is still a very deeply divided society with very large backlogs, even larger inequalities and clear evidence of what can be called an "underclass" which contains deprivation and social fragmentation as serious as that to be found in any other African society. The evidence of rapidly growing inequality *within* race groups and the society at large, the growing unemployment, the very large sector of the population which is still marginal to the modern formal sector of the economy and the persistence of a massive, low productivity subsistence sector in the black rural areas all combine to suggest that if trends continue along current lines, South Africa will be called an "enclave" society. The competitive sector of the formal economy will grow, as will the relative welfare of the unionised formal sector working class and the modern public bureaucracy, along with their consumer-based lifestyles, but the marginal sectors will grow faster, with an increasing social distinction between these insiders and outsiders as the social networks within each sector became more crystallised and internally convergent. This is a familiar pattern in many parts of the developing world, but it could become South Africa's major distinguishing feature.

Getting rid of apartheid may have been the easy part, therefore; avoiding the new "apartheid" of a non-racial "enclave" society will be more difficult. If the economy enjoys very high growth rates the challenge will be manageable. If its growth rates continue to be relatively sluggish, however, the future scenario of an enclave society is virtually guaranteed.

There are, however, some areas of socio-economic progress, and the almost new government has been rather quicker than most other post "liberation" administrations to realise that the "transformation" which it promised its supporters up to 1994 is an impossible ideal. A very comprehensive centrally-planned development mobilisation initiative launched by government soon after it came to power, the

Reconstruction and Development Programme (RDP), has been dismantled in all but name and its concrete goals incorporated into normal line functions in government, much to the dismay of some of the more centralist government alliance partners.

Further, the government, in recently adopting an economic policy based on fiscal discipline and deficit reduction – the Growth, Employment and Redistribution (Gear) plan, has in fact imposed on itself the rigour and the political pain of "structural adjustment" which the IMF has had to force on so many other cases of failed populist transformation in recent years. It is this realism and the signs that the new voters did not completely fall for the promises made in the election campaign that give the society most hope. Whether this sense of realism will be sufficient to help South Africans to endure the fact that many of South Africa's indicators will get worse before they start to improve, remains to be seen.

ACKNOWLEDGEMENTS

The authors thank colleagues Amanda Jackson and Mandy Lamprecht in the Quality of Life Research Unit at the University of Natal for assistance with the compilation of indicators and typing. The financial support of the Human Sciences Research Council for the Unit's Quality of Life Project is gratefully acknowledged. Views are those of the authors and do not in any way reflect those of sponsors or other persons or organisations.

REFERENCES

Central Statistical Service (CSS), Republic of South Africa: 1995; 1996, October Household Survey 1994; 1995, Statistical Release P0317 (Pretoria, South Africa).

de Kock, C., C. Schutte, N. Rhoodie, and D. Ehlers: 1994, 'The legitimacy of the Government of National Unity', Information Update, Ad hoc issue, No. 1, pp. 1–20 (Human Sciences Research Council, Pretoria, South Africa).

Institute for Democracy in South Africa (Idasa): 1996, 'Opinion Poll', 2 (1 September).

NEDCOR: 1996, NEDCOR project on Crime, Violence and Investment (Johannesburg, South Africa).

Ministry in the Office of the President: 1996, Children, Poverty and Disparity Reduction (Pretoria, South Africa).

Republic of South Africa: 1995, National Social Development Report. Report prepared for the World Summit on Social Development, Copenhagen, Denmark (Government Printer, Pretoria).

Møller, V.: 1995. 'Waiting for utopia: Quality of life in the 1990s', Indicator South Africa 13(1), pp. 47–54.

Møller, V.: 1997, 'Quality of life in South Africa: post-apartheid trends', Social Indicators Research (in press).

Mostert, W.P., B.E. Hofmeyr and J.S. Oosthuizen: 1997. Demographie: Handboek vir die Suid-Afrikaanse Student (Demography: Handbook for the South African student) (Human Sciences Research Council, Pretoria) (in press).

Schlemmer, L.: 1996, 'New Evidence on Unemployment', South African Institute of Race Relations, Fast Facts 9/96 (September), pp. 2–6.

South African Institute of Race Relations (SAIRR): 1984; 1988; 1989; 1993; 1995; 1996, Race Relations Survey 1987/88; 1988/89; 1992/93; 1994/5; 1995/96 (Johannnesburg, South Africa).

Van den Berg, S.: 1994, Issues in South African social security (Unpublished background paper prepared for the World Bank, Department of Economics, University of Stellenbosch, Stellenbosch, South Africa).

United Nations Development Programme (UNDP): 1996, Human Development Report 1966 (Oxford University Press, New York).

Whiteford, A. and M. McGrath: 1994, Distribution of Income in South Africa (Human Sciences Research Council, Pretoria, South Africa).

World Bank: 1996, World Bank Development Report 1996 (Oxford University Press, New York).

Visiting Researcher   Lawrence Schlemmer
South African Institute of Race Relations
P.O. Box 31044
Braamfontein 2017
South Africa

Quality of Life Research Unit   Valerie Møller
Centre for Social and Development Studies
University of Natal
Durban 4041
South Africa
E-mail: moller@mtb.und.ac.za

STEPHAN KLASEN[1]

POVERTY, INEQUALITY AND DEPRIVATION IN SOUTH AFRICA: AN ANALYSIS OF THE 1993 SALDRU SURVEY

ABSTRACT. This paper analyses poverty and inequality in South Africa based on data from a comprehensive multi-purpose household survey undertaken in 1993 to provide baseline statistics on poverty and its determinants to the new government. The paper shows that South Africa has among the highest levels of income inequality in the world and compares poorly in most social indicators to countries with similar income levels. Much of the poverty in the country is a direct result of *apartheid* policies that denied equal access to education, employment, services, and resources to the black population of the country. As a result, poverty has a very strong racial dimension with poverty concentrated among the African population. In addition, poverty is much higher in rural areas, and particularly high in the former homelands. Poverty among female-headed households and among children is also higher than average. Moreover, poverty is closely related to poor education and lack of employment. The poor suffer from lack of access to education, quality health care, basic infrastructure, transport, are heavily indebted, have little access to productive resources, and are heavily dependent on remittances and social transfers, particularly social pensions and disability grants. The paper uses an income-based definition of poverty for most of the analysis. In addition, it develops a broad-based index of deprivation including income, employment, wealth, access to services, health, education, and perceptions of satisfaction as its components. While on average the two indicators correspond fairly closely, the income poverty measure misses a considerable number of people who are severely deprived in many of the non-income measures of well-being. This group of severely deprived not identified by the income poverty measure consists predominantly of Africans living in rural areas, concentrated particularly in the province of KwaZulu/Natal.

1. INTRODUCTION

In 1990, South Africa embarked on a transition from white *apartheid* rule to a democratic regime open to all members of the population. This transition culminated in the first democratic and all-inclusive elections of April, 1994 and the installation of a Government of National Unity under President Mandela in May, 1994.

A critical element of the mandate of the new government has been to address poverty and inequality. In fact, the White Paper

Social Indicators Research **41**: 51–94, 1997.

on Reconstruction and Development states unequivocally that "at the heart of the Government of National Unity is a commitment to effectively address the problems of poverty and the gross inequality evident in all aspects of South African society" (Government of South Africa, 1994).

This determination to address poverty and inequality necessitated more and better background information on the problem and its root causes. Official statistics had excluded four of the poorest nominally independent 'homelands' since 1970 (which are home to about 20% of the population and about 30% of South Africa's poor) and under-sampled poor peri-urban areas and were therefore of limited value. Other information available was often not representative and mostly qualitative in nature (e.g. Ramphele and Wilson, 1989).

At the request of the government-in-waiting, and with technical assistance of the World Bank and funding from the Governments of Denmark, Netherlands, and Norway, the Southern African Labour and Development Research Unit (SALDRU) at the University of Cape Town was commissioned to undertake the first nation-wide, representative household survey in South Africa. This survey sampled 9,000 households in late 1993 and included a broad range of information on family composition, income, employment, health status, education, transport, housing, agriculture, as well as questions on perceptions and aspirations of the population (RDP, 1995). While since 1993, the Central Statistical Services has conducted two annual household surveys, the latter of which has not been published yet (CSS, 1994; 1995), the so-called SALDRU survey has to date still been the most comprehensive source of poverty-related data. Future analyses of the CSS household surveys and other surveys will, however, serve as important means to monitor progress in the implementation of the government's new programmes and policies to combat poverty.

This paper summarises the key findings of the survey as they relate the poverty, inequality and deprivation in South Africa. The next section discusses methodological issues, while the three following sections discuss, respectively, South African poverty in an international perspective, a profile of South Africa's poor, and the burden suffered by the poor in South Africa. A part of these sections summarises results first presented by a World Bank paper produced for the government (RDP, 1995)[2]; the remainder extends the analysis to include new data and new indicators of income-based and non-income measures of deprivation. The final section develops a composite indicator of well-being and deprivation to identify and describe the most deprived groups in South Africa.

2. METHODOLOGY

Before discussing the results of the survey, a brief discussion on the nature and measurement of poverty is critical. Many countries define poverty using a fixed level of household income below which the household is considered poor. Since these methods are focused on income, they omit many other important characteristics of human well-being, such as health, education, mobility, and the like, that are not necessarily closely correlated with income (UNDP, 1996). Moreover, income only constitutes an important *input* to well-being, but it does not measure the level of well-being itself. In order to avoid these short-comings, Sen (1992, 1995) has proposed to use a capability concept in the definition and measurement of well-being and hence of poverty. The capability concept focuses on measuring well-being directly by examining the ability to achieve certain states of 'doings' and 'beings' or so-called 'functionings' (Sen, 1992), such as the ability to be healthy, well-fed, well-educated, mobile, and well-integrated into a community.[3] While this is a superior concept to a simple focus on income and income poverty, there have been few satisfactory attempts to measure capabilities and capability shortfalls directly due to the enormous information requirements. The UNDP Human Development Index is one such attempt, but has been criticised for its rather arbitrary choice of indicators, weights, and implicit trade-offs (Ravallion, 1996).

The first parts of this paper will stick to a more conventional income-based definition of poverty. At the same time, the analysis will describe other critical capability-related measures such as health, education, access to employment, transport, services, as well as perceptions and aspirations, and relate them to income poverty. In addition, the final section of the paper will develop a composite indicator of deprivation with measures of income, employment, education, access to services, health, and satisfaction levels as its components, which will help determine whether broader conceptions of deprivation yield significantly different results.

Poverty levels were measured using monthly household expenditure since this measure is usually more reliably reported and more stable than household income, especially among poor people. In order to account for differences in household size, composition, and economies of scale, total consumption was divided by the number of 'adult equivalents' (which was calculated using nutrition requirements of children and adults)[4] and adjusted to take into account economies of scale.[5] In addition, adjustments were made to account for differences in prices in different locations. Since prices, which were also collected by the survey, were found to be higher in rural than in urban or metropolitan areas, this adjustment increased the poverty of rural households, compared to others. The households were then ranked according to their adult equivalent expenditure and divided into five quintiles, ranging from the poorest to the richest 20% of households (quintile 1 being the poorest and quintile 5 being the richest).[6]

Bearing in mind that the definition of poverty depends on largely local circumstances, two definitions of a poverty line in South Africa are used. For international comparisons in poverty, Chen, Dhatt, and Ravallion (1996) have defined a crude international poverty line, based on the purchasing power parity-adjusted equivalent of 1 US-$ per capita per day (in 1985 prices). This line is roughly equivalent to India's poverty line and should be considered the bare minimum for subsistence. In South Africa, 24% of the population lives below that line (Table I).

For all other purposes, it is critical to take into account local conceptions and constructions of poverty. In South Africa, an upper middle-income country boasting considerable material wealth with corresponding high aspirations of the population, even people having somewhat more than $1 a day are considered poor using local poverty definitions. The two poverty lines used most in the country are the household subsistence level (HSL, see e.g. Whiteford et al. 1995) and the Minimum and Supplemental Living Levels (MLL and SLL, respectively). Applied to the SALDRU survey data, they yield poverty rates between 44 and 57%, which is in the same range but slightly higher than poverty rates based on caloric intake require-ments (Table I).

While these local measures have been useful in focusing the dis-cussion on poverty, both have considerable short-comings. The HSL distinguishes between a lower rural and higher urban poverty line and thus implicitly assumes that rural people have fewer needs, an urban-biased and ethically very dubious assumption (see Lipton, 1977). The MLL and SLL are per-capita based measures that cannot easily be adapted to account for the different family compositions through the adult equivalency calculations described above. There-fore, and in the absence of a nationally agreed poverty line, this paper follows the method used by the World Bank in its summary paper on poverty (RDP, 1995) which simply assumes that the poor-est 40 percent of households, measured in terms of adult equivalent expenditures, are considered poor; similarly, the poorest 20% of households are considered ultra-poor. In 1993, these lines stood at about R 300 and R 178 monthly expenditure per adult equivalent. Since poor households tend to be larger, the number of *people* below the poverty line is larger than the number of *households* (53% of the population are considered poor and 29% are ultra-poor, see Table I). This poverty line yields similar results to the locally used poverty lines, while the ultra poverty line generates results closer to the much lower international poverty line.[7]

This paper uses two different concepts to examine the distribution of poverty. One is simply the share of the population with a certain characteristic that is below the poverty line, which is the well-known concept of the poverty rate as used above (e.g. what percentage of the rural population is poor?).

The other measure is called the poverty gap and refers to the amount of monetary transfer that would be necessary to lift the income[8] of a poor person exactly to the poverty line.[9] Since it specif-ically incorporates the depth of poverty in the assessment (since a poorer person requires a higher transfer than a less poor to reach the poverty line), it gives a more accurate picture of the magnitude of the problem. Using the poorest 40% of households as the poverty line, the total poverty gap, i.e. the total amount of money poor people need to reach the poverty line, stood at R20.022b in 1993, equivalent to about 4% of GDP.

TABLE I
Comparison of Selected Poverty Lines for South Africa - 1993

Types of Poverty Lines	R. Amount/Month Cut-Off	Percentage of Population Below the Poverty Lines
1. Population cut-offs at the:		
Poor: 40th percentile of households ranked by adult equivalence	301.0	52.8
Ultra-Poor: 20th percentile of households ranked by adult equivalence	177.6	28.8
2. Minimum per capita caloric intake (at 2000 Kcal per day)	143.2	39.3
3. Minimum caloric-adjusted per capita intake (at 2500 Kcal per day)*	185.4	42.3
4. Minimum and supplemental living levels per capita set by The Bureau of Market Research, University of South Africa**		
Supplemental Living Level (SLL)	220.1	56.7
Minimum Living Level (MLL)	164.2	44.7
5. Per adult equivalent household subsistence level (HSL) set by The Institute for Planning Research, University of Port Elizabeth***	251.1	45.7
6. International poverty line (US$ 1 per capita per day)	91.4	23.7

* The adjustment takes into account the energy requirements by age and gender as in the calculations for the adult equivalence figures, but does not include adjustments due to economies of scale (of items consumed within the household).
** For the minimum and supplemental living level, we utilised the values given for a family of five (the average family size in South Africa).
*** HSL is an "absolute poverty" line which provides two separate lines: one for urban areas where the minimum level of welfare required by a family of 2 adults and 3 children is specified as R. 825.1 per month; and a rural line where the minimum level of welfare for a family of 2 adults and 4 children is taken to be R. 723.1 a month.
Source: RDP (1995), Whiteford et al. (1995), Ravallion and Chen (1996).

In the following sections, two ways of presenting this poverty gap are used. The first is the gap between the poverty line and the income of the average poor household of a certain characteristic (e.g. by how much must the average income of poor Africans increase to reach the poverty line), thereby directly measuring the depth of poverty among that group. The other is the share of the total national poverty gap that is made up of people with these characteristics (e.g. what share of the total poverty gap is made up of the poverty gap among Africans; equivalently, what share of the transfer to lift all poor people to the poverty line would have to go to the African poor). This gives an indication of which groups of the population should receive the highest priority for government if it wishes to have a maximum impact on poverty.

The final section will look at a broader indicator of well-being to determine whether other measures of deprivation yield results that are different from a focus on income. The deprivation measure is a composite index of 12 indicators, including income, health, education, household wealth, access to services, transport, and perceptions of quality of life. The twelve areas of focus were chosen based on their close relation to important basic capabilities, such as the ability to be healthy, well-fed, adequately housed and the like. For each indicator, each household is assigned a score of 1 to 5 with one being the lowest and five the highest, corresponding to the characteristic of the household regarding this measure.[10] Table II describes the indicators and the scores attached for each characteristic. In doing the scoring it was aimed to roughly ensure that a score of five represents the best possible standards or condition, a score of three should allow a basic level of welfare to lead a simple, but reasonably safe and healthy existence, while a score of one is an indication of severe deprivation, severe health hazards, and few physical and human resources. The total deprivation index is a simple average of all individual scores.[11]

Clearly, such a measure is subject to the same criticism that has been levelled against the HDI and similar composite indicators. The purpose of this section is not to argue for this particular indicator (or each particular scoring) as a definitive measure of well-being. Instead, it is merely illustrating the differences of such a broader measure to a pure income-based measure and its use in identifying particularly deprived groups.

TABLE II
Components of a Composite Measure of Deprivation

Component	Description of indicator used	Score (1 signifying most deprived, 5 least)				
		1	2	3	4	5
Education	Average years of schooling of all adult (16+) household members	<2	3–5	6–9	10–11	12+
Income	Expenditure quintiles (as used throughout paper)	Poorest quintile	Quintile 2	Quintile 3	Quintile 4	Richest quintile
Wealth	Number of household durables (appliances, vehicles, phone, etc.)	0–1	2–4	5–7	8–10	11+
Housing	Housing characteristic	Shack	Traditional dwelling, hostel, outbuilding	Combination of buildings	Flat, maisonette	House
Water	Type of water access	River/Stream, Dam, Standing Water	Rainwater, Protected spring, well, borehole	Public Standpipe, water tanker/carrier	Piped water on premise	Piped water inside house
Sanitation	Type of sanitation facilities	No toilet	Bucket	Latrine	Imp. latrine, chem. toilet, flush toilet outside	Flush toilet inside

TABLE II
Continued

Component	Description of indicator used	Score (1 signifying most deprived, 5 least)				
		1	2	3	4	5
Energy	Main source of energy for cooking	Wood	Dung	Paraffin, coal	Gas from bottle, dry battery	Electricity from grid, town gas
Employment	Share of adult members of households employed	0–19%	20–39%	40–59%	60–79%	80–100%
Transport	Type of transport used to get to work	Walk	Bicycle	Bus, train, taxis		Car
Nutrition	Share of children stunted in household*	80–100%	61–80%	40–59%	20–39%	0–19%
Health Care	Use of health facilities during last illness*	None	Family, friend, trad. healer	Clinic, public hospital, shop	Pharmacy, visit by PHC nurse	Private doctor
Perceived Well-Being	Level of satisfaction of household	Very Dissatisfied	Dissatisfied	Neither/Nor	Satisfied	Very Satisfied

* only applies to households that have children under six or have used health services in previous two weeks, respectively.

3. SOUTH AFRICA IN AN INTERNATIONAL PERSPECTIVE

a. Social Indicators

Before turning to an in-depth discussion of poverty and inequality in South Africa, it is useful to place South Africa's poverty and social deprivation in an international context by comparing social indicators in South Africa to countries with similar levels of incomes. Table III shows that in all of the most important social indicators, including life expectancy, infant mortality, illiteracy, fertility and access to safe water, South Africa fares poorly against comparable middle income countries. On all indicators except infant mortality (where it is close to the worst), South Africa has the worst performance. These results are a direct legacy of the *apartheid* system where inequalities in opportunities and services were intentional, thereby ensuring that the majority of the population was not sharing in the considerable wealth of the country.

In fact, South Africa fares only slightly better on some of these indicators than much poorer countries in Sub-Saharan Africa (Table III). If South Africa's indicators were restricted to include only the African population, black South Africa fares as badly as a much poorer country like Kenya.

b. International Poverty and Inequality Comparisons

Using the international poverty rate (share of population having less than US$ 1 a day), South Africa's poverty rate stands at about 24%. This is considerably higher than many comparable middle-income countries except Brazil, while it is less than much poorer African countries (see Table IV).

Table IV also shows that this high poverty in South Africa despite fairly high average incomes is closely related to income inequality. The middle-income countries with the lowest poverty rates (Thailand, Tunisia, Poland) are also those that have the comparatively lower rates of income inequality. Conversely, South Africa's high poverty rate is closely related to its high inequality, which is among the highest in the world. The Gini-coefficient, which measures the degree of inequality,[12] stands at 0.61, close to the figure for Brazil, which has the highest level of inequality. A disaggregated analysis of inequality shows that between-race inequality

TABLE III
Comparative Social Indicators: Selected Countries

	Middle-Income Countries							Sub-Saharan Africa		
	Thailand	Poland	Venezuela	Brazil	South Africa[c]	Malaysia	Chile	Kenya	Nigeria	Tanzania
GNP per capita US$ (1994)	2,410	2,410	2,760	2,970	**3,040**	3,480	3,520	250	280	140
Life expectancy (years) (1994)	69	72	71	67	**64**	71	72	59	52	51
Infant Mortality Rate (1994)	36	15	32	56	**50**	12	12	59	81	84
Adult Illiteracy Rate (%) (1995)	6	..[b]	9	17	**18**	17	5	22	43	32
Total Fertility Rate (1994)	2.0	1.8	3.2	2.8	**3.9**	3.4	2.5	4.9	5.6	5.8
Access to Safe Water (%) 1993[a]	77	100	89	96	**76**	78	86	49	40	52

[a] Some data are for 1990.
[b] no comparable data are available.
[c] The South African data is an average of all races. There are large differences between the races in these social indicators.
Source: RDP (1995), World Bank (1996), World Bank (1994), DBSA (1994).

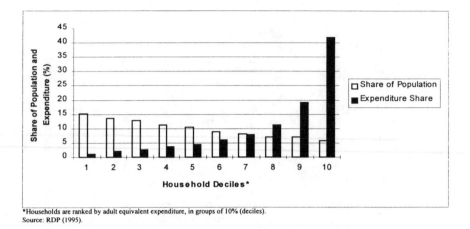

*Households are ranked by adult equivalent expenditure, in groups of 10% (deciles).
Source: RDP (1995).

Figure 1. Inequality in South Africa

is, as expected, considerable. Using the Theil-T measure, between-race inequality accounts for 52% of total inequality. At the same time, within-race inequality, especially among the African population is also fairly substantial and accounts for between 25–42% of total inequality, depending on the measure chosen.[13] As a result of changes since 1993, including the appointment of Africans to high positions in government and business, within-African inequality is likely to have increased further.

Another way to illustrate the degree of inequality in South Africa is to examine the expenditure shares of deciles of households (Figure 1). The poorest 40% of households, equivalent to 53% of the population, account for less than 10% of total consumption; in contrast, the top 10% of households, with only 5.8% of the population, account for over 40% of consumption.

4. CHARACTERISTICS OF SOUTH AFRICA'S POOR

a. The Locations of Poverty

As shown in Figure 2, poverty is worst in rural areas. The poverty rate in rural areas stands at 73%, more than three times the rate prevailing in metropolitan areas.[14] Moreover, the poor in rural areas are much poorer than their urban or metropolitan counterparts. As the 'gap to poverty line' in Figure 2 shows, the average poor household in

TABLE IV
Poverty and Inequality: South Africa and Comparable Countries

| | Middle-Income Countries | | | | | | | | Sub-Saharan Africa | | |
	Tunisia	Thailand	Poland	Venezuela	Brazil	South Africa	Malaysia	Chile	Kenya	Nigeria	Zambia
GNP pc ($) (1992)	1,790	2,410	2,410	2,760	2,970	**2,770**	3,480	3,520	250	280	350
Gini-Coefficient*	0.40	0.43	0.27	0.44	0.63	**0.61**	0.51	0.58	0.57	0.45	0.46
International Poverty Rate (%)	3.9	0.1	6.8	11.8	28.7	**23.7**	5.6	15.0	50.2	28.9	84.6

* All Gini-coefficients are based on income, except for those for Sub-Saharan Africa which are based on expenditure (a Gini of 0 signifies absolute equality, and 1 absolute concentration). Gini coefficients and poverty rates are for different years in the late 80's or early 90's.
Source: RDP (1995) Poverty rates are based on a recent revision of the data (Ravallion and Chen, 1996).

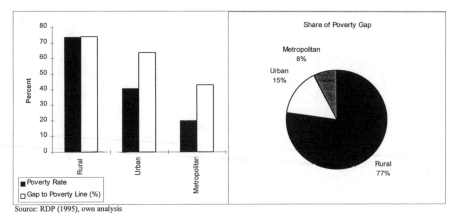

Source: RDP (1995), own analysis

Figure 2. Poverty Rate and Poverty Gap by Location

rural areas would need an increase in income of over 70% to reach
the poverty line, compared to a little more than 40% in metropolitan
areas. The combination of a high poverty rate and deep poverty
among the poor in rural areas ensures that 77% of the total poverty
gap is accounted for by poverty in rural households, although they
only make up 53% of the population.[15]

Poverty is also distributed very unevenly among South Africa's
nine new provinces. Figure 3 shows that the Eastern Cape and the
Northern Province have by far the highest poverty rates. In these
provinces, more than 75% of the population are poor. In contrast,
the poverty rates in Gauteng and Western Cape are both only around
20%.[16] Similarly, poverty is deepest in the Eastern Cape, the Free
State, and Northern Province. In these provinces, poor households
would need to boost their incomes by 95%, 83%, and 76%, respectively, to reach the poverty line.

As a result, these three provinces account for a disproportionate share of the total poverty gap; while having only 35% of the
population, poor households in these provinces generate 58% of the
total poverty gap. Together with KwaZulu/Natal, the most populous
province, they make up three-quarter of the total poverty gap. In contrast, Gauteng and Western Cape make up only 8% of the national
poverty gap, despite having 26% of the population.

The provincial distribution of poverty is closely linked to the
old administrative structures of the *apartheid* era, where public and
private resources were concentrated in the former provinces largely

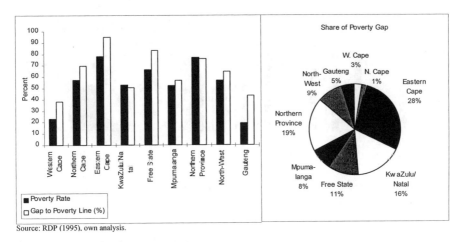

Source: RDP (1995), own analysis.

Figure 3. Poverty Rate and Poverty Gap by Province

reserved for whites.[17] Provinces such as Northern Province and Eastern Cape, which are largely made up of the former 'homelands' for
Africans (i.e. the former self-governing territories and the former
nominally independent TBVC states: Transkei, Bophuthatswana,
Venda, and Ciskei) suffer from a much higher burden of poverty.
Figure 4 shows poverty rates and gaps using the old administrative
boundaries. It shows the disproportionately high poverty rates in
most of the former homelands, which reaches a peak of 92% in the
former Transkei. Transkei (now in the Eastern Cape) is also the one
former homeland where the average expenditures of poor households is less than half the poverty line so that poor households need
their incomes increased by 108% in order to reach the poverty line.
As a result, the share of the poverty gap in the former homelands
is nearly 70%, despite having only 50% of the population. Among
them, the former Transkei and Lebowa together account for fully
36% of the gap (21% and 15%, respectively) despite having only
19% of the population (10% and 9%, respectively).

b. Race and Poverty

Many of the *apartheid* measures, including the extensive welfare
system available to white people, the higher quality of education
available to white students, and the formal and informal job reservations for white workers (at the expense of other population groups),
was specifically designed (and largely successful) in preventing

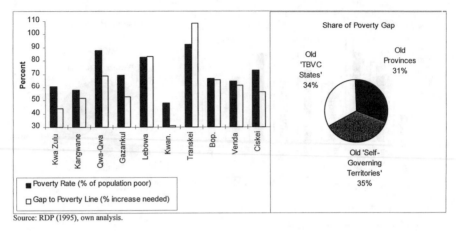

Source: RDP (1995), own analysis.

Figure 4. Poverty Rates and Poverty Gap by Former Administrative Boundaries

poverty among the white population group. As shown in Figure 5, poverty among whites is close to zero. In contrast, poverty among Africans, the most disadvantaged group in the *apartheid* state, stands at 64%, compared to 33% for coloureds, and 3% for Indians. Similarly, poverty is more severe among Africans than other population groups. It is interesting to note, however, that the very few poor Indians and whites also seem to be at a considerable distance below the poverty line.

With Africans making up 77% of the population, their high incidence and depth of poverty ensures that they account for 96% of the poverty gap, with the remaining 4% largely accounted for by poverty among coloureds. The differences in poverty by race also contribute to the distribution of poverty by location since the racial groups were unevenly distributed in the country.[18] At the same time, among Africans, the group comprising nearly all the country's poor, the pattern of much higher poverty in rural areas and the concentration of poverty in the former homelands and some of the provinces still holds.

c. Household Structure, Age, Gender, and Poverty

A household survey which collects most information for the entire household and not its individual members, cannot say much about the distribution of poverty among categories that cut across households since it does not collect any information on intrahousehold

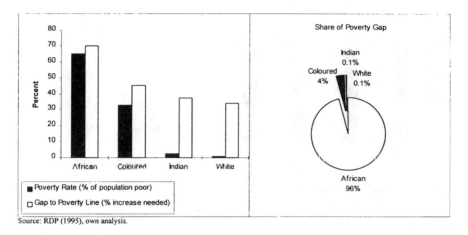

Source: RDP (1995), own analysis.

Figure 5. Poverty Rates and Poverty Gap by Race

resource allocation. For example, it is not possible to say with much precision how many females, or children, or seniors are poor, since a household survey cannot tell how many females or children who live in non-poor households receive so few resources that they should be classified as poor.[19] Instead, it is only possible to determine how many females or children live in poor households. In addition, it is possible to examine whether particular household *types* are more prone to poverty than others.

Such an analysis yields that household size and poverty are closely related. Large households with many dependants are disproportionately represented among the poor. The average household size among the poor is 5.9, compared to 3.5 among the non-poor. Children, who predominate in large households, therefore suffer from higher poverty than average, with 60% of children living in poor households.

In addition, female-headed households are overrepresented among the poor. Figure 6 shows that the poverty rates among female-headed households, both *de jure* (where the head is officially female) and *de facto* (where the head is in practice female, since the official male head is absent for most of the year), are much higher than for households with a resident male head. In rural areas, *de jure* female-headed households have an 82% poverty rate, making this group one of the most deprived of all.

At the same time, the distance to the poverty line does not differ much between household types suggesting that household struc-

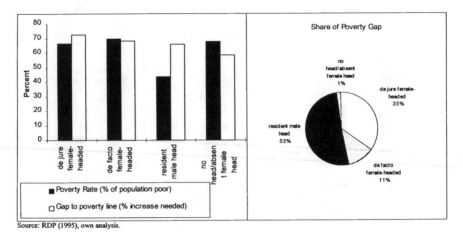

Source: RDP (1995), own analysis.

Figure 6. Poverty Rates and Poverty Gap by Household Structure

ture, while correlated with the *incidence* of poverty, is not a very good predictor for the *severity* of poverty. Female-headed households account for about 46% of the poverty gap, while making up 37% of the population.

Slightly more women than men live in poor households which is mostly due to female-headed households having, on average, more females than males living in them.[20] 52% of the elderly live in poor households, equal to the national average. The lack of disproportionate poverty among the elderly is due to the fact that the majority of elderly (esp. among Africans, coloureds, and Indians) do not live alone, while those that do either have access to sufficient private resources or the non-contributory social pensions which are sufficient to lift a single elderly above the poverty line (Case and Deaton, 1996).[21]

d. Education and Poverty

One of the factors resulting in the high poverty among blacks has been their much-reduced access to quality education during the *apartheid* years. To illustrate the importance of this factor, Figure 7 shows poverty rates in households according to the education levels of the household head.[22] Households whose heads have no education have a poverty rate of nearly 80%, compared to only 7% among those households where the head has at least a completed secondary education. Moreover, poverty is much deeper among households

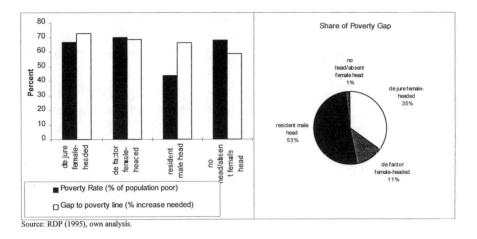

Source: RDP (1995), own analysis.

Figure 7. Poverty Rates and Poverty Gap by Education of Household Head

with poorly educated heads; those with no education would require a boost of over 80% of incomes in order to reach the poverty line. The importance of lack of education as a cause of poverty is powerfully demonstrated by the share of the poverty gap: 84% of the poverty gap is accounted for by households whose heads have less than completed primary education.

e. Employment, Wages, and Poverty

Poverty and unemployment are closely linked. Using the broad definition of unemployment (all people not working who would like to work and are either actively seeking work or have given up looking)[23], Table V shows that the unemployment rate among the poorest quintile (the ultra-poor) is 53%, compared to only 4% among the richest 20% of households. Among racial groups, Africans have a much higher unemployment rate than all other groups. In addition, the female unemployment rate is at 36%, much higher than the male rate (26%).[24] Finally, unemployment in rural areas is nearly twice as high as in metropolitan areas. The SALDRU survey finds an overall unemployment rate of 30%; the CSS October 1994 Household Survey found an unemployment rate of 33%, with similar differences by race, gender, and location.

In addition, labour force participation also differs by quintile with many working-age poor being out of the labour force due to illness, disability, catching up with education, or domestic responsibilities. Less than half of the poor are in the labour force. Since more than half of those are unemployed, less than 23% in the poorest quintile are actually working (Table V).

Since many households contain several working-age adults, high unemployment would not be so drastic if at least one person was working in every household. The last line of Table V shows, however, that this is not the case for many poor households. Nearly half of the population on the poorest quintile lives in households where no one is working, i.e. every adult member of those households is either unemployed or out of the labour force.

With such high unemployment and, in many cases, not a single household member working, many of the poor and ultra poor have to rely for their survival on multiple sources of income as a coping strategy with wages being just one element (May, 1996).

Figure 8 calculates the average shares of income sources for ultra poor (poorest 20%) and poor (poorest 40%) households. Social pensions and remittances each play a role as important as wages[25] in ultra-poor households (the poorest 20%). The reliance on transfers, both public (pensions and other government grants including disability grants, poor relief, workmen's compensation) and private (remittances) is very large among very poor households, exceeding 50% of total income in the average ultra-poor households and 45% in poor households. The dependence on remittances is particularly strong among the rural poor where it accounts for 24% of households income alone.

A combination of factors account for this high dependence levels of poor households. They include the *apartheid* migrant labour system which separated the employment and home for many households which explains the importance of remittances, particularly in rural areas; an economy that ceased to generate employment since the early 1980s, leading to ever-increasing unemployment rates (Da Silva, 1994); and the equalisation of pensions to all population groups in the early 1990s, making social pensions an increasingly important safety net (Ardington and Lund, 1995; Case and Deaton, 1996).

In addition to high unemployment and high reliance on private and public transfers, low wages plague those among the poor who

TABLE V

Unemployment and Participation Rates by Race, Gender, and Location (%)*

	All South Africans	Households Ranked by Consumption Quintiles				
		Quin. 1 (Poorest)	Quin. 2	Quin. 3	Quin. 4	Quin. 5 (Richest)
Race						
African	38.3	54.3	44.2	32.0	19.7	13.1
Coloured	20.8	34.3	32.5	21.2	14.5	6.8
Indian	11.3	**	**	23.3	12.6	3.7
White	4.3	**	**	25.8	9.4	2.8
Gender						
Female	35.1	56.7	46.2	37.2	23.3	5.8
Male	25.5	50.2	40.5	24.4	13.2	3.3
Location						
Rural	39.7	53.7	44.3	30.6	13.2	5.9
Urban	25.6	49.9	38.5	30.3	16.1	4.2
Metropolitan	21.3	58.3	45.0	30.3	19.5	4.2
Total	29.9	53.4	43.3	30.4	17.1	4.4
Participation rate	61.1	49.5	55.4	62.5	69.5	76.5
Working	42.7	22.9	31.3	43.3	57.6	73.0
Share of People living in households with no one working	29.5	49.0	36.5	21.5	10.5	6.3

* The unemployment rate is calculated by dividing the number of people aged 16–64 who are not working but would like to work (and are either actively seeking work or have given up looking) by the number of people in the labour force (defined as those currently employed plus those not working who would like to work).
** too few observations in these cells to calculate reliable rates.
Source: RDP (1995), own analysis.

are employed (Table VI). Particularly in rural areas, these jobs are characterised by low productivity, little job security, and vastly fluctuating demand, so that they represent a poor and rather unstable source of income. Thus while more jobs and employment opportunities is clearly important to reduce poverty, better jobs for those that are employed is another high priority.[26] Table VI also shows that there is a considerable racial wage gap which is mostly linked to a discriminatory education and training system as well as the effects of past labour market discrimination against blacks.

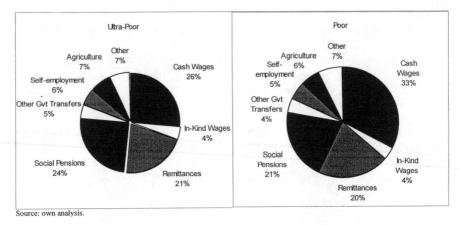

Source: own analysis.

Figure 8. Sources of Income (%) for Poor and Ultra-Poor Households

TABLE VI

Average Household Total Monthly Wage by Race and Expenditure Quintile (in Rand)*

	All South Africans	Households Ranked by Consumption Quintiles					
		Poorest Quin. (Ultra)	Quin. 2	**Poorest 40% (Poor)**	Quin. 3	Quin. 4	Quin. 5 (Richest)
African	757	281	519	**397**	859	1254	2652
Coloured	1744	485	862	**745**	1500	2292	3165
Indian	3371	**	1081	**1081**	1148	2496	5661
White	4695	**	1073	**1073**	1091	2620	5055
All	1598	287	546	**417**	930	1611	4689

* Includes households who reported regular or casual wage incomes.
** Too few observations in these cells to calculate reliable rates.

5. POVERTY AND OTHER DEPRIVAATIONS

a. *Access to Services*

Access to services such as water, electricity, and sanitation is an important indicator of well-being, as it directly improves quality of life. It also has great instrumental significance for health outcomes and the time available for employment and income-earning activities.

There is a great disparity in the living conditions and access to services between the poor and the non-poor population. Table VII

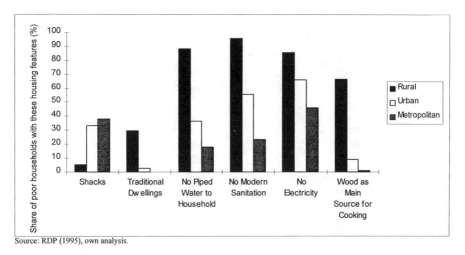

Source: RDP (1995), own analysis.

Figure 9. Housing Characteristics of the Poor by Location

details some of the most serious shortcomings for poor households, including the high incidence of poor housing and crowding, and the little access to piped water, modern sanitation, or electricity. This lack of access is particularly severe among the rural poor who are considerably worse off in most indicators of service access than their urban and metropolitan counterparts (Figure 9).

The poor access to services has a direct negative impact for well-being. In addition, it places a great burden on women who have to spend long hours fetching water and wood. A detailed analysis shows that about 80% of poor rural African households spend an average of four hours a day fetching water and firewood. More than 80% of the people fetching the water and wood are women (RDP, 1995). Finally, the poor access to clean water, and proper sanitation has a negative impact on health through its effects on the spread of communicable diseases.

b. Access to Land and Irrigation in Rural Areas

About 42% of the rural poor are dependent to some extent on crop or livestock production (Table VIII). Due largely to *apartheid* land policies, the rural poor have very little access to land. Only about 28% of the rural poor have access to some land for crop production, 80% of which is communally owned and much of it is of poor quality. The inequality in cropland access and use between quintiles

TABLE VII
Selected Housing Characteristics of South African Households by Expenditure Quintile

| | All South Africa* | Poorest Quin. (Ultra) | Quintile 2 | Households Ranked by Consumption Quintiles | | | |
				Poorest 40% (Poor)	Quintile 3	Quintile 4	Quintile 5 (Richest)
Percent Living in Shacks or Traditional Dwelling**	22.6	39.0	31.6	35.3	25.4	15.2	1.6
Persons per Room (Crowding)	1.4	2.3	1.7	2.0	1.4	1.0	0.5
% of Households with:							
Electricity[27]	53.4	15.1	27.7	21.4	49.4	77.3	97.5
Piped Water to Household***	58.9	18.9	36.4	27.5	59.9	82.0	97.6
Flush Toilet and Improved Latrine	53.0	11.3	25.5	18.4	50.2	80.8	97.5
Wood as Main Source for Cooking	23.7	59.9	35.3	47.6	16.8	4.1	0.2

* the CSS 1994 October Household Survey found very similar results on all these items.
** some observations in the housing data were adjusted to align the house type classification with data on wall and ceiling materials.
*** this refers to internal or yard taps.
Source: RDP (1995).

TABLE VIII
Crop Land Access and Use in Rural Areas

	All Rural South Africa	Households Ranked by Consumption Groups Quintiles				
		Quin. 1 (Ultra)	Quin. 2	Quin. 3	Quin. 4	Quin. 5 (Richest)
Percentage of Households in Crop and/or Livestock Production	36.8	42.3	42.7	32.1	21.9	22.0
Percentage of Households with Access to Land	26.2	27.5	28.1	25.8	18.4	28.1
Average Size of Land Per Capita Used Last Year (hectares)	4.6	0.3	0.4	0.8	4.5	63.7
Percentage of Available Land Communally Owned	69.2	84.5	70.0	65.6	55.0	15.5
Percentage of Available Land Privately Owned	26.8	13.5	26.0	29.1	44.0	70.6
Main Source of Water for Croplands (% households)						
–Rain/River	92.7	97.4	98.3	94.6	84.4	45.6
–Irrigation (borehole, dam, municipality)	5.8	2.3	1.2	2.2	12.5	46.5

Source: RDP (1995).

is considerable, ranging from 0.3 hectares per capita for the ultra poor to 64 hectares for the richest quintile. In addition, there is large inequality in the access to irrigation.

c. Households Debt and Financial Services

Due to the seasonality and irregularity of many of their income sources, many poor households are forced to carry a considerable debt burden. On average, poor households spend 10% of their monthly income on debt service and have a debt load of about 35% of monthly expenditures (Table IX). While richer groups have much higher levels of debt, relative to their incomes, they also pay around 10% of their monthly income on debt service. This suggests much worse terms of credit for poor households, including higher interest rates and shorter repayment periods. This is not surprising given that

TABLE IX
Debt Burden and Source of Credit

	All South Africa	Households Ranked by Consumption Quintiles				
		Quin. 1 (Ultra-Poor)	Quin. 2	Quin. 3	Quin. 4	Quin. 5 (Richest)
Amount Owed (% of monthly expenditure)	161.0	33.4	40.7	56.6	104.4	226.0
Debt Service (% of monthly expenditure)	8.7	9.8	7.8	8.0	10.3	8.7
Source of Credit:						
Banks	8.4	0	0.4	1.8	6.1	27.0
Hire Purchase	30.4	17.5	29.4	39.5	33.9	27.6
Shopkeepers	33.7	48.2	37.4	31.6	32.3	25.7
Relatives/Friends	12.9	21.2	16.0	12.0	12.3	7.0
Other*	14.6	13.1	16.8	15.1	13.4	12.7

* includes government schemes, NGOs, money-lenders, stokvels, burial societies, employers, and miscellaneous sources (none of which exceed 5% individually).
Source: own analysis.

the poor have no access to formal financial services with the exception of limited access to hire-purchase. Instead, they rely mostly on shop-keepers and informal sources of credit.

d. The Burden of Transport To and From Work

Due to the *apartheid* policies regarding the spatial segregation of the various racial groups and the lack of a commensurate public transport system, transport has become a major constraint for the poorer population. Consequently, the working poor (as well as middle-income groups) spend a large amount of time and money on transportation (Table X). This reduces their take-home earnings, increases their cost of living, and reduces mobility for the poor, an important indicator of well-being. In addition, high accident rates pose an additional safety risk for those forced to commute long distances.

More than 60% of the ultra poor walk to work,[28] another 27% use buses or taxis. Among middle-income groups (quintiles 3 and

TABLE X
Transportation Modes, Times, and Costs*

	All South Africa	Households Ranked by Consumption Quintiles				
		Quin. 1 (Ultra)	Quin. 2	Quin.3	Quin. 4	Quin. 5 (Richest)
Types of Transport Used to go to Work (%):						
Bus	11.5	11.3	15.5	15.0	12.1	5.7
Taxi	24.5	16.3	28.9	38.6	33.3	7.0
Car/Motorbike	30.1	6.5	7.3	9.8	26.1	76.7
Walk	28.3	62.1	42.3	28.6	21.3	8.1
Other	5.6	3.8	6.0	8.0	7.2	2.5
Transport Time (min.)**	72.5	66.3	76.6	83.7	79.7	57.4
Av.Transport Cost (R.)**	5.4	3.0	4.0	4.5	5.3	7.2

* The CSS October 1994 Household Survey found very similar results.
** people who walk to work are excluded in the calculation of average transport costs. Transport times and costs are per return trip.
Source: RDP (1995).

4), buses and taxis are used much more frequently, while the richest rely predominantly on car. All income groups, with the exception of the richest quintile, spend more than one hour in transit to and from work, with transport times being particularly high for middle-income groups who have to rely on buses and taxis to get to work. While transport costs rise with income, they constitute a much larger share of expenditure (more than 30% in some cases) among the working poor.[29]

e. Education

Education has important instrumental significance for well-being through its impact on earnings and employment (see above). At the same time, it has considerable intrinsic value as one of the most basic capabilities.

The history of lack of access to basic education for blacks and large differences in the quality of schooling has led to significant differences in the educational attainment of the various racial and income groups (Table XI). About 50% of the poor have no education

TABLE XI

Highest Educational Attainment by Quintile (% of individuals 16+ who have achieved each level)*

	Quin. 1 (Ultra- Poor)	Quin. 2	**Poorest 40% (Poor)**	Quin. 3	Quin. 4	Quin. 5 (Richest)	Total
No Education	23.9	17.5	**21.3**	12.9	7.3	5.6	14.7
Primary-Incomplete	30.5	24.8	**28.1**	20.1	13.5	3.3	20.0
Primary-Complete	11.3	11.0	**11.2**	10.0	7.4	1.5	8.8
Secondary-Incomplete	30.1	38.4	**33.6**	44.6	48.6	27.3	37.5
Secondary-Complete	3.7	7.3	**5.0**	10.4	16.7	32.5	12.6
Tertiary- Incomplete	0.5	0.9	**0.8**	7.3	5.5	19.5	4.7
Tertiary Degree	0.0	0.0	**0.0**	0.2	0.6	10.3	1.8

* The CSS October 1994 Household Survey found very similar results.
Source: RDP (1995).

or only incomplete primary education, and only 7% have completed secondary or higher education. In contrast, among the richest quintile, 62% have at least completed secondary education. The rural poor are, once again, worse off than their urban and metropolitan counterparts. 53% of poor rural adults have less than primary education, compared to 31% for the metropolitan poor. As already shown in Figure 8, these large discrepancies in educational attainment have a major impact on the differences in employment opportunities and wages between the rich and poor (Schultz and Mwabu, 1995).

While educational attainment affects the labour market opportunities of today's adults, net enrolment rates give an indication of future income-earning opportunities of today's youth (Table XII). While people in richer quintiles have higher net primary enrolment rates[30] than people in poorer quintiles, the differences are not very large, suggesting that there has been a considerable expansion of education at the primary level in recent years (Fuller, Pillay and Sirur, 1995). Secondary and tertiary enrolment rates are, however, closely associated with income, showing that educational opportunities at these levels continue to be very uneven. In addition, great differences in the quality of education available to different income and racial groups further exacerbate differences in future income-earning opportunities than those suggested by the enrolment data.

TABLE XII

Net Enrolment Rates by Quintile (% of Relevant Age Group who are Enrolled)

	Primary*	Secondary	Tertiary
Quintile 1 (Ultra-Poor)	85	46	4
Quintile 2	87	57	5
Quintile 3	88	67	8
Quintile 4	89	78	20
Quintile 5 (Richest)	90	83	38
Total	87	60	11

* Due to some children entering school later than normal and some children accelerating their education (i.e. moving to secondary education although they still are primary school age), net enrolment rates of 100% are unlikely to be achieved (see note 30). For the calculation of primary school enrolment, the school age was assumed to be 6–12 years, for secondary 13–17, for tertiary 18–23.
Source: RDP (1995).

Thus education has not only been found to be a major cause of poverty (see above), but a consequence of poverty is lower access to quality education, thereby serving to reproduce poverty inter-generationally.

There are no significant differences in the school achievement and school enrolment by gender. In fact, among the poorer quintiles, girls have higher primary and secondary enrolment rates.

f. Health

Good health is another basic capability and is, in addition, of critical importance for employment and income-earning opportunities. Unfortunately, differences in health status are difficult to measure without a physical examination or reference to objectively measured morbidity and mortality rates. In the absence of this, reliance on respondent's own perception of their health status often leads to biases since better educated and objectively healthier people are typically more concerned about their health status and report being sick even if they suffer from comparatively minor ailments. In contrast, health awareness among poorer groups is often lower and leads to a lower reported incidence of ill health, despite objectively worse health indicators (Sen, 1992).

TABLE XIII
Proportion Suffering from Each Illness among those who were Ill in Two Weeks
Prior to Survey (%)*

	Quintile 1 (Ultra-Poor)	Quintile 2	Quintile 3	Quintile 4	Quintile 5	Total
Tuberculosis	4.0	3.5	3.8	1.7	0.6	2.9
Diarrhoea	9.3	7.5	5.0	3.5	3.3	6.0
Fever	9.7	7.5	7.7	5.5	2.5	6.9
Physical Disability	4.0	4.9	4.1	2.0	2.3	3.6
Mental Disability	6.8	5.5	4.8	1.4	0.0	4.0

* % of individuals reporting an illness in the two weeks prior to survey, who
complained of a particular symptom.
Source: RDP (1995).

The SALDRU survey methodology fell victim to this bias and
found that the wealthy reported a higher prevalence of ill health
than the poor. Despite this, the nature of the health problems listed
gave some clue towards the true state of health among the poor.
The health problems listed in Table XIII are all related to poverty
and demonstrate the higher prevalence of diseases of poverty among
lower income groups, including tuberculosis, diarrhoea, and fever.
In addition, the much higher rates of mental disability among the
poor are an indication of poor mental health facilities as well as the
likely influence of violence and trauma on many poor people.

The survey did undertake a physical examination of the heights
and weights of a subsample of children which allows a more objective assessment of their health status. It shows that poor children
suffer from much higher rates of chronic undernutrition (stunting,
i.e. insufficient height for age, Figure 10). Among ultra-poor children below the age of five, 38% suffer from stunting. This rate is
only 6% for the richest quintile.[31]

There are also clear differences in the type of treatments available
for different expenditure groups (Table XIV). While the richer segments of the population rely mostly on private doctors for treatment,
the poor have much more limited options: 26% seek no treatment
at all. Of those, more than half cite high costs of treatment and/or
transport as the major reason for not seeking treatment for their illness, suggesting a clear lack of affordable health care for the poorest

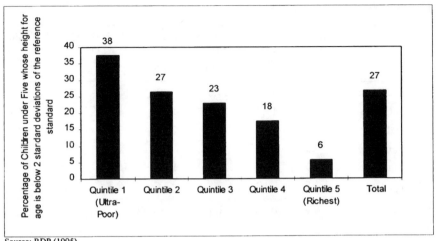

Source: RDP (1995).

Figure 10. Stunting Rates by Quintile (%)

segments of the population. Another 40% rely on health centres and hospitals, while less than a quarter seek help from a private doctor. This heavy use of hospitals suggests low availability of quality primary health care at the level of clinics/health centres; consequently, this is a major cause for very high health care costs to the State, since hospitals use their expensive and specialised facilities for primary health care for the poor.[32]

The treatment options available not only affect the quality of the care received, but also cost of treatment, transport and waiting time. While costs of treatment for richer groups are much higher, due to their predominant reliance on the private sector, even the poor have to pay substantial amounts for care (esp. those that use the private sector due to the perceived lack of availability of quality care in the public sector) In relation to monthly income, the treatment costs exceed 10% of monthly income for the ultra-poor (RDP, 1995).

In addition, the poor have to travel and wait much longer. The poorest travel for nearly two hours to and from the place of treatment and spend, on average, another 45 minutes waiting for medical attention (RDP, 1995).

TABLE XIV
Type of Treatment Sought* (%)

	Quin. 1 (Ultra-Poor)	Quin. 2	**Poorest 40% (Poor)**	Quin. 3	Quin. 4	Quin. 5	Total
Private Doctor	23.4	31.3	**27.6**	41.0	52.6	72.8	43.6
Health Centre	17.9	17.4	**17.6**	16.4	9.3	2.3	12.9
Hospital	27.7	26.3	**27.0**	24.8	17.9	6.2	20.9
Traditional Healer	3.5	2.6	**3.0**	1.9	1.0	0.5	2.0
No Treatment	24.9	19.4	**22.0**	12.6	16.4	14.6	17.7
Other	2.5	2.9	**2.8**	2.4	2.3	3.7	2.7

* % of individuals reporting ill who obtained treatment from a particular provider.
Source: RDP (1995).

g. *Poverty, Levels of Satisfaction, and Need for Government Support*

The survey, which was conducted in late 1993, asked questions regarding people's own perception of their quality of life. The contrasts by levels of expenditure are considerable and closely related to income (Table XV). While rich people are predominantly satisfied with their current living situation, poor people are predominantly dissatisfied. The high dissatisfaction among the poor could be a result of their poor absolute living conditions as well as a result of their position in a highly unequal society.

The vast majority of the poor also indicate that they are poorer than their parent's generation (Table XV). What is most striking is that all quintiles, with the exception of the richest, state that this generation is poorer than the previous one, suggesting a strong sense of economic decline among the vast majority of the population.

There is an important difference in the levels of satisfaction between the rural, urban, and metropolitan poor. While all poor are predominantly dissatisfied with their current living situation, Figure 11 shows that the metropolitan poor have a much higher rate of respondents being 'very dissatisfied' which may translate into more vocal calls to address their needs over those of the many more numerous rural poor.

TABLE XV
Perceived Quality of Life (% in each Quintile who have the following perceptions)

	Quin. 1 (Ultra-Poor)	Quin. 2	Poorest 40% (Poor)	Quin. 3	Quin. 4	Quin. 5 (Richest)	Total
Very Satisfied	2.2	3.3	**2.8**	5.2	8.3	21.2	8.0
Satisfied	14.3	19.0	**16.7**	23.9	30.4	48.5	27.1
Neither/Nor	9.3	8.8	**9.1**	8.8	9.1	9.9	9.2
Dissatisfied	44.8	40.9	**42.3**	36.0	26.2	13.5	32.4
Very Dissatisfied	29.3	28.0	**28.7**	26.1	26.0	6.9	23.4
Compared with Parents:							
Richer	12.1	19.4	**15.3**	24.2	26.0	42.9	24.9
The Same	18.9	21.3	**19.7**	24.8	26.0	25.1	23.2
Poorer	69.0	59.3	**65.0**	51.0	48.0	32.0	51.9

Source: RDP (1995), own analysis.

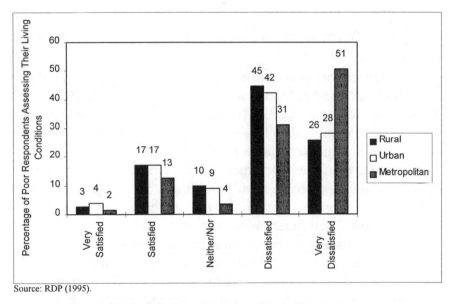

Source: RDP (1995).

Figure 11. Satisfaction Levels among the Poor by Location

The survey also asked for the three most important things government could do to help. The results, presented in Table XVI, show that the poor want the government to help the most with jobs, piped water, housing, food aid, electricity, and schools. The greatest concern for the richest, however, are jobs, housing, peace, and

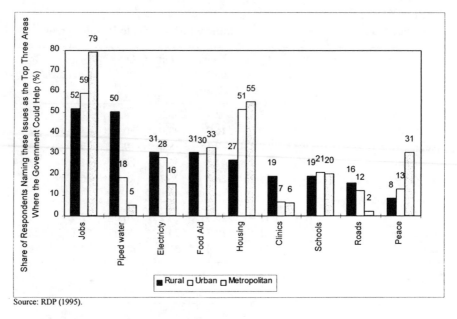

Source: RDP (1995).

Figure 12. Where Government could help the Poor the Most by Location

schools; the importance of peace as a concern may be largely due
to the high levels of political violence prevailing in late 1993 when
the survey was conducted. It is interesting to note that housing,
while high on everybody's list, appears to be a particularly pressing
concern among middle-income groups (quintiles 3 and 4).

The majority of the poor expect the government to improve conditions for them. Overall, most households expect government to
improve their economic conditions; only in the richest quintile does
a majority fear a deterioration of their situation.

Figure 12 disaggregates the concerns for government action by
location. Jobs are a top priority for rural, urban, and metropolitan poor. At the same time, housing and peace are more pressing
concerns for the metropolitan poor, reflecting the current housing
shortage and the security situation (in late 1993) in metropolitan
areas. For the rural poor, piped water is as important as job creation. Moreover, electricity, clinics, and roads are much more pressing concerns for the rural poor than their urban and metropolitan
counterparts.

TABLE XVI

Where Could the Government Help Most? (% in each Quintile who name the following issues among the three items the government could help most with)

	Quin. 1 (Ultra-Poor)	Quin. 2	Poorest 40% (Poor)	Quin. 3	Quin. 4	Quin. 5 (Richest)	Total
Jobs	57.8	54.0	**55.9**	57.5	58.6	˙56.6	57.3
Housing	32.1	36.1	**34.1**	42.8	42.7	37.1	38.6
Food Aid	34.3	26.6	**30.6**	17.2	13.5	10.6	19.9
Piped Water	44.2	37.0	**40.6**	25.1	9.2	7.8	24.2
Electricity	27.3	30.1	**28.7**	24.7	13.2	9.8	20.4
Schools	19.9	19.8	**20.1**	22.3	18.5	19.9	19.2
Clinics	18.1	13.9	**16.0**	12.1	7.9	8.3	11.8
Peace/End of Violence	9.2	13.8	**11.5**	24.9	39.2	35.0	27.1
Predicted Effect of New Government on Household:							
Better	72.0	68.9	**70.6**	62.5	57.3	17.7	56.0
The Same	14.8	15.4	**15.0**	15.4	16.6	28.0	18.0
Worse	13.2	15.8	**14.4**	22.2	26.1	54.4	26.0

The totals exceed 100% since people were asked to name the 3 most important things government could do.
Source: RDP (1995), own analysis.

6. IDENTIFYING THE MOST DEPRIVED: INCOME AND NON-INCOME MEASURES

As discussed above, this section examines results based on a composite indicator of deprivation, including income, health, education, access to services, and perceptions of well-being. While the average scores need to be disaggregated carefully for a detailed interpretation, scores above 4.5 suggest a very high living standard similar to the ones prevailing among the middle class and above in first-world countries, scores above 3 are sufficient for a life with moderate prospects, resources, and services, and scores below 2.5 suggest severe deprivation, multiple threats to health and welfare, and very poor human resources and prospects.

The average score for the entire population is 3.03. About 8.7% have a score below 2 suggesting extreme deprivation, 53.1% a score below 3 needed for a basic levels of resources, services, and well-

TABLE XVII

Comparing Expenditure Quintiles to Composite Deprivation Index

	Quin. 1 (Poorest)	Quin. 2	Quin. 3	Quin. 4	Quin. 5 (Richest)	Total
Composite Deprivation Index:						
Average	2.27	2.68	3.12	3.69	4.45	3.03
Share of population (%):						
< 2	24.4	6.0	1.3	0.1	0	8.7
2–3	68.1	64.8	37.9	12.0	0.6	44.4
3–3.5	6.8	22.2	30.7	20.9	2.2	26.6
3.5–4.5	0.7	7.0	29.9	62.1	39.4	26.0
>4.5	0	0	0.1	4.9	57.8	6.9

Source: own analysis.

being. 6.9% of the population score 4.5 or above suggesting that they are doing very well in all the components included in the indicator.

Table XVII shows that there is, on average, a close correlation between income poverty and the composite index of deprivation. People in the richest quintile score nearly twice as high as people in the poorest quintile. This is not surprising given the close correlation between income and non-income measures such as education, health, access to services, and the like. While true on average, it is far from a perfect correlation with people in the various quintiles spread across several categories of deprivation scores (Table XVII).

For the purposes of analysing poverty and deprivation, it may be most important to compare the most deprived groups as measured by income poverty and by the composite index. Table XVIII takes the 29% worst off in terms of income poverty (the poorest quintile of households) and the composite deprivation index (scores up to 2.4) and compares their characteristics. While, by definition, all of the income poor are drawn from the poorest quintile, about 35% of the most severely deprived are actually drawn from quintiles 2,3, and even 4. This amounts to about 3.7 million severely deprived people who are apparently 'missed' by the income poverty measure.

Their average income is higher than that of people in the poorest quintile (R.190 vs. R.117), suggesting that their higher incomes are more than off-set by other deprivations. This is borne out by all the other indicators where the worst off in the deprivation measure do much worse than the people in the poorest quintile. A significantly larger number of people is drawn from households with no one in employment; more depend on pensions and remittances; their housing and access to water, sanitation, and energy sources is significantly worse; a much higher rate of children is stunted and the average education levels are much worse; finally, they are considerably more dissatisfied than people in the poorest quintile.

When it comes to race and location of the most deprived group, there are also considerable differences between the two indicators. While both indicators put over half of the worst-off people in Eastern Cape and Northern Province, the deprivation index finds that KwaZulu/Natal is home to about 24% of the most severely deprived, as opposed to 'only' 14.5% in the poorest quintile. Conversely, the deprivation index has much lower shares for all other provinces. The reason for the much higher share of KwaZulu/Natal in the deprivation index than in the poorest income quintile is mostly due to the much worse levels of housing and services (water, sanitation, energy sources) available in the rural areas of the province, while prevailing income and employment levels are slightly better than in rural areas of other provinces. Finally, the deprivation index suggests that virtually 100% of the most severely deprived are Africans, while the income poverty measures finds 3% coloureds among the worst off.

This discussion suggests that, while corresponding relatively closely, there are significant differences between the two methods of identifying the most deprived groups. The income poverty measure seems to miss groups of people who have slightly higher incomes, but are deprived in multiple other ways. About 90% of the group 'missed' by the income poverty indicator are Africans from rural areas, drawn to a large extent from KwaZulu/Natal (41% or 1.5 million of the about 3.7 million 'missed'). This suggests that Africans in rural areas, particularly in KwaZulu/Natal, are more deprived on a broader scale than their expenditure levels would suggest.

The considerable differences in income-based and broader measures of deprivation indicates the need to examine broader measures of deprivation for policy and targeting purposes. In household surveys such as the SALDRU surveys, the data for such broader measures is readily available and can be used to develop such broader indicators of well-being and deprivation.

TABLE XVIII

Characteristics of the Most Deprived using Income-Based Measure and Deprivation Index (share of people living in households with the following characteristics)

	Income Poverty (Poorest Quin.)	Deprivation Index (up to 2.4 average score)
1. Expenditure, employment, and income sources		
Average monthly adult equivalent expenditure (R.)	117.3	190.9
% in poorest expenditure quintile	100.0	65.1
% in quintile 2	0	26.4
% in quintile 3 or above	0	8.5
% of people with no one in household employed	49.0	58.6
% of income from pensions and remittances	47.1	54.6
2. Housing and Access to Services		
% living in shacks or traditional dwellings	54.0	73.9
% without piped water to household	81.2	95.4
% without modern sanitation	88.6	98.4
% using wood as main source of fuel for cooking	63.6	79.7
3. Education, health, and satisfaction		
% with less than two years of average education per adult	23.6	30.1
% with less than five years of average education	80.6	86.1
% of households with all children stunted	16.8	24.5
% dissatisfied or very dissatisfied	73.0	80.2
4. Race and location		
% living in rural areas	80.7	90.1
% living in metropolitan areas	5.3	2.6
% living in Eastern Cape and Northern Province	52.0	52.4
% living in KwaZulu/Natal	14.5	23.6
% living in North-West, Free State, and Mpumalanga	27.0	20.5
% living in Gauteng, Western Cape, and Northern Cape	6.6	3.3
% African	97.1	99.3
% Coloured	2.9	0.7

Source: RDP (1995), own analysis.

7. CONCLUSION

The SALDRU survey gives a comprehensive picture of poverty and inequality in South Africa on the eve of the inauguration of the new government. As such, it provides an important baseline against which to monitor the progress of the new government in its determination to reduce poverty and inequality in coming years.

The analysis has shown that the legacy of *apartheid* has left the majority of the population in poverty, with little access to employment, education, health, or other basic services. It enforced a spatially unsustainable residential pattern, leaving a majority of the poor in economically marginal areas of the country, dependent on transfers and whatever incomes they could eke out of the available resource base. While the racial nature of poverty is obvious and ever-present in all indicators, there are also important gender differentials. Women suffer from higher unemployment, less access to services, a high burden associated with carrying water and wood, and higher dependence on uncertain transfers. Unfortunately, a household survey does not permit a more precise disaggregation of gender differentials at the household level, thereby leaving the potentially most important source of gender bias unexamined.

The analysis also shows that income poverty is closely related to other capability failures such as poor health, poor mobility, poor education, and poor access to services. This is not altogether surprising, since many of these inequalities are a result of past government policy. While a comparison between the broader index of deprivation and income poverty bears out this close correlation, it also identified important differences. In particular, the broader measure of deprivation, which is readily available in a comprehensive household survey such as the SALDRU survey, is able to identify a group of people that is suffering from far higher levels of deprivation than suggested by the income poverty measure alone.

It should also be pointed out that the close correlation between income poverty and broader deprivation does not mean that income poverty reduction alone will solve the problem of multiple deprivations. While the reduction of income poverty is one of the important ways to reduce many of these deprivations, there are other possible strategies that focus directly on reducing the specific non-income deprivations suffered (Dreze and Sen, 1989). The challenge will be to find the right mix of strategies to have the maximum impact.

A particularly important aspect of the survey are the perceptions and aspirations of the population. In contrast to the often-heard suggestion that the poor may be just as satisfied and happy as the wealthy, South Africa's poor are deeply dissatisfied with their current situation which left them in a position worse off than the previous generation. They expect government to assist them over the coming years to improve their economic position, and are confident that the government will do so. To what extent the government will be able to meet these expectations, will, to a considerable degree, determine the success of the current transition.

NOTES

[1] From January 1995 to October 1996, the author was working for the World Bank in Johannesburg and participated in the analysis of the SALDRU survey, including the document produced for the government summarising the results of the survey (RDP, 1995). He would like to thank Debbie Budlender, David Dickinson, Valerie Møller, Clive Pintusevitz, Emma Rothschild, Amartya Sen, Meena Singh, and Ingrid Woolard for helpful comments and discussions on earlier versions of this paper.

[2] The poverty rate and most of the quintile analysis is based on RDP (1995), while the poverty gap analysis and the composite indicator of deprivation is newly developed in this paper.

[3] Also, some may argue that poverty has, to a certain extent, take into consideration local conceptions and definitions of poverty which may differ in different communities. For a discussion, see May (1996).

[4] Since adult and elderly females require less nutrition than adult and elderly males, the implication of this method is that those females need less in general, which is a problematic assumption. It turns out, however, that adjusting for this bias has a negligible effect on the measured poverty rates (less than 2% increase in the relative poverty rate of females), including those of females or female-headed households, so that this bias does not alter the results by much.

[5] For details, refer to Collier (1986).

[6] In order to avoid double-counting, in most of the analysis, households were defined to exclude those who were away for more than 15 of the last 30 days prior to the survey.

[7] In order to measure progress in combating absolute poverty, analyses of future surveys will either have to apply the absolute cut-off implied by this definition (share of people below R.300 and R.178) and compare it to the share of poor in the SALDRU survey, or apply another absolute poverty line.

[8] As discussed earlier, throughout the paper expenditure levels are used as more reliable proxies for income (rather than reported income levels).

[9] The transfer concept is simply a way to conceptualise the depth of poverty; it is not intended as a policy proposal.

[10] Due to data limitations, all measures are applied at the household level and thus do not necessarily measure individual welfare within a given household adequately. Moreover, none of the measures include community characteristics that may have an impact on well-being and deprivation.

[11] There is a difference in treating missing observations among the indicators. For most indicators, the very few missing observations are assigned the average of the indicator. For stunting and health service utilisation, however, the many missing observations are excluded and the average will therefore exclude those components.

[12] with a Gini-coefficient of 0 signifying absolute equality and 1 indicating absolute concentration.

[13] The difference depends on whether within-race inequality is weighted by population (42%) or income (25%). The analysis is based on incomes, not expenditures.

[14] The classification of areas into rural, urban (towns and cities), and metropolitan (the four largest metropolitan areas including Johannesburg/Pretoria/Vereeniging, Cape Town, Durban, and Port Elizabeth) are made according to the CSS definitions.

[15] Whiteford et al. 1995 who uses an income-based HSL finds that only 66% of the total poverty gap is accounted for by rural areas, while 14% is due to poverty in metropolitan areas. This finding is largely dependent on the use of a poverty measure that assumes that rural people need less, the failure to adjust for the higher prices prevailing in rural areas, and a peculiar adjustment for remittance expenditures that artificially increases poverty in metropolitan areas. Despite these differences, it still finds disproportionate poverty in rural areas.

[16] Small differences in poverty rates (e.g. Northern Province versus Eastern Cape) are not always statistically significant and should be treated as indicative only. Also, the data for Northern Cape are based on a small sample and should be treated with some caution.

[17] Coloureds and Indians were allowed to live in the old provinces in specially designated areas, while Africans were only permitted to reside in the provinces if they had a pass, usually linked to employment, that entitled them to also reside in designated areas.

[18] Whites, coloureds, and Indians are concentrated in urban and metropolitan areas, where they together constitute nearly half the population, while Africans constitute 97% of the rural population. Whites reside predominantly in Gauteng, Western Cape, and the Free State, while coloureds reside predominantly in Western Cape, and Indians reside predominantly in KwaZulu/Natal.

[19] Due to the paucity of interracial households in South Africa, poverty by race can still, with considerable reliability, be determined at the household level. This is likely to change as interracial households are bound to increase.

[20] On average, 50% of children are female, 50% male; thus if the male head of household is absent, the sex ratio of the household will, on average, be tilted towards females. In addition, female-headed households include single women households which are, by definition, entirely female.

[21] The social pension (R370 per month in 1993) would put an individual elderly above the poverty line. In fact, the generosity of this transfer has led to many poor people to live with their elderly relatives to partake in this benefit (see Figure 8).

[22] This analysis excludes about 1% of households which reported no household head.

[23] Most countries use a narrower definition of unemployment which excludes from the unemployed those who have given up looking. Using this narrower definition, the survey found that the unemployment rate in South Africa is 12.8%.

[24] In addition, the unemployment rate for women may be an underestimate, since many women who declared that they were housewives and therefore out of the labour force would actually like to work outside of the home and should therefore properly be counted among the unemployed.

[25] In-kind wages include food, travel, and housing support. While important for the poor, their share in total income is much larger among the non-poor (over 7% of household income).

[26] Sender (1996) and ILO (1996) argue that this survey as well as others have undercounted poor employed people and thereby overstated the unemployment rate, esp. in rural areas. While there may have been a small undercount of some employed people (including miners and some farmworkers), the evidence presented does not convincingly suggest that all available surveys (which are quite consistent with each other) erred to a significant extent in the same way.

[27] This figure is higher than that reported by DBSA in its regional human development profile (DBSA 1994). One reason for the discrepancy may be that the DBSA figure refers to an earlier time period, after which ESKOM launched a major electrification campaign; another is that the household survey included illegal hook-ups, which are not counted in most other available data. The CSS October 1994 Household Survey found an electrification rate of 50%.

[28] This is only partly a reflection of the absence of any affordable transport. In many rural areas, people live on the farms they work on or within walking distance of their place of work so that other forms of transport (to and from work) are not necessary. At the same time, it does reflect considerable difficulties to get to places other than work.

[29] None of these estimates include the long and costly commutes many working poor have to make on weekends or holidays to their more permanent places of residence.

[30] Net enrolment rates refer to the share of people of a certain age group who are in the school-level prescribed for that age group, e.g. the number of 6–12 years old children who are enrolled in primary school divided by the total number of 6–12 years old children. The gross enrolment rate refers to the number of students (regardless of age group) divided by the age cohort that should be in that school-level. The difference between gross and net enrolment rates is particularly large in South Africa due to the presence of many older students in schools and universities who are trying to make up for their earlier lack of educational opportunities.

[31] Since stunting is determined based on 95% confidence that the child in question is malnourished (rather than simply a well-nourished but unusually short child), one should always expect 5% of children to be wrongly classified us stunted which is the reason for the 6% stunting rate among the richest quintile.

[32] The percentage seeking treatment from traditional healers is quite low; this is in contrast to findings from the CSS October 1994 Household Survey which showed that 23% of people have consulted a spiritual or traditional healer in the past month. One reason for this discrepancy could be that the SALDRU survey asked who the people consulted when they were ill (i.e. their first contact), while the CSS Household Survey asked everyone whether they consulted a traditional or spiritual healer in the past month (regardless of whether they stated that they had been ill and regardless of whether it was their first contact in response to that illness). This discrepancy might therefore suggest that people consult modern

practitioners first when they are ill, but continue to rely heavily on traditional and spiritual healers as well.

REFERENCES

Ardington, E. and F. Lund: 1995, 'Pensions and Development: Social Security as Complementary to Programmes of Reconstruction and Development', Development Southern Africa 12: 557–577.

Central Statistical Services: 1994, 1995 October Household Survey (CSS, Pretoria).

Case, A.C. and A. Deaton: 1996, Large Transfers to the Elderly in South Africa, Mimeographed (Princeton University, Princeton).

Chen, S. Dhatt, and M. Ravallion: 1996, Is Poverty Increasing in the Developing World (The World Bank, Washington, DC).

Collier, P., S. Radwan, S. Wangwe, and A. Wagner: 1986, Labor and Poverty in Rural Tanzania (International Labor Office/Clarendon Press, Oxford).

Development Bank of Southern Africa: 1994, South Africa's Nine Provinces: A Human Development Profile (DBSA, Midrand).

Dreze, J. and A. Sen: 1989, Hunger and Public Action (Clarendon Press, New York).

Fuller, B., P. Pillay, and N. Sirur: 1995, Literacy in South Africa: Expanding Enrollments while Re-Inforcing Inequality? Mimeographed (Harvard University, Cambridge).

Government of South Africa: 1994, White Paper on the Reconstruction and Development Programme (Pretoria, Government Printing Office).

International Labour Office: 1996, South African Labour Market Review (ILO, Geneva).

May, J.: 1996, The South African Participatory Poverty Assessment-Synthesis Report (DRA, Durban).

Lipton, M.: 1977, Why Poor People stay Poor: A Study of Urban Bias in World Development (Temple Smith, London).

Pereira da Silva: 1994, South Africa: Economic Performance and Policies, Informal Discussion Paper No. 7 (The World Bank, Washington, DC).

Ramphele, M. and F. Wilson: 1989, Uprooting Poverty: The South African Challenge (Norton, New York).

Ravallion, M.: 1996, Good and Bad Growth: The 1996 Human Development Report. Mimeographed (The World Bank, Washington, DC).

Ravallion, M. and S. Chen: 1996, What can New Survey Data Tell us About Recent Changes in Living Standards in Developing and Transitional Economies? Policy Research Department mimeographed (The World Bank, Washington, DC).

RDP Office: 1995, Key Indicators of Poverty in South Africa (RDP Office, Pretoria).

Schultz, P. and Mwabu: 1995, Returns to Education in South Africa, mimeographed (Yale University, New Haven).

Sen, A. K.: 1992, Inequality Re-examined (Harvard University Press, Cambridge).

Sen, A.K.: 1995, Commodities and Capabilities (North-Holland, Amsterdam).

Sender, J.: 1996, Rural Poverty and the Labour Market in South Africa, SOAS mimeographed (School of Oriental and African Studies, London).

United Nations Development Program: 1996, Human Development Report (Oxford University Press, New York).

Whiteford, A., D. Posel, and T. Kelatwang: 1995, A Profile of Poverty, Inequality, and Human Development in South Africa (Human Science Research Council, Pretoria).

World Bank: 1995, A Detailed Poverty Profile, Mimeographed (The World Bank, Washington, DC).

World Bank: 1996, 1994, World Development Report (Oxford University Press, New York).

Centre for History and Economics
King's College
University of Cambridge
Cambridge, CB2 1ST
United Kingdom
E-mail: sk242@cam.ac.uk

JULIAN MAY and ANDY NORTON

"A DIFFICULT LIFE": THE PERCEPTIONS AND EXPERIENCE OF POVERTY IN SOUTH AFRICA[1]

ABSTRACT. The purpose of this article is to provide a fuller and more integrated understanding of poverty based on the results of a nation wide participatory study recently completed in South Africa. A surprisingly consistent view of poverty emerges from the study which includes social isolation, malnourished children, crowded homes, the use of basic energy sources, no employment, and fragmented households. A clear image of what results from extreme poverty also emerges comprising continuous ill health, arduous and often hazardous work for virtually no income, no power to influence change, and high levels of anxiety and stress. The article concludes that conventional definitions of poverty do not fully describe the experience of poverty as analysed by the poor themselves. Instead, the multi-dimensional nature of poverty suggests that three basic concepts would be useful in any analysis of extent, nature and persistence of poverty. These are sufficiency, access and vulnerability.

INTRODUCTION

Despite the relative wealth of South Africa in terms of the country's per capita Gross Domestic Product, the experience of the majority of South African households is either one of outright poverty, or of continued vulnerability to becoming poor. Although, in common with many countries, this inability to satisfy essential needs stems from many sources, the specificity of poverty in South Africa has been the impact of apartheid. One aspect of this system was a process of active dispossession whereby assets, such as land and livestock, were stripped from the black majority, while simultaneously, opportunities to develop these assets, such as markets, infrastructure and education, were denied them. As such, apartheid, and the legislation through which this ideology was implemented, operated to both produce poverty and to compress social and economic class.

Measuring Poverty in Post-Apartheid South Africa

An adjunct of apartheid has been the absence of credible and comprehensive social indicator data which could assist in policy formu-

Social Indicators Research **41**: 95–118, 1997.

lation. As a starting point to address this, the Project for Statistics on Living Standards and Development (PSLSD) was undertaken in 1993 which provided a quantitative base-line survey. In 1995, this survey was following by a complementary qualitative research project.

The purpose of this study, referred to as the South African Participatory Poverty Assessment (SA-PPA) was to provide a fuller and more integrated understanding of poverty from the perspective of those who are poor and to fill the gaps which the quantitative study could not readily explain.[2] In particular, the multi-dimensional experience of being poor, and the perceptions of "the poor" towards the causes and relief of their poverty could not be assessed.

Eventually, the SA-PPA included fifteen linked studies and involved some 45 researchers from 20 organisations. In addition, the SA-PPA covered sites in all provinces of South Africa with the exceptions of Gauteng and the Free State. Work was undertaken with 25 communities, 10 of which were located in KwaZulu-Natal, 7 in the Eastern Cape and 4 in the Northern Province. Judging the number of participants in the studies is difficult, since a large group does not necessarily imply that all who attended the workshops and meetings actually participated. Nonetheless a rough estimate suggests that about 1400 people were included in the SA-PPA.

This article discusses findings from the SA-PPA which show the experiences of the poor themselves and the indicators by which they perceive and evaluate their lives. The emphasis placed on Participatory Appraisal methodologies allows for a discussion of social indicators as analysed by communities and individuals, and provided new insight into the measurement of poverty as seen by the poor.

Participatory Appraisal Methodologies

The most commonly used research methodologies in the SA-PPA were explicitly based on Participatory Rural Appraisal (PRA).[3] These methodologies draw on various traditions of research including applied anthropology, Participatory Action Research, Rapid Rural Appraisal and agro-ecosystems analysis. Although the origins of the methodologies are predominantly rural, and generally related to participatory planning of natural resource management, they are increasingly used in a wide variety of contexts, including urban research and poverty research. Much of the early development of these approaches took place within a context of participatory community development rather than policy research, and was carried out by NGOs in Africa and South Asia. The methodologies place emphasis on the following dimensions:

- *local people as analysts rather than informants* – whether for the purposes of local level planning and action or participatory policy research, a key element of PRA is that research participants play an active role in generating analyses and directions for action, rather than being seen purely as informants providing information that outsiders will analyse

- *outsiders act as facilitators* – stimulating examination of issues by local research participants, but striving to avoid adopting a dominant mode in behaviour or attitudes

- *group contexts for research*, often differentiated according to different social categories (women, men, elders etc.) – a process of generating consensus yields information and stimulates examination of key problems facing the social group or community in question

- *visual sharing of information* – a process of generating visual representations (maps, institutional diagrams, causal flow diagrams, seasonality diagrams, matrices) allows for transparency, cross-checking by a number of participants, and enhanced participation in the process of analysis

- *empowering weaker, marginal members of communities* – to participate in the research process (Chambers, 1993a; Norton et al., 1995)

In contrast to previous "extractive" research initiatives, where the information that is generated in local areas is often processed, analysed and disseminated outside of the areas in which the research was originally conducted, the goal of PRA is "to enable rural people to do their own investigations, to share their knowledge and teach us, to do the analysis and presentations, to plan and to own the outcomes" (Chambers, 1993a: 5). Insights which are generated during PRA sessions are graphically illustrated and can be interrogated, which can subsequently enhance local-level information generation and planning while creating "arenas for discussion and analysis" that are understood and, when properly facilitated, directed by participants.

EXPERIENCE AND PERCEPTIONS OF POVERTY

One of the central premises of the SA-PPA was that understanding the lived experience of poverty is an essential element to formulating policy which will be effective in assisting the poor to improve the quality of their lives and security of their livelihoods. In the sphere of policy analysis and research, definitions of poverty are usually constructed by the non-poor. As Chambers (1993b) has noted these definitions show a bias to what is measurable, comparable, and conforms to the concepts and realities of professionals from dominant disciplines and regions of the world. In the process the multi-faceted experience of the rural and urban poor is reduced to measures based purely on constructs of household-level income and consumption – what Chambers terms 'income-poverty'. In the following section we present material from the studies undertaken in this project on the local level understanding of what poverty, vulnerability and ill-being mean in poor rural and urban communities.

Views of Poverty

Despite the wide divergence in the circumstances of the various communities which were included into the SA-PPA, a surprisingly consistent view of poverty emerges from the various studies. The essential features of the 'poor' were:

- Isolated from the community being unable to mix easily with other people;
- The children are malnourished and the food that is served is of poor quality;
- The homes are crowded and are not maintained;
- The most basic forms of energy are used and the family is frequently energy insecure;
- Nobody in the household is employed;

- Families are split, with fathers not present, and children living elsewhere.

For example, looking only at malnourished children as a feature of poverty, a mapping exercise undertaken by Chopra and Ross (1995) indicated that the following characteristics were perceived by the participants as common to the poorest homes in their village:

- female headed (all but one were female headed);
- homesteads are in bad repair;
- crowded;
- little or no food;
- many children;
- not part of the community gardens or crèche;

In contrast, wealth was perceived to be characterised by:

- good housing;
- the use of gas or electricity;
- ownership of a TV, radio or fridge;
- and in extreme cases, ownership of a motor vehicle.

Two aspects of this characterisation are striking: firstly poverty is perceived to encompass a number of key dimensions with income not mentioned.[4] Thus poverty is manifested by too little food, large numbers of children, inadequate and crowded shelter, and finally, exclusion from community self-help structures. In contrast, wealth is manifested by good housing and the ownership of appliances and the use of more efficient forms of energy. Secondly, the perception of wealth is extremely modest, suggesting that although the income gap between the poor and the wealthy may be vast by the standards of the community, the 'wealthy' in rural villages would be considered to be extremely poor in other communities. As such, the wealthy are a modest 'elite' who have managed to achieve little more than a working class life-style.

Well-Being/Ill-Being

Frequently, concepts used in ranking exercises coincided more closely with an idea of 'well-being/ill-being' than 'wealth/poverty'.

For example Black Sash conducted a ranking exercise in one community where poorer households were those judged as 'unhappy'
and the most secure category were described as 'happiest'. In this
listing those people, especially women, who were socially isolated
featured strongly as 'unhappy':

*"Some of the poorest and unhappiest people are unemployed or casually employed
women with children. These are widows, mothers deserted by the fathers of their
children, grandmothers struggling to support abandoned children and women
looking after other people's children, all without support from fathers or maintenance grants from the state"* (Tiexara and Chambers, 1995: 23–4).

Social Isolation

The theme of social isolation as a major component of poverty and
ill-being also emerges very clearly from wealth ranking exercises
carried out by the Elim Care Group/HelpAge International study of
older peoples' needs in a rural area of Northern Province (HelpAge
International, 1995):

*"Both men and women gave family care as the main criteria for well-being
in old age. Having a sympathetic daughter-in-law is the main ingredient for a
comfortable life within the family, since it is the duty of the son's wife to care for
his parents In Tsonga culture, married women live with their husband's family
and are expected to care for his parents, accepting them as her own. A 'bad' or
'rude' daughter-in-law is a main cause of unhappiness for older people, and can
damage household relations ... Unlike women, all men stated that the presence
of a spouse was a main positive factor of well-being. Having sons with income
was another important source of well-being, as well as being well cared for by
daughters-in-law. The presence of grandchildren was seen as a positive factor,
provided there were other sources of support for these children. Loneliness was a
main criteria of unhappiness, even for older people with pensions. One man gave
the example of people who live alone and are compelled to use their pensions to
'buy' the services of extended family members and neighbours to cook or fetch
water for them."*

Experiencing Poverty

The experience documented in the various SA-PPA reports provides
a very clear image of what results from extreme poverty. Generally,
the picture which emerges comprises continuous ill health, arduous
and often hazardous work for virtually no income, no power to
influence change, and high levels of anxiety and stress.

Illustrations of ill health are numerous: Murphy (1995) discusses
the life history of Mrs. Dlamini between 1984 and 1995. During

this 10 year period, her brother-in-law died from an asthma attack, her sister-in-law died during an operation, her mother-in-law died of a stroke, her fourth child "... grew with difficulty – there was no milk", her husband was killed by gangsters and her father died. All of the other women who participated in Murphy's study reported that they or members of their family suffered from ill health.[5]

Arduous work is also well illustrated, and was often reported to have lead to ill health. Once again the life histories gathered by Murphy provide useful material. The husband of Mrs. Msane was earning R125 per month for farm work in 1979, before leaving work because he became ill. Mrs Mchunu's foster child broke his leg in an accident in the mines and in the case of Mrs. Silangwe, her husband first broke his arm on his farm job, and was later killed when a tractor fell on him.

The absence of power is almost a defining characteristic of the poor. Clearly, powerlessness is linked to gendered power relations as is illustrated by Murphy within the household: *"My husband is demanding money. I have no choice, I must give him. I am alone. No-one is helping me"*; and by Roodt (1995) within community leadership:

"In our culture, women tend to feel very small. Men have always been the leaders, their voice is final." "Another thing that makes me very unhappy. Everybody is allowed to voice their opinion. In many cases, I'm cut off while I am voicing my opinion" [female South African National Civics Organisation members in the Eastern Cape].

Finally, the constant emotional stress of being poor and of the struggle for survival is revealed in many of the studies. This is most extreme in the case of the street children. Here, analysis of self-portraits drawn by the children indicates stress, anxiety, emotional regression and the lack of a real connectedness with the world (Bedford, 1995: 20). Violence and sexual abuse is also a part of the lives of these children, as is graphically depicted in the drawings produced by the children.

Violence and sexual abuse is by no means confined to the extreme example of street children. The case studies documented by Black Sash describe the rape of teenage girls, women being afraid to press child maintenance claims on the fathers of children for fear of being beaten and a argument between a drunken couple leading to the women being stabbed and as a result, crippled. For two of the women interviewed by Murphy, violence had had a profound impact on the lives of the poor. The husband of Mrs. B. Dlamini had been murdered 'by gangsters' in Durban leaving her little option other than limited farming and the support of her father's pension. In the case of Mrs Msane, political violence had resulted in her house being burnt, the family being dispersed between relatives, and to the family having to relocate to a new area.

Amongst other reactions, the emotional stress produced by the struggle, uncertainty and extreme living conditions can be linked to the resignation that little will change. This is well summed up by Mrs. C. Dlamini:

"Since birth I have had a difficult life. Things did not improve after my marriage. Through my experience, I have got used to the difficulties."

In urban areas, poverty produces other forms of reaction:

"I am so behind with my rent (service charges) that I can't even sleep at night" (Tiexara and Chambers, 1995: 38).

For street children, sniffing glue is not a problem. Rather sniffing glue relieves the pain of cold and hunger. Taking alcohol or marijuana relieves boredom and enables the child to become part of a supportive group (Bedford, 1995: 44).

The link between stress, the responses to stress and health are self-evident, and show the inter-related nature of the causes of extreme poverty and how poverty is experienced.

Gender, Generation and Poverty

The notion that the experience of role and power is differentiated by gender, generation and social identity is widely acknowledged. Much of the debate has been concentrated on the roles and activities expected of women, and their limited ability to take control over these roles, and the resources with which they are expected to perform these activities. In more recent years, research has moved from a blanket concern that all women were disadvantaged and poor, to a more focused approach that acknowledges that certain groups of women face particular constraints. This differential experience and roles within poverty, in terms of gender, age and social group was evident in many of the input studies.

Roles of breadwinners and household management are often given as being unambiguous: In the villages of Patensie and Krakeel in the Eastern Cape, men are expected to undertake the role of bringing money into the family, whereas women were largely said to be responsible for juggling household resources in order to ensure that the little money the family has is used to cover their most pressing needs:

"If there is a man in the household who is working, it is our tradition that he will bring home the money and give it to his wife to spend. If there is not enough in the month, she will have to run around borrowing or making a plan to ensure that her children's needs are met. Women make plans to get what they want. When I was young I went into the bush and picked prickly pears to sell. I also went to white farmers and asked for old clothes to sell. In this way I managed to educate my children" (Tiexara and Chambers, 1995: 43).

However, this ideal functioning of the poor household seems to be infrequently encountered. Instead, households with no breadwinner, or in which the breadwinner is not a male, or in which there is conflict over resources are more often encountered. This is particularly important in terms of decisions over income. The impact of a sudden change in external socio-economic position of an individual on their internal status within the household is described by a female respondent:

"My husband and I are no longer as close as we used to be when I was working – I think it is because he knows that I am solely dependent on him especially because the children are still young. I am scared of him because he has even started to abuse me, but I know that I have to do my best and listen to what he tells me to do, for the sake of the children" (Tshabalala, 1994).

In general, however, women who did not have control over their own income source were largely excluded from such decision making:

"But the husband is also stingy and makes a fuss. The husbands do not show us their wages, they hide the money from us and give us less money and let themselves spend more money" (Chopra and Ross, 1995).

Indeed, a 'good husband' was perceived to be a man who revealed what he earned and who limited his personal expenditure.

The threat of violence remains a major form of control by men over women. In discussions around obtaining child maintenance, women repeatedly stressed that they were reluctant to insist on pressing for support, even when this was a legitimate claim to be backed up by court action as this would put them at risk: *"it is dangerous to go looking for him, you might get hurt"* (Tiexara and Chambers, 1995: 70).

Interestingly, the limiting of roles for women transcend gender, and have an inter-generational element as well. Bank (1995: 51) describes the case of Pumla, who, whilst pregnant, confronted the new lover of Thobile, her child's father. In this instance, the parents of Thobile insisted that she had no right to approach the other woman, and that such matters should be dealt with by the parents of both parties. This argument resulted in the collapse of Pumla's relationship, and her moving out of the home of the Thobile and his parents with her baby. It was not clear whether this meant that Thobile no longer provided support for his child.

As an example of inter-generational control, Chopra and Ross illustrate that the decision making role of the older women in the husband's family is important:

"Gogo (grandmother) does not like – yes I spoke about her – the gogo is the supervisor in taking care of the baby. The gogo asks if we have given the baby food and she is the one who is giving instructions. Gogo is the one giving instructions. The gogo is the one who tells you to stop whatever you are doing and go and feed the baby, no matter how busy you are" (Chopra and Ross, 1995: Appendix: 11).

Generational differences are not confined to women. Operation Hunger describe how younger people in Klipfontein in the Northern Cape feel that they are discriminated against by older people. Younger men felt that while they are engaging in migrant labour on the farms and mines in the Northern Cape, older men are able to plough their fields. The younger men felt that this arrangement undermined their ability to accumulate and use assets. In addition, younger men felt that they were not allowed to participate in local decision making committees and forums, and as a result, were marginalised from local development processes. In support of this, it was noteworthy that despite the emphasis placed on "the youth" in many of the communities included in the LRG (1995) study in the Northern Province, the youth were notable for their absence in terms of participation in the work which was undertaken.

Nonetheless, while the outcome of such cross generational conflict is by no means set, the power of the male earner appears to be final:

Thozamile . . . claimed that his father was constantly nagging him to invest more money in livestock. His wife, on the other hand, did not favour this idea. She wanted

better things for her house and proper education for her children. **Thozamiloe
said he always had to weigh up these demands before he spends his money**
(Bank, 1995: 58).

What is clear is that the household is far from a co-operative unit,
and instead, people have competing needs, and place pressure on
those who have access to resources.

Social Differentiation

Social differentiation is another aspect of poverty which emerged
from the SA-PPA. A wealth ranking exercise carried out on a social
map by Murphy (1995) with community members who were also part
of the research team gave relative proportions of people belonging
to the different strata in the community of Nhlangwini in KwaZulu-
Natal as well as some criteria for placing households in the different
groups. They found that:

- Of the 76 houses drawn on the map 50% (38) were classified in
  the poor category. Criteria included: no-one working for cash,
  doing cheap labour, the household head living alone (especially
  women with no husbands), ill health, mental illness, pensioner,
  no parents and farmworkers.[6]

- 30% (21) were placed in the average category. These were households where members were waged workers (e.g. teacher, police-
  man, nurse, work in Durban) or got an income from farming,
  owning an informal 'tuck' shop or a taxi. In many cases there
  was more than one member having a regular job.

- 20% (17) were classified as rich. Some of these households ran
  more than one business (e.g. shops, taxis, tractors, traditional
  healer) while others had a number of members in salaried work.

When all the three groups had been filled in on the map (as
different coloured 'houses') it became obvious that all three groups
had a very mixed distribution – which the team attributed to the fact
that the area was 'betterment planned' in the apartheid era.[7] This has
meant that people of different income groups live in close proximity,
which in turn, has affected the survival strategies of the poorest.
The six poor women who participated in depth in the study reported
that doing domestic tasks for wealthier neighbours (such as fetching

water, doing washing and cleaning clothes) was an important source of income for many of them.

Breslin and Delius's (1996) research shows that common characteristics in the definition of the poor relate to particular 'life situations' which are not necessarily simply related to characteristics of gender or age, but involve more specific characteristics. In terms of characteristics of the poor which came up regularly in the fieldwork in different provinces they list female single parents, pensioners supporting grandchildren, and the homeless as well as the unemployed. For example, a resident of the community of De Doorns in the Western Cape described the following groups as different categories within the poor:

- *Generally Poor People* – " one can get confused in the process of identifying these people. There are many who pretend to be poor but who are not. Poor people do not wear a uniform. Some can be easily seen and some are not. Many poor people still have their pride although they may be poor."

- *Employed, but poor* – "poverty to such people is caused by the lack of financial management in their homes" Discussions on the choices people make around how to spend their money ensued, with questions raised about the control that some members of the household (male) have and how this money is spent on alcohol and tobacco instead of food and clothes. The poverty of this group is "caused by themselves."

- *Vagrants* – "with this group one must be careful – many of them are not poor. Many of them are alcoholics and drug abusers."

- *Single, female parents* – "the person cannot go out for work (because they must look after a baby)"

- *Pensioners* – who often do not receive their grants and have to look after grandchildren

- *Unemployed men* – who often survive by living with girlfriends who work.

In Kwa-Jobe, KwaZulu-Natal, the productive means used for farming was a major characteristic for defining the richer and poorer for two groups of women. The poorest are seen to be those who 'work for others, then plough', 'plough by hand', were 'pensioners without

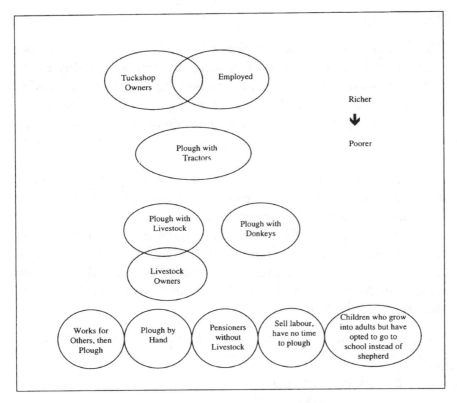

Figure 1. Social groups in Kwa-Jobe (Breslin and Delius, 1995)

livestock', 'sell labour and have no time to plough', and 'children who grow into adults but have opted to go to school instead of being shepherds' (Breslin and Delius, 1995). The less poor ploughed with tractors, cattle, donkeys, and owned livestock. The wealthiest of all, however were shop owners or those employed with steady jobs. This social structure is shown in the Venn Diagram exercise reproduced in Figure 1.

The transition between livelihoods based on rural assets, and those based on the labour market, is visible in changing generational views of the key assets which prevent someone from being poor:

"Many young people in Tambo Village (Eastern Cape) explain that poverty means you can not purchase things that you want whereas the older generations claim that poverty means that you cannot purchase cattle. The middle age groups argued that the condition of one's child and the number of children that one had were all indicators of poverty and wealth" (Breslin and Delius, 1995).

Poverty Traps

Recent quantitative research in South Africa has explored the factors which lead to a persistence of poverty in rural areas (May et al., 1995). In essence this research concluded that the lack of access by rural households to complementary assets and services resulted in a "poverty of opportunity", whereby individuals were unable to take full advantage of the few assets that they did have access to. Further to this, rural households also experienced "time poverty", whereby the time required to undertake essential 'reproductive' tasks meant that individuals, especially women, had insufficient time to engage in additional income earning activities.

A wide range of other factors emerge from the participatory research methods which combine to produce a poverty trap from which the poor find it difficult to escape. For example, the poor women in Murphy's study saw the main 'things that kept them struggling' as the following:

- they got little or no financial assistance (e.g. from husbands or urban remittances)

- their work is poorly paid

- furthering their children's education requires cash that they find difficult to raise (pay school fees and buy uniforms)

- they do not have enough money to improve the quality of their housing

- obtaining enough food throughout the year is difficult

- to farm successfully requires cash that they find difficult to save (pay for ploughing, fertiliser and seed).

ICA/RF (1995) report that groups of boys in the village of Maromufase, Northern Province also highlighted the theme of social isolation as being associated with poverty. Wealth, by contrast was associated with various forms of income-generating capacity – including engaging in criminal activity:

"Generally poverty is associated with unemployment, lack of food and water, as well as being orphaned, and old women living alone. Generally wealth is associated with informal sector trade, being educated, employed and being involved in criminal activities" (ICA/RF, 1995: 11).

Nduli's presentation of the results of three discussions in rural areas of KwaZulu-Natal on the causes and effects of poverty shows three different conceptions of the nature and impact of poverty. A group of women saw the causes of poverty in relation to lack of employment and education, and the effects predominantly in terms of sufficiency of various consumption items at the household level (food, shelter, clothing). A mixed group of men and women showed a high level of concern with security issues – seeing violence, a high crime rate and unemployment as consequences of poverty – while relating causes to 'political power struggles' as well as lack of jobs and discriminatory policies. A third group perceive poverty largely in terms of lack of access to basic social infrastructure in rural areas (roads, electricity, water, hospitals) – as well as stressing the lack of job opportunities raised by the other groups (Nduli, 1995: 36). Finally, the theme of 'irrational use of money' – referring primarily to male use of money for alcohol, drugs and tobacco – also emerged as one of the main defining categories of the poor in Klipfontein in the Northern Cape (Breslin and Delius, 1995).

Seasonality

Seasonal stress has long been recognised as a feature of the livelihoods of the rural poor in many contexts (Swift 1989, Norton et al. 1995). An assumption has prevailed in South Africa, however, that due to the relatively smaller statistical importance of own account agriculture, even for the rural poor, this would be less the case. The material from these studies, however, indicates that this is a major issue for the rural poor in all areas where these studies were carried out. This is borne out from the following seasonality diagram below which is one woman's analysis of the pattern of labour, food supply, expenses and income over a year (see Figure 2).

All of the other five women who were the main participants in Murphy's research indicated similar experiences in which the months that they 'struggled the most' were identified as being September, October, August and July (in that order). The components of this recurring crisis were lack of home produced food, especially maize, which is exhausted in this season, combined with low levels of income from casual work, and high levels of expenditure required for buying seeds, fertiliser and obtaining tractor ploughing services.

	JAN	FEB	MAR	APR	MAY	JUN	JUL	AUG	SEP	OCT	NOV	DEC
WORK	weeding fields	fewer jobs			"mudding"	"mudding" and harvesting		ploughing, weeding	ploughing, more work	ploughing	ploughing, weeding	ploughing, weeding, planting
FOOD	some food		some food pumpkins, imifino, green maize dry	some food pumpkins starting to dry	eating maize from fields harvesting	harvesting dry maize	harvesting dry maize finish	problem- no food	buy food from shops	problem-no food from garden plantings	have some food	more food because holiday food
EXPENSES	school fees, school uniform, no food	minor problems, still have food		preparing for Easter	have food-harvesting; Easter Food	harvesting food has temporary work	harvesting food has temporary work	buying seeds, fertilizer, tractor for ploughing				ploughing, Xmas, plastering houses, kids clothes
INCOME	weeding	less weeding	less weeding	less weeding	harvesting	more harvesting	harvesting, mudding	"mudding" plant first potatoes	planting (more)	planting	weeding eg. Potatoes	weeding

Figure 2. Seasonality chart of Mrs. C. Dlamini, Nhlangwini Ward, KwaZulu-Natal

This means that cash resources have to be split between the purchase of food, and investment into the forthcoming season. There is also a minor crisis at the beginning of the year, in January/February when school fees are due, and income is low.

The ICA/RF material on seasonality bears witness to the same cycle in terms of the 'lean season' in the winter months with malnutrition rising to a peak in July and August .

Seasonality goes beyond the availability of food and peaks in expenditure. Ill health also follows a seasonal pattern, as does workload:

The participants felt that late spring/early summer were the hardest months and this was when they were hoeing, weeding and working hardest in the fields. It was also the time of greatest sickness for the children with increased rates of diarrhoea and chest infections. Hospital records reflect this picture with increasing rates of admission for diarrhoea and respiratory infection during the period of the first rains (September–December) (Chopra and Ross, 1995).

In an earlier study, Murphy (1991) notes that as the providers of water, seasonal water shortages become women's burden in South Africa. Women in her study in Southern KwaZulu have to "queue at springs that are heavily utilised, flood in summer and dry up in winter."

Farmers also experienced seasonality in terms of the ability of their cattle to provide sufficient draught power. Nduli points out that the ploughing season coincides with the time when draught animals are in the weakest condition after the winter months when feed is in short supply.

Finally, Operation Hunger note that the juxtaposition of seasonal work on mines and farms with the planting season prejudices the younger men who take up work opportunities as they are unable to engage in agriculture.

The combination of ill health amongst children and high work load is particularly problematic for women, as caring for sick children is extremely time consuming, and limits the time that women have for their efforts to ensure food in the future. Chopra and Ross (1995) also note that the planting season coincides with that time of the year when there are the greatest number of child-births. This is probably linked to those households in which migrant labour still occurs, and to which men return on a annual basis.

Seasonality also has differing implications for different segments of the poor as well as a spatial specificity. In the case of those dependent upon casual or seasonal labour, the time of greatest work is also the time when such employment is most available, and hardship occurs when such opportunities are not available. As a result, the first seasonality chart indicates that income is least in February to April, and highest when harvesting occurs in June, and when production takes place: planting in September, and weeding in December and January. In contrast, seasonal farm and factory workers in the village of Krakeel in the Eastern Cape faced the greatest hardship from the end of June, when the factory and farm work becomes scarce, until the beginning of October, when the soft fruit harvesting begins and work on the farms becomes abundant (Tiexara and Chambers, 1995: 34).

Seasonality also has an urban dimension. In the case of the street children, Bedford (1995) notes that the winter months were a time of hardship due to the weather and reduced income in the absence of tourists. The summer months saw incomes increase. It is also likely that the incidence of fire in shack settlements discussed by Bank would increase during the winter months when households use volatile fuels for heating. From this, it would seem that the impact and extent of seasonality will vary by area as well as according to the income generating tactics used by different groups of the poor.

CONCLUSION

Although not all of the studies commissioned by the SA-PPA dealt with the issue of the perception of poverty at the local level there are still some themes that emerge from this material. These can be summarised as follows:

- a sense of *isolation* from institutions of kinship and community powerfully characterises the experience of poverty in the studies represented here: old people isolated from kin and without care from younger family members are 'poor' even if they have an income from a pension that is high by the standards of local incomes; the poor are often isolated from community level institutions as well – unable to participate in community gardens and other self-help initiatives; young single mothers without the support of older kin or husbands are also always listed as a category among the poor. Indeed, Hambridge (1995) reports that a major fear associated with HIV/AIDS is the fear of social isolation that would result for a household and individual if the knowledge of infection became public. This causes many to hide the fact of infection – thereby hampering efforts to bring the issue into the open to further public education.

- *income* alone is a factor in local definitions of poverty – but rarely the dominant factor. Within a purely economic sphere *low wages* for the kind of work they do, *lack of security* in their employment/income situation (casual, seasonal labour) and *lack of employment opportunities* are more frequently cited as characterising the experience of poverty than lack of income *per se*.

- *poor nutrition, lack of capacity to educate children*, and *lack of access to water* are the most frequently cited dimensions of poverty which relate to household level consumption. Having many children is also frequently seen as a cause of poverty – and it should be noted that the type of household suffering this is not necessarily the parents. Grandparents and other relatives frequently find that they have to take on responsibility for children – especially those from single daughters.

- there are strong *generational* and *gender* dimensions to the perceptions and experience of poverty – but in both cases these are frequently tied to other specific situations. For old people, for example, being the primary source of support (through the pension) for grandchildren when the parents are absent is a specific misfortune. Old people without pensions are also uniformly seen as poor. For women a state of single motherhood without access to support from older kin or husbands/fathers of their children is generally seen as denoting a state of poverty. Male misuse of resources is often blamed for a household's poverty – which generally refers to alcohol and drug abuse, as well as wasting money on tobacco.

- *vulnerability* emerges as an important concern of the poor and refers to potential circumstances rather than to concrete conditions. As a concept, vulnerability tends often to capture the concerns of the poor to a greater extent than other concepts concerned with the analysis of deprivation, as it speaks to the prevailing insecurity of livelihoods which characterises the experience of poor South Africans. Vulnerability is thus about the dynamic aspects of well-being, refering to the negative outcomes for households, individuals and communities of various kinds of change over time.

Re-Conceptualising Poverty

Poverty is generally characterised by the inability of individuals, households, or entire communities, to command sufficient resources to satisfy their basic needs. Despite the obviously large numbers of people living in such circumstances in rural South Africa, the best method of objectively measuring the extent of poverty has been the subject of some debate amongst poverty researchers in the past. However, what has emerged from recent quantitative research is a broad agreement that some 40 to 50 percent of people in South Africa can be categorised as being poor, whatever the measure that is employed.[8]

The information presented in the SA-PPA suggests that this definition does not fully describe the experience of poverty as analysed by the poor themselves. Instead, the multidimensional nature of poverty suggest that three basic concepts would be useful in any analysis of extent, nature and persistence of poverty. These are:

- **Sufficiency** – having (or not having) *enough* food, income and essential services as well as non-material needs such as safety and opportunities. This requires some understanding of what constitutes sufficient resources.

- **Access** – being able (or unable) to actually *acquire* sufficient food, income, services and so on. This introduces the notion that poverty is related to access to assets and rights, and the processes which allow these to be converted into the commodities and services that people require for subsistence.

- **Vulnerability** – having (or not having) secure and sustainable access to essential commodities, services and other conditions for an acceptable life (e.g. physical safety of the person). This stresses that poverty is not only about being poor, it is also about the risk of becoming poor or poorer in the face of change.

Actually measuring these concepts can be approached in different ways. 'Objective' approaches, particularly access to income, have been the most commonly used approach to monitoring quality of life. In essence, poverty is analysed by weighting elements that indicate real purchasing power and average productivity, and tracing a poverty line. This form of analysis approaches the analysis of poverty in a manner that is essentially static in nature. Importantly, it often looks upon poverty as a disease whose symptoms can be treated by appropriately targeted transfers. Furthermore, although such methodologies may offer useful analytical insights, they are not geared towards active or collaborative research. Instead, the research often operates in comparative isolation, both from the communities in which the research takes place, as well as from the policy makers for whom the research is intended. As such, while poverty profiles can provide key indicators of poverty, they do not offer policy makers sufficient information in the way of concrete issues for policy geared towards reducing the vulnerability of individuals and households to poverty.

An approach based specifically on the perceptions, experiences and aspirations of the poor, such as the SA-PPA, can complement more conventional research approaches to fill in this gap. Specifically, the iterative and flexible mode of enquiry involved is particularly suited to highlighting the historical and process dimensions of poverty, which are particularly critical to understanding the current South African situation. Moreover, rapid appraisal methodologies assist in the more timely delivery of research, and when coupled with participatory techniques, can also bring policy maker, researcher and community more directly in contact. The SA-PPA shows that such methodologies can both complement quantitative analysis, as well as offer unique policy insights which are missed by more conventional methodologies.

NOTES

[1] The research upon which this article is based was a collaborative exercise involving many organisatons, individual researchers and communities. Specifically, the work of the other co-authors of the final report must be acknowledged:

Heidi Attwood, Peter Ewang, Francie Lund and Wilfred Wentzal. This research was made possible by funding received from the World Bank and Overseas Development Agency.

[2] Participatory Poverty Assessments have been carried out in connection with World Bank country Poverty Assessment exercises in a number of other countries in Africa including Zambia, Ghana, Kenya, Madagascar and Mozambique. For further information see Norton and Stephens (1995).

[3] A number of studies used a combination of conventional qualitative research techniques combined with disciplinary perspectives based on sociology or social anthropology. Methods used in these studies included participant observation, focus group discussions, and various forms of conversational and semi-structured interviewing.

[4] This is consistent with Sen's (1981) point that income is an input to well-being whereas commodities and capabilities are the critical outputs that people care about.

[5] Mrs Mbhele: "husband's feet swelled up"; Mrs Mchunu: "daughter died at two, son died at 42, foster child mentally disturbed"; Mrs. Silangwe "two children passed away"; Mrs Msane "twins died after a home delivery."

[6] Extensive quantitative research has produced an almost identical result, see: RDP (1995), May et al. (1995).

[7] Betterment Planning was a policy of the previous South African government which was pursued in the 1950's and 1960's. It meant that previous dispersed residential patterns were consolidated into distinct residential, arable and grazing areas.

[8] The RDP report "Key Indicators of Poverty in South Africa" concludes that 39 percent of people consume less than a minimum intake of food of 2000 Kcal per day, and between 36 and 45 percent of people are living in households which are below an income poverty line.

REFERENCES

Bank, L.: 1995, 'Poverty in Duncan Village, East London: A Qualitative Perspective', report commissioned for the South African Participatory Poverty Assessment, Institute for Social and Economic Research, Rhodes University, East London.

Bedford, L.: 1995, 'Ondeleni Children on Their Way: 'Street Children' in Durban Pasts, Presents and Futures, Constraints and Possibilities', report commissioned for the South African Participatory Poverty Assessment, Independent Development Research, Durban.

Breslin, N. and P. Delius: 1995, 'A Comparative Analysis of Poverty and Malnutrition in South Africa', report commissioned for the South African Participatory Poverty Assessment, Operation Hunger, Johannesburg.

Chambers, R.: 1993b, 'Participatory Rural Appraisals: Past, Present and Future.' Forests, Trees and People Newsletter 15/16, p. 5.

Chambers. R.: 1993a, Challenging the Professions: Frontiers for Rural Development (Intermediate Technology Publications, London).

Chopra, M. and Ross, F.: 1995, 'A Qualitative Investigation into the Cause of Malnutrition in a Rural Area of South Africa', report commissioned for the South African Participatory Poverty Assessment, Vusi Impilo, Hlabisa.

Guijt, I. and Cornwall, A, (1995): 'Editorial: Critical Reflections on the Practice of PRA', PLA Notes 24, International Institute for Environment and Development, London.

Hambridge, M.: 1995, 'Constructing Vulnerability to HIV/AIDS in Rural and Urban Youth', report commissioned for the South African Participatory Poverty Assessment, Department of Social Anthropology, University of Natal, Durban.

HelpAge International: 1995, 'Assessment of the Needs of Older People in Shihimu, Northern Province, South Africa', report commissioned for the South African Participatory Poverty Assessment, HelpAge International and the Elim CARE Group, Johannesburg.

ICA/RF: 1995, 'Access to Health Services in Lenyenye', report commissioned for the South African Participatory Poverty Assessment, Itusheng Community Association and Rural Foundation, Stellenbosch.

LRG: 1995, 'Access to Land and Services in an Ex-Homeland in the Northern Province', report commissioned for the South African Participatory Poverty Assessment, Land Research Group, Pietersburg.

May, J.D., Carter, M.R. and D. Posel: 1995, 'The Composition and Persistence of Poverty in Rural South Africa', Land and Agricultural Policy Centre, Working Paper No 14, Braamfontein.

Murphy, C.: 1991, 'Gender Constraints to Increased Agricultural Production – A Case Study of Women in Rural KwaZulu', investigational report Number 45. Institute of Natural Resources, University of Natal Pietermaritzburg.

Murphy, C.: 1995, 'Implications of Poverty for Black Rural Women in KwaZulu/Natal', report commissioned for the South African Participatory Poverty Assessment, Institute for Natural Resources, University of Natal, Pietermaritzburg.

Nduli, N.: 1995, 'Farming Systems Suitable for Small Scale Farmers to Alleviate Poverty in KwaZulu/Natal', report commissioned for the South African Participatory Poverty Assessment, Mangusotho Technikon, Durban.

Norton, A. and T. Stephens: 1995, 'Participation in Poverty Assessments', ENVSP Participation Series no .020 World Bank, Washington, D.C.

Norton, A., Bortei-Doku, E., Korboe, D. and T. Dogbe: 1995, Poverty Assessment in Ghana: Using Qualitative and Participatory Research Methods, PSP Discussion Paper Series No. 83, World Bank, Washington.

RDP: 1995, Key Indicators of Poverty (South African Government Printer, Pretoria).

Roodt, M.: 1995, 'The Effect of State Restructuring at Provincial and District Level, and Local Politics, on Service Provision to Rural Villages and Small Towns in the Eastern Cape', report commissioned for the South African Participatory Poverty Assessment, Department of Sociology, Rhodes University, Grahamstown.

Sen, A.: 1981, Poverty and Famines: An Essay on Entitlement and Deprivation (Clarendon Press, Oxford).

Swift, J.: 1989, 'Why are some people vulnerable to famine', IDS Bulletin, Vol 20, No. 2.

Tiexara. L and F. Chambers: 1995, 'Child Support in Small Towns in the East-
    ern Cape', report commissioned for the South African Participatory Poverty
    Assessment, Black Sash, Port Elizabeth.
Tshabalala, V. L.: 1994, 'The Effects of Retrenchment on Family Life: an Assess-
    ment of Frame Textile Company Workers in the Greater Durban Area', M Soc.
    Sci. Thesis. Durban: University of Natal.

Julian May
Data Research Africa
Suite 10, Strathmore Park
305 Musgrave Rd.
Durban 4000
South Africa

Andy Norton
West and North Africa Department
Overseas Development Agency
94 Victoria Street
London SW1E 5JL
United Kingdom

ROS HIRSCHOWITZ and MARK ORKIN

INEQUALITY IN SOUTH AFRICA: FINDINGS FROM THE 1994 OCTOBER HOUSEHOLD SURVEY

ABSTRACT. This paper argues that inequality and relative deprivation are the main problems to be addressed in the country, based on the denial of access to facilities and equal opportunities by the previous apartheid government. It focuses on the stark contrasts in living conditions and life-styles between blacks and whites, males and females, urban and non-urban people, the employed and the unemployed, and those doing formal versus those doing informal work. It is based on the findings of the 1994 *October Household Survey* (OHS) of South Africa's Central Statistical Service. The findings show that Africans, who constitute 76% of the population, are more likely to be affected by inequality and relative deprivation. As many as 64% of Africans of all ages, and 70% of Africans aged between 0 and 15 years, live in non-urban areas. Africans are more likely than other population groups to live in shacks in urban areas and in traditional dwellings in non-urban areas, and to have less access to domestic infrastructure such as water, sanitation and electricity. They have also received less education, and are therefore less able to compete with others for jobs in the formal economy. The informal economy consists mainly of service and trade businesses, with little scope for new employment creation. The UNDP's Human Development Index is much lower for Africans, compared to whites. On the basis of the findings, it is argued that large-scale development programmes are required to overcome the inequalities of the past. If this does not happen, there is a danger that there will be insufficient high-level skills in the country to sustain economic growth.

INTRODUCTION

In South Africa, after many years of struggle for liberation, a government elected by all the people is at last in place. But the years of apartheid have taken their toll. South Africa has a highly distorted socio-economic structure, polarised into urban and non-urban, "black and white, privileged and oppressed" (Turock, 1993: p. 28).

This paper aims to supply selected indicators against which to measure change in growth and development over time. To compile it, we used the data contained in the 1994 *October Household Survey* (OHS) conducted by the Central Statistical Service (CSS, 1995). The

Social Indicators Research **41**: 119–136, 1997.

OHS is conducted annually. It gives detailed information about the living conditions and life circumstances of all South Africans.

A programme of household surveys makes it possible, not only to describe the situation in a country at a given point in time, but also to measure change in people's life circumstances as and when new government policies are implemented. In South Africa, the first comprehensive CSS household survey in the country was conducted in October, 1993. It was repeated, with modifications to the questionnaire, in 1994 and 1995. The former "TBVC states"[1] were originally excluded, but in 1994 and 1995, the entire country was included.

THEORETICAL ORIENTATION

In this paper, we focus on stark contrasts in life-styles between different groups of people. In international statistics, the differences in life circumstances between rich and poor countries are generally stressed, while the differences between rich and poor within a country tend to be downplayed (Townsend, 1993). To remedy this deficiency, the focus here is on the extent of inequality between black and white, males and females, urban and non-urban, the employed and the unemployed, and those doing formal and informal work within South Africa.

Relative deprivation is an essential concept underlying the selection and interpretation of the data in this paper. People are relatively deprived "if they cannot obtain . . . the conditions of life – that is the diets, amenities, standards and services – which allow them to play the roles, participate in the relationships and follow the . . . behaviour which is expected of them" (Townsend, 1993). Inequality in South Africa is based on denial of access among the vast majority to amenities, standards and services. South Africans have been denied equal access not only to basic resources such as water and sanitation (Hirschowitz and Orkin, 1995), but also to social investments such as education (Chisholm, 1992) and health-care (De Beer, 1992).

South Africa is a middle-income developing country (Ministry in the Office of the President: Reconstruction and Development Programme (RDP), 1995). It is not the under-development of the country as a whole that characterises it, but rather the skewed and uneven distribution of access to resources that enable people to lead productive lives. By identifying these patterns, we can help policy makers set the targets to be met by strategies such as the RDP, and the more recent growth, employment and redistribution (Gear) strategy; and by tracking these patterns over time, to help to monitor the extent to which the targets are being met. Comparisons of the data in this paper with the forthcoming 1995 OHS will be a topic for further research.

METHODOLOGY

We now describe the method of sampling, the questionnaire design and weighting of the sample. As far as the sample is concerned, information was obtained from 30 000 households in 1 000 enumerator areas in the country (30 households per enumerator area). The sample was stratified by province, urban and non-urban areas[2] and race. The 1991 population census was used as a frame for drawing the sample. However, this census has certain shortcomings. Firstly, the former "TBVC states" were excluded in the 1991 Census. Consequently, their size had to be estimated when drawing samples of households from these areas. Secondly, certain parts of the country, particularly rural areas in the former "self-governing territories"[3], were not demarcated into clearly defined enumerator areas, and the households in these districts were not listed. Instead, a "sweep census" was done, covering an entire magisterial district. Thirdly, in other areas of the country, particularly informal settlements, aerial photography was used to estimate population size.

The questionnaire used in the survey contains questions about the household as a whole, as well as on all individual members. In the household section, questions are asked about type of dwelling or dwellings in which the household lives, access to facilities such as electricity, tap-water, toilets and regular refuse removal, access to health and social welfare services, and the safety and well-being of the household. In the section for individuals in the household, questions are asked on age, gender, education, marital status, migration, use of health services, employment and self-employment.

Data concerning households were weighted back to the estimated number of households in the country in the various provinces, according to the proportions found in urban and non-urban areas, and by the race of the head of the household. Data on individuals within households were weighted by age, race and gender, according to 1994 CSS estimates of population size in urban and non-urban areas in the nine provinces.

LIMITATIONS OF THIS ANALYSIS

The following limitations should be borne in mind when interpreting this paper. The poor quality of the 1991 population census and exclusion of the former "TBVC states" from the statistics that were collected by the CSS prior to the 1994 elections have meant that numerous estimates have been made regarding the size of the population, the size of the economically active population and the number of jobs available in the formal sector. The data presented here should therefore be regarded as showing possible trends rather than as definitive.

It should also be noted that the household survey programme by its design focuses on "outcome" measures, such as household income, employment status and level of education. Policy makers will also need to take "input" measures, such as state budget allocations to education, health and water supply, or "process" measures, such as mechanisms for the distribution of resources, into account. To monitor change in the quality of life in South Africa, all three types of measures are required.

DEMOGRAPHIC PROFILE OF SOUTH AFRICA

When examining the results of the 1994 *October Household Survey*, we situate them in a context of the demography of the country. This gives a clear indication of the relative size of the various population groups to each other, and the number of people affected by inequality.

The size of the population of the country has been increasing steadily during the apartheid era. It has grown from a mid-year estimate of 23.4 million people in 1971 to a mid-year estimate of 41.2 million by 1995. During that time, the proportion of Africans[4] in the population has steadily increased from 71% to 76%, while the proportion of whites has steadily decreased from 17% to 13% (Bureau of Market Research, 1993).

More than half of the population (52%) lives in non-urban areas. However, the urban – non-urban distribution varies substantially by population group. Relatively few coloureds (17%), Indians (4%) or whites (9%), but almost two thirds of Africans (64%) are found in non-urban areas.

Two provinces, Gauteng and the Western Cape, are largely urban, while the other provinces tend to contain large proportions of non-urban populations. In the Northern Province, more than 90% of the population of 5.3 million people are living in non-urban areas. Seven in every ten African children aged between 0 and 15 years (70%) live in non-urban areas.

AGE DISTRIBUTION OF THE POPULATION

Among Africans, the age distribution of the population resembles the pyramidal structure of developing countries. Fifteen percent of all African males and 14% of all African females are aged between 0 and 4 years. Relatively few people (3% of African males and 4% of African females) are aged 65 years or more. Among whites, we find that only 7% of both males and females (less than half the proportion of the African population) are aged between 0 and 4 years, while 8% of males and 11% of females (more than double the proportion of the African population) are aged 65 years or more. This age distribution of whites is very similar to the age distribution pattern in developed countries. There are relatively few white children, particularly babies, while the proportion of older people is relatively large.

TYPE OF ACCOMMODATION IN WHICH SOUTH AFRICANS LIVE

73% of all households in South Africa are found in formal structures such as a house or part of a house, a flat or townhouse, while 14% of households are found in traditional dwellings, 9% in shacks, 3% in hostels and 1% in other accommodation such as hotels and institutions. However, while 86% of urban households are situated in formal housing structures, only 57% of households in non-urban areas are found in these types of structures.

Inequality and type of housing are indeed closely related. People living in traditional dwellings, hostels and shacks are poorer than those living in formal structures. For example, almost half of all households living in traditional dwellings live on R 410 per month (the lowest income category) or less, compared to fewer than a quarter (24%) of those households in formal dwellings. Shack dwellers tend to fare better economically than inhabitants of traditional dwellings, even though there is a great deal of poverty amongst them, since one third (34%) of these households earn an income of R 410 or less.

ACCESS TO INFRASTRUCTURE AND SERVICES

The lack of domestic infrastructure such as water, sanitation and electricity, and domestic services such as regular refuse removal, varies by race and in urban versus non-urban areas. The overall pattern of inequality and relative deprivation is clear.

Table I indicates that almost all Indian (98%) and white households (98%), and the vast majority of coloured households (76%) have taps inside their dwellings, compared with only 27% of African households.

Among African households, those in urban areas are more likely to have taps inside the dwelling (54%) compared with non-urban areas (8%).

Access to electricity for cooking also varies by race, and by the urban – non-urban divide. Table I shows that 99% of Indian, 98% of white and 76% of coloured households use electricity for cooking purposes, compared with only 31% of African households. Among African households, 58% of those in urban areas use electricity for cooking, compared with only 11% in non-urban areas. More than half of all non-urban African households (53%) use wood for cooking.

A similar pattern can be found for toilet facilities. Among African households, 13% have no toilet facilities at all. The absence of a toilet facility applies to only 2% of African urban households, but to as many as 20% of African rural households.

We find that Africans living in the more urban provinces, for example Gauteng and the Western Cape, have more access to services, compared to those living in more rural provinces, for example the Northern Province, the North West or the Free State.

TABLE I

Access to water and energy for cooking

Facility	Total %	Africans %	Coloureds %	Indians %	Whites %
Number of households (000)	8 688	5 991	711	233	1 752
Domestic water: Total					
Tap in dwelling	47.6	27.4	76.0	97.7	98.4
Tap on site	18.8	25.1	17.5	0.6	0.2
Public tap/tanker	12.8	18.1	3.5	0.4	0.0
Borehole	7.9	11.0	0.4	0.4	1.2
Rainwater tank	0.7	0.9	0.5	0.5	0.0
Stream, river, dam, etc.	12.2	17.5	2.1	0.4	0.2
Domestic water: Urban					
Tap in dwelling	74.7	54.3	84.0	99.2	99.8
Tap on site	17.6	31.5	12.2	0.4	0.0
Public tap/tanker	6.5	11.8	3.7	0.1	0.0
Borehole	0.7	1.3	0.0	0.0	0.0
Rainwater tank	0.0	0.0	0.0	0.0	0.1
Stream, river, dam, etc.	0.5	1.1	0.1	0.3	0.1
Domestic water: Non-urban					
Tap in dwelling	12.1	8.0	42.9	60.0	81.4
Tap on site	20.4	20.4	39.3	5.9	0.9
Public tap/tanker	21.0	22.6	2.7	6.5	0.1
Borehole	17.4	18.0	2.4	10.4	14.9
Rainwater tank	1.6	1.5	2.5	14.2	0.5
Stream, river, dam, etc.	27.5	29.5	10.2	3.0	2.1
Energy – cooking: Total					
Electricity	49.8	30.6	76.1	98.5	98.4
Gas	4.8	6.1	5.7	0.5	0.9
Paraffin	17.3	24.2	5.6	0.5	0.3
Wood	22.8	31.7	11.6	0.4	0.3
Coal	5.2	7.3	1.0	0.2	0.1
Other	0.1	0.1	0.0	0.0	0.0
Energy – cooking: Urban					
Electricity	76.0	57.8	83.6	99.5	98.9
Gas	4.1	6.4	5.2	0.0	0.6
Paraffin	12.5	23.0	5.6	0.2	0.3
Wood	2.1	3.0	4.7	0.1	0.1
Coal	5.2	9.8	0.9	0.2	0.1
Other	0.0	0.0	0.0	0.0	0.0

TABLE I
Continued

Facility	Total %	Africans %	Coloureds %	Indians %	Whites %
Energy – cooking: Non-urban					
Electricity	15.4	11.0	45.9	72.8	92.2
Gas	5.8	5.8	7.7	11.7	4.5
Paraffin	23.4	25.1	5.6	6.5	0.5
Wood	50.0	52.5	39.7	8.5	2.2
Coal	5.1	5.5	1.3	0.5	0.6
Other	0.2	0.2	0.0	0.0	0.0

Rural domestic infra-structural development, is therefore a high priority for the government, particularly if we recall that 70% of African children live in rural areas.

LEVEL OF EDUCATION

Inequality and relative deprivation affect not only households but also the individuals within them. Educational opportunities have been meagre or absent for many South Africans in the past. When examining the education level of the population as a whole aged 20 years or more, we find that 13% of the population have received no education, while 19% have received some primary school education and a further 8% a complete primary school education. This means that four in every ten (40%) of South Africans aged 20 years or more have received seven or fewer years of schooling, if any.

Among Africans, 17% of those aged 20 years or more have not received any formal education, while a further 4% have received three or fewer years of schooling. In addition, 18% have received between four and six years, and 9% seven years of schooling. This means that almost half (48%) of the African population have received seven years or less schooling. Among whites, this proportion is only 1%.

Nevertheless, over time, the proportion of Africans who have received at least some schooling has increased. In 1994, 55% of Africans aged 65 years or more had not received any education, compared to 17% of those aged between 40 and 49 years and fewer than 1% of those aged 20 to 24 years.

EMPLOYMENT AND UNEMPLOYMENT

While the size of the population of South Africa has been steadily increasing over time, so has the size of its economically active population, defined here as those who are available for paid work, including both the employed and the unemployed. Full-time students, housewives, retired people, pensioners and the disabled who are unable to work are therefore excluded from this definition. Between 1970 and 1995, the economically active population has increased from an estimated 8.1 million people to an estimated 14.3 million people.

THE RATE OF UNEMPLOYMENT IN THE COUNTRY

Of the estimated 14.3 million economically active people in the country in 1995, some 9.6 million people were employed. It is estimated that 8.0 million (56%) of these economically active people are working in the formal sector, while 1.6 million (11%) are found in the informal sector, and 4.7 million people (33%) are unemployed (CSS, 1995).

Unemployment is indeed a complex issue, particularly in relation to poverty and under-development characteristic of the African population in South Africa. Wield (1992) states that "unemployment statistics by themselves do not allow us to get a good picture of how people do make a living nor (crucially if they want to avoid hunger, ill-health and famine) how people stop being able to sustain themselves." He points out that in Bangladesh, India and the Philippines, for example, unemployment rates are calculated in different ways in each country.

At least two definitions of unemployment are used in South Africa – the strict and the expanded definition. Both definitions include people who are aged 15 years or older, and who are not employed, but who are available for work. But they differ from each other in the following way. A requirement of the first or strict definition is that a given individual has taken specific steps to seek employment in the four weeks prior to a given point in time, Using this definition, we calculate the unemployment rate to be 20% of the economically active population. The second or expanded definition focuses on the desire to work, and the availability for work, irrespective of whether or not the person has taken active steps to find work. In other words, there are people who would readily accept work, but who have given up seeking it, because it is often too costly to do so. The World Bank (Ministry in the Office of the President: RDP, 1995) call these people "the discouraged" unemployed. In terms of this definition, the unemployment rate was calculated to be 33%. There are good reasons why people stop seeking employment. "If there are few jobs to be had then it is well known that the number of people seeking them goes down" (Wield, 1992: p. 59). In addition, if there are few jobs, the expense of job-seeking such as travel expenses, clothing and food may further discourage job-seeking.

The unemployment rate is therefore defined here in terms of the expanded or discouraged definition. It is the proportion of the economically active population (all those aged 15 years or older who are available for work) who are not in paid employment or self-employment in the seven days prior to a given point in time, but who are available and want to be employed or self-employed.

Unemployment affects Africans more severely than it affects members of other population groups. Half (50%) of all economically active African females and one in every three (34%) economically active African males are unemployed, compared with one in ten (9%) economically active white females and one in every twenty (5%) economically active white males. The effects of inequality on the ability to find work are therefore again clearly visible.

In Table II we examine the extent of unemployment among Africans in the nine new provinces of South Africa by gender. Provinces were chosen for analysis because they reflect additional inequalities. For example, in the Eastern Cape, which contains the former "independent states" of Ciskei and Transkei, unemployment among Africans is as high as 52% of the economically active population, while in Western Cape, which contains no former "homelands" or independent states, it is 28%. In the non-urban areas of the Western Cape, where people live and work on commercial farms, Africans were prevented from job-seeking on these farms during the apartheid era, and coloureds, rather than Africans, were given jobs. The unemployment rate of 10% reflects the situation where the absences of a job is linked to the absence of accommodation.

TABLE II

Unemployment among Africans by province and gender, in urban and non-urban areas

Province	Total %	Male %	Female %
South Africa:			
Total	41.1	33.6	50.2
Urban	39.0	35.0	44.4
Non-urban	43.2	32.1	55.3
Western Cape:			
Total	27.8	21.2	40.7
Urban	31.1	24.4	42.2
Non-urban	10.0	8.4	19.4
Eastern Cape:			
Total	52.3	47.7	56.7
Urban	40.5	41.6	39.4
Non-urban	58.8	51.2	65.7
Northern Cape:			
Total	39.4	34.0	49.0
Urban	50.8	49.7	52.5
Non-urban	17.4	9.7	38.7
Free State:			
Total	27.6	18.7	38.1
Urban	36.9	30.8	43.0
Non-urban	16.7	6.5	31.0
KwaZuluNatal:			
Total	38.0	31.2	45.3
Urban	36.7	32.8	41.4
Non-urban	38.7	30.2	47.5
North West:			
Total	39.3	30.7	51.7
Urban	37.5	31.8	46.2
Non-urban	40.3	30.0	54.3
Gauteng:			
Total	40.1	35.9	46.5
Urban	41.1	37.3	46.8
Non-urban	19.9	12.0	37.3

TABLE II
Continued

Province	Total %	Male %	Female %
Mpumalanga:			
Total	41.4	32.1	54.2
Urban	40.8	33.7	49.9
Non-urban	41.7	31.4	56.2
Northern Province:			
Total	49.6	35.7	61.4
Urban	31.1	25.9	37.1
Non-urban	51.6	37.0	63.7

This table shows that unemployment is higher among African females (50%) than among African males and it is slightly higher among Africans in non-urban (43%) than in urban (39%) areas. This finding of high unemployment in non-urban areas is surprising in relation to other developing countries, where agricultural non-market production activities sustain many households. However, as a result of forced removals from their land during the apartheid era, many non-urban Africans cannot engage in these activities. We do not fully understand, at present, the extent of non-urban lack of access to land, and how the large numbers of landless non-urban people sustain themselves. Further CSS research, planned for 1997, should start to give some answers to these questions.

When examining the monthly household income among the unemployed, we find that, overall, 36% live in households with an average monthly disposable income of R 410 or less (the lowest quintile), while only 8% live in households with an average monthly income of R 2 573 or more (the highest quintile, CSS, 1995).

Amongst the unemployed, the lower the level of education of the individual, the more likely he or she is to live in a low-income household. Thus 46% of those with no education who are unemployed live in households with average disposable incomes of R 410 or less per month (the lowest quintile), compared to 25% of those with a Standard 10 or higher level of education who are unemployed. Only 1% of those who are unemployed with no education live in households with average disposable monthly incomes of R 2 753 or more per month (the highest quintile), compared with 16% of the unemployed who have a Standard 10 or higher level of education. Therefore the unemployed with lower levels of education are more likely to live in impoverished circumstances than those with higher levels of education.

THE DISTRIBUTION OF FORMAL EMPLOYMENT

The low level of education, if any, that Africans have received is directly reflected in the type of work that they do. Among employed Africans, 35% of males and 52% of females are in elementary occupations such as farm work or cleaning or unskilled labour requiring relatively little, if any, education or training. Only 3% of employed African males and 2% of employed African females are in management posts. While Africans tend to work in jobs requiring relatively low level skills, the educational advantages that whites have enjoyed during the apartheid era are clearly evident in the type of work that they do. As many as 18% of employed white males and 7% of employed white females are in managerial posts, while 11% of employed white males and 12% of employed white females are in professional jobs. However, white working females tend to cluster into clerical posts (45%).

We have seen in the demographic section of this report, that whites constitute only 13% of the population. Therefore the pool from which people have been drawn to occupy jobs requiring high-level skills is a small one. The proportion of whites in the population is decreasing, and the white population is an aging one.

If we examine the vacancies in the formal employment market (CSS manpower surveys), we find that, overall, between 1991 and 1994, there were approximately 350 thousand vacant jobs in each year, while in 1994, approximately 4.6 million people required employment. There are extremely few vacant posts to meet the huge demand for employment. The vacancies that exist are to be found mainly in professional jobs, for which a high level of education is required.

THE INFORMAL SECTOR

Altogether, in 1994, there were 1 575 000 workers in the informal sector, 991 000 (63%) of whom were African. Approximately 1 300 000 people in this sector were classified as workers for their own account. More than half (58%) are in community, personal and social services, while a further 22% are in trade. Only 7% are in manufacturing, and 4% in transport businesses. The income generated in these businesses tends to be lower than in the formal sector. The average monthly income among Africans in this sector in 1994 was R 1 196.

HUMAN DEVELOPMENT INDEX

The *Human Development Index* (HDI) has been generated by the United Nations Development Programme (UNDP) as a way of measuring and ranking the extent of human development in a country in relation to other countries. It takes into account life expectancy at birth, adult literacy and level of education in the population, and per capita GDP.

The overall HDI for South Africa is 0.677 which is comparable to other middle-income countries. However, among whites it is extremely high (0. 901) and comparable to countries ranked in the top twenty in the world on the basis of this instrument such as Finland and Luxembourg. For Africans, it is rather low (0.50), and comparable to other African countries such as Swaziland and Zimbabwe. There are therefore vast differences between whites and Africans in the quality of life. Among Africans, however, there are vast differences in the HDI between provinces. While Africans living in Gauteng have an HDI of 0.659, equivalent to the HDI of a middle-income country, those living in Northern Province (0.442) or the Eastern Cape (0.440) have an HDI comparable to some of the poorer countries in Africa.

In general, the HDI for Africans is lower in those provinces that are largely rural, and higher in the two provinces that are essentially urban in character.

POVERTY

In this section we examine the extent of poverty in the country in terms of income distribution, based on the 1994 October Household Survey.

To calculate the extent of poverty, we divided household incomes into quintiles. However, the first quintile contained more than 20% of households because it contained all households in the country who are dependent on an old age pension as the sole income for their survival as well as those households where there is no regular income.

The recent publication *Key indicators of poverty in South Africa*, prepared for the Office of the Reconstruction and Development Programme by the World Bank (Ministry in the Office of the President: Reconstruction and Development Programme, 1995), gives a detailed picture of the extent of poverty in the country. The following description complements the above-mentioned report by highlighting inequalities.

Poverty mainly affects African households, and African households have a lower income on which to live than coloured, Indian or white ones. More than half (52%) of African households were surviving on R 726 or less on average per month (the first two income categories) in 1994 compared to 34% of coloured, 21% of Indian and 12% of white households.

On the other hand, 53% of white households had average incomes above R 2 752 a month (the top income category), compared with 32% of Indian, 20% of coloured and 9% of African households.

Non-urban households survive on lower incomes than urban households. Six in every ten non-urban households (60%) have an average household income of below R 727 a month (the lowest two quintiles), while three in every ten urban households (35%) fall into this category.

Female-headed households are likely to survive on lower incomes, compared to male-headed ones and six in every ten female-headed households (59%) live on incomes below R 727 per month, on average, compared to one in three (35%) male-headed ones.

Poverty in South Africa is also unequally distributed by province. Proportionately more households in the Eastern Cape and the Northern Province have average monthly incomes in the lowest two quintiles. However, Gauteng (28%) and the Western Cape (27%) have relatively few households in these categories.

CONCLUSIONS

The findings of this report strongly support the contention that inequality and the resultant relative deprivation are important factors to take into account in future planning for South Africa. The effects of inequality are clearly evident in the difference in life circumstances between blacks and whites, males and females, urban and non-urban dwellers, the employed and the unemployed and those doing informal work. The benefits of economic growth in a country very rarely filter down (Grindle and Thomas, 1989), unless such growth is linked to the development of the productive potential of all South Africans. Poverty alleviation, employment creation, the supply of infrastructure and human resource development are all part of the same process. Low-income households require access to education and training, to income generating activities or to formal employment and to adequate domestic infrastructure.

The findings outlined in this paper indicate that a holistic, integrated, developmental approach is required. The fact that the majority of people, particularly children, live in rural areas has implications for the delivery of infrastructure, education and training, and the creation of employment opportunities. Land reform and rural development are essential components of any future planning strategy.

Poverty alleviation, human resource development and employment creation should therefore be seen as different components of the same process. Interventions directed at one component are likely to affect the other components.

We have shown in this paper that there is an urgent need for human resource development to take place in the country as a whole to overcome the inequalities of the past and to build up the capacity that will be required to obtain and sustain economic growth. Adult education and training among Africans is particularly important to enable Africans to participate fully in the economy of the country. If we fail to develop the potential of all South Africans, there may be insufficient high-level skills in the country to obtain or to sustain economic growth.

Tackling development means addressing past inequalities, and we have used the HDI to indicate the extent to which unequal development has taken place in the country, not only between population groups, but also between provinces. Among Africans, the quality of life of those living in the more rural provinces, as measured by the HDI, has lagged far behind the quality of life of those living in more urban provinces.

NOTES

[1] The Transkei, Bophutatswana, Venda and Ciskei were deemed to be "independent states" by the apartheid regime. They were therefore excluded from official South African statistics.
[2] An urban area is defined as one where there is a fully established local government. A non-urban area, on other hand, does not have an established local authority. The area could, for example, be run by a tribal authority or a regional authority.
[3] In addition to the "TBVC states", there were also largely rural "self-governing territories" into which people were forcibly removed during the apartheid era.
[4] The terms African, coloured, Indian and white are used here as classification variables to enable us to study the extent of racially-based inequalities that exist in South Africa.

REFERENCES

Bureau of Market Research: 1993, 'A projection of the South African population 1991-2011', Research Report No. 196 (University of South Africa, Pretoria).
Central Statistical Service: 1995, 'October Household Survey 1994 ', Statistical Release PO317 (CSS, Pretoria).
Chisholm L.: 1992, South African education in the era of negotiation, in G. Moss and I. Obery (eds.), South African Review 6: From 'Red Friday' to CODESA (Ravan Press, Johannesburg).
De Beer, C.: 1992, 'Health policy in transition? The limits to reform', in G. Moss and I. Obery (eds.), South African Review 6: From 'Red Friday' to CODESA (Ravan Press, Johannesburg).
Grindle, M.S. and Thomas, J.W.: 1989, 'Policy makers, policy choices and policy outcomes', Policy Studies 22, pp. 213–248.
Hirschowitz, R. and Orkin, M.: 1995, A national household survey of health inequalities in South Africa (Henry J. Kaiser Family Foundation, Washington, DC).
Ministry of the Office of the President: Reconstruction and Development Programme: 1995, Key indicators of poverty in South Africa (Office of the President, Pretoria).

Townsend, P.: 1993, The international analysis of poverty (Harvester Wheatsheaf, London).

Turock, B.: 1993, South Africa's skyscraper economy: Growth or development?', in B. Turock, D. Kekana, M. Turock, E. Maganya, J. Noe, B. Onimode, J. Chikore, M. Suliman and M. Khor (eds.), Development and reconstruction in South Africa: A reader (Institute for African Alternatives, Johannesburg).

Wield, D.: 1992, 'Unemployment and making a living', in T. Allen and A. Thomas (eds.), Poverty and development in the 1990s (Oxford University Press, Oxford).

Central Statistical Service
Private Bag X44
Pretoria 0001
South Africa

ANTOINETTE LOUW

SURVIVING THE TRANSITION: TRENDS AND PERCEPTIONS OF CRIME IN SOUTH AFRICA

ABSTRACT. Crime and violence have dominated South Africa's transformation over the past two decades. High crime rates cause widespread feelings of insecurity and fear which undermine popular confidence in the democratisation process. Considering both trends and public perceptions, this paper explores changing crime levels over the past decade, elaborating on the problems associated with crime statistics in South Africa, and the salience of the transition for current crime levels. Data is drawn from official police statistics and from victimisation and other surveys. Crime has been increasing gradually in South Africa since 1980. It is, however, since 1990 and not more recently as is popularly believed, that levels have risen sharply. An examination of the statistics shows that despite general increases, not all crimes have been committed with equal frequency and not all areas of the country are similarly affected. These trends are a product of the political transition and are associated with the effects of apartheid and political violence, the breakdown in the criminal justice system and more recently, the growth in organised crime. High crime levels are taking their toll on South Africans. Surveys show that crime rather than socio-economic issues now dominates people's concerns, and that fear of crime is increasing. Currently, fewer people feel safe and believe the government has the situation under control than in previous years. Faced with widespread unemployment on the one hand, and the prospects of development on the other, levels of property crimes will probably continue to increase. While violent crime levels should decline over the medium term, improved relations with the police and a culture of reporting crimes like rape and assault may result in more crime being recorded.

INTRODUCTION

The most significant feature of South Africa's transition from a racially divided apartheid government to democracy has been the peaceful nature of the transformation in the form of negotiation as opposed to revolution. But for many South Africans, one of the dominant features of the transformation process over the past two decades has been, and continues to be, crime and violence. South Africa's recent history has been characterised by violence, emanating in varying degrees of intensity from the state, from the liberation

Social Indicators Research **41**: 137–168, 1997.

REPORTING AND RECORDING CRIME

Problems associated with measuring crime and interpreting crime statistics, particularly over long periods of time, are well known and not restricted to South Africa. But the effects of the apartheid system on the recording process created additional problems, many of which still influence the data.

The reliability of official crime statistics is largely subject to: the relationship between the public and the police, and the internal practices and procedures of the police. Most incidents of crime only come to the police's attention after being reported by the public, and events then have to be recorded by the police and processed before being reflected in the official crime database. In most countries, most crimes are recorded, but even in Britain where the crime recording system is fairly sophisticated, official records do not reflect the actual extent of crime (Bottomly and Pease, 1986).

Glanz (1995a: p. 7) has summarised several of the most important determinants of crime reporting. Crimes of varying levels of seriousness have different reporting patterns, for example, petty theft and rape or wife abuse tend not to be reported. In addition, whether or not crimes are covered by insurance affects reporting behaviour, while insurance in turn, varies according to socio-economic status. The ease with which crimes can be reported is also a factor, such as the distance to the nearest police station, access to transport and to telephones, particularly for less serious crimes.

Police practices and the level of police staffing may also influence the recorded incidence of crimes such as drug related offences, gambling and prostitution. Furthermore, differences in levels of police staffing across geographical areas also affects crime statistics, as does police management and control. For example, certain crimes which are hard to solve may be recorded less often than others in order to inflate the rate at which crimes are solved by the police.

Many of these determinants have been complicated in South Africa by factors associated with the apartheid government. In terms of the public's willingness to report crime, the police have historically functioned more as an army enforcing and maintaining a particular system of government (often brutally), rather than protecting the rights of the country's citizens. This created deep animosity between people and the police, which undoubtedly affected crime reporting and recording. Today, the legacy of this divide still constitutes one of the biggest obstacles to effective policing and prosecution. In addition, the perception – which is more recent for white than for black South Africans – that the police and justice system are unable to effectively arrest, convict and incarcerate criminals, undermines public confidence and may encourage the belief that reporting crime is not worthwhile.

In terms of police practices and their recording of crime, the apartheid order generated crime rather than controlling it, and the police acted as agents of a state in which apartheid offences were classified as crimes in an effort to erect moral, economic and political boundaries between the races (Brewer, 1994a). This not only influenced the nature of crimes recorded, but also meant that the policing of apartheid was prioritised over crime detection and investigation. This is illustrated by the fact that "the South African Police's (SAP) official historian concedes that during the apartheid era, only one in ten members of the force were engaged in crime detection and investigation" (Dipenaar, 1988 quoted in Shaw, 1995a: p. 11).

Since the beginnings of transition in 1990 and the election of a new government in 1994, this situation has changed, but the implications both in terms of public perceptions and crime statistics are still important. One result of the apartheid era which continues to have dramatic consequences for crime statistics, is the historical exclusion of the so-called bantustans, or 'independent black homelands', from the SAP's records. While these bantustans no longer exist, and police from these regions have been integrated into the SAPS, police data up to 1996 still presents analysts with 'black holes' where data is completely absent for these areas.

The implications of all these factors for crime statistics are that the figures, particularly for the 1980s are problematic. The universal problem of the 'dark figure' of unrecorded crime is probably more pronounced in this country, but more seriously – and of consequence for crime statistics even in the 1990s – data simply do not exist for large areas of South Africa. Beyond the obvious drawbacks of an absence of data, this has implications for the calculation of crime rates – the most reliable measure for comparative purposes – since it takes into account the number of crimes committed per head of population.

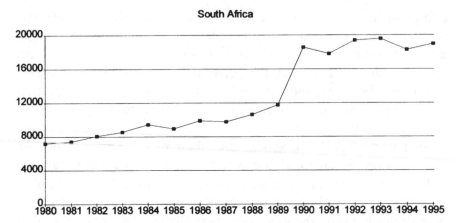

Figure 1. The number of murders reported to police in South Africa annually from 1980-1995.

Before 1994 when the former provincial boundaries were still in place, the calculation of crime rates would have excluded the population of the former homelands. Population figures for the new provinces now include former homelands, but official crime data for these areas are still absent. Because both accurate census data and crime data are absent for large parts of the country, estimating the real crime rate, and predicting future trends, is difficult.

Despite these problems with the statistics, generalised crime patterns can and indeed should be discerned if crime trends during the transition in South Africa and since 1994 are to be understood. Moreover, it is not useful to discount these statistics altogether since there are few other resources available to measure changes in crime patterns over the past decade and during the transition (Shaw, 1995a).

CRIME BEFORE THE TRANSITION: 1980–1990

A breakdown of the recorded annual incidence of crime in South Africa between 1980 and 1990 shows a general increase in most crimes, with dramatic increases occurring in 1990. Violent crimes, and in particular levels of murder and rape, escalated noticeably during this period (Figures 1 and 2).

Serious assault maintained a fairly steady level throughout the decade, dropping slightly in 1986 and 1990 (Figure 3). The two major

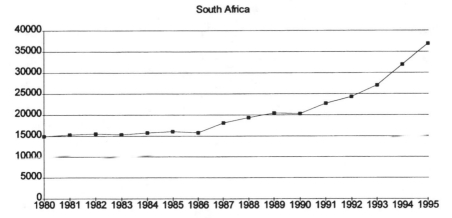

Figure 2. The number of rapes reported to police in South Africa annually from 1980-1995.

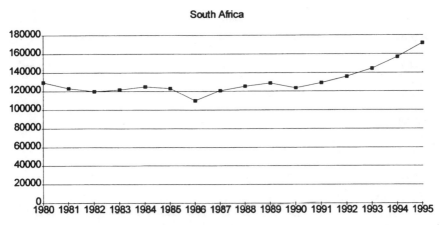

Figure 3. The number of serious assaults reported to police in South Africa annually from 1980-1995.

property crimes reflected overall increases during this period, but did not rise consistently. Housebreaking dropped quite substantially in 1988 and 1989, resuming high levels again in 1990 (Figure 4). Robbery declined slightly between 1980 and 1984, and after increasing in 1986, levels dropped again in 1988 (Figure 5).

Shaw (1995a) suggests that these trends reflect broader changes in society which impacted on the nature of crime once the political transition began, and can be linked to increased criminality during the 1990s. This argument is based largely on the fact that some

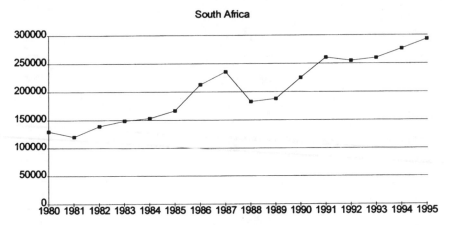

Figure 4. The number of housebreakings reported to police in South Africa annually from 1980-1995.

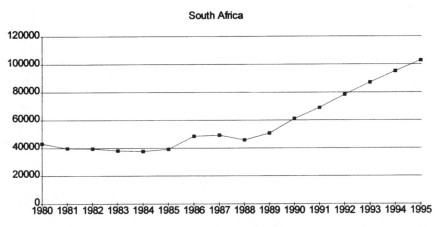

Figure 5. The number of robberies reported to police in South Africa annually from 1980-1995.

crimes did not increase consistently over the decade – a trend which he attributes to factors related to reporting and recording on the one hand, and to the political struggle and the state's response, on the other.

The decline in some crimes may be attributed to the failure of the police to record crime from 1985 to 1990 when the States of Emergency – declared in response to the intensified political activity in black townships after the formation of the United Democratic Front in 1983 – focused police resources on policing these laws rather than on solving crimes in black residential areas in particular. The repressive nature of policing during this period may also have disinclined people to report crimes to the police, although the same would not have applied for crimes committed in white areas. Shaw (1995a) also notes that forms of "people's justice" increased in the 1980s, and that offences handled by these people's courts would probably not have been reported to the authorities.

More interesting, although much harder to assess, is the effect of the political struggle and the attendant political violence on the crime rate. One argument is that the crime rate escalated in conjunction with political violence from the mid-1980s (Brewer, 1994b). The statistics suggest that this argument applies most clearly for murder levels: according to figures compiled by unofficial sources, 9 130 murders occurred between 1985 and 1990 in South Africa in incidents related to political violence. While it is difficult to determine what proportion of the official murder figures provided by the police account for political violence related deaths, the dramatic increase in murders particularly from 1986 to 1990 (and indeed beyond) is in all likelihood related to political violence.

However, based on the fact that not all crimes increased consistently throughout the 1980s (notably assault, housebreaking and robbery), Shaw (1995a) argues that the political struggle may actually have suppressed certain crime rates. Drawing on comparative experiences in Northern Ireland, he points out that the threat of political violence meant a consistently higher presence of armed security forces on the streets. In addition, state repression may have increased community control and cohesiveness during the 1980s, which would have made committing crime more difficult (Shaw, 1995a). With the lifting of restrictions in 1990, these bonds probably began to weaken as the perception of threat decreased, thus contributing to the dramatic increases in crime during and after 1990.

The States of Emergency probably suppressed certain crime levels up to 1990, while the effects of these laws contributed to high rates thereafter. In terms of reducing levels, several of the laws limited freedom of movement and association, and afforded the security forces unlimited powers of search, seizure, arrest and detention without trial. This would have restricted people's ability to commit crime in general. This is illustrated by statistics supplied by official sources which show the effect of the 1986 State of Emergency on curbing levels of political "unrest", which excluded ordinary crime, but included a wide range of events from "illegal gatherings" to murder (Olivier, 1992: p. 2).

Under these circumstances in which people were pitted against the security forces, and given the legacy of apartheid policing which developed more brutal overtones during the Emergency, crimes that did occur during this period were probably less likely to be reported than ever before. In terms of the rising crime levels after 1990, the effects of the States of Emergency on policing practices played an important role. For five years, policing was unchecked and unrestricted, enabling the investigation, arrest and incarceration of "criminals" without following accepted procedures of criminal justice. Without the freedom that the Emergency laws afforded them, police have since 1990 struggled to combat the escalating crime rate. Other pressures brought about by the internal reform of the police and the amalgamation of all police forces into one service, have added to these strains.

TRANSITION TO CONSOLIDATION: CRIME FROM 1990 TO 1996

After the elections in 1994, media coverage of conflict issues shifted noticeably away from political violence towards monitoring the new government's first steps and the obstacles it faced in building a new South Africa (Louw, 1996). Crime was quickly, dramatically (and accurately) identified as one central obstacle. The shift in media, government and public attention towards crime in 1994 – which the figures show was mis-timed rather than misplaced – created the impression that the new government promised not only a new era of democracy, but was part of a process which unleashed a "crime wave" throughout the country.

The statistics confirm the notion that crime has increased during the transition, but it is important to note that on the whole, crime levels escalated markedly in 1990, four years before the new government was elected. Furthermore, not all crimes have been committed with equal frequency and not all areas of the country are similarly affected. To illustrate this, the following section presents first, the changing patterns of crime from 1990 to 1996 over time for the whole country, and second, the spatial distribution of various crime types between the new provinces in South Africa. Because provincial boundaries changed after the new government was elected in April 1994, this section analyses data for the period 1994 to 1996 only.

The dominant arguments in explaining these trends suggest that the rising crime rate is linked in complex ways to the political, economic and social transition. The effects of more than a decade of political violence are also important. This questions the notion that the "crime wave" is the recent product of policies or peculiarities of the new government.

Crime levels over time

Since 1990, crime generally has increased, although patterns for certain crimes vary. Due to limitations of space, only the main violent and property crimes will be considered. These are also the crimes which present the most serious threat to people's lives and property on a daily basis, and which exhibit particularly high levels in South Africa.

One of the most worrying features of the crime scene in South Africa is the propensity for violence. The Nedcor Project reports that the average international murder rate is 5.5 per 100 000 people. South Africa's rate is 45, making this one of the most murderous countries in the world. Comparisons of assault rates are equally disturbing – especially when considering that assault is an underreported crime type: South Africa's rate is 840 per 100 000, compared with an international average of only 142 (Nedcor Project, 1996: p. 7).

The number of murders increased dramatically in 1990 (Figure 1). In the years that followed levels continued to climb until 1994, when, unlike other crimes, the number of murders dropped to around their 1990 levels. Deaths attributable to political violence – which are included in these general murder statistics – probably account for both the increase in murder in 1990 and the decrease in levels in 1994. Political violence largely subsided after the country's first democratic elections in April 1994 (Figure 6). Political conflict has probably contributed substantially to South Africa's high murder figures, and while levels are high, they do not seem to be increasing.

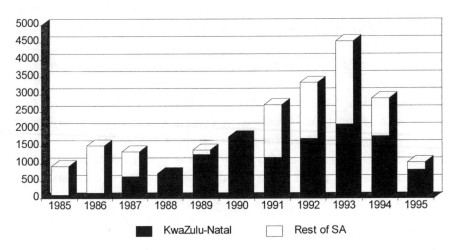

Figure 6. The number of murders comitted in the course of political violence in KwaZulu-Natal province and in the rest of South Africa annually from 1980-1995.

Unlike murder, increases in other serious violent offences like rape, assault with intent to do grievous bodily harm, and robbery have been unwavering – and like murder, substantial – since 1990 (Figures 2, 3, 5). Rape statistics are particularly prone to underreporting: Rape Crisis estimates that only one in every 35 cases are reported to the police (Steenkamp, 1996). The trend in Figure 2 may be explained by women's growing propensity to report rape in recent years, but the consistent nature of the increase suggests that rape itself is escalating. Based on the Rape Crisis estimate, about 3 500 women were raped every day in 1995, which amounts to 146 women every hour.

Property crimes have also increased since 1990, but less consistently than violent crimes. After levelling off between 1991 and 1993, the number of housebreakings has begun to climb again (Figure 4). Unlike the other crimes mentioned here, the most pronounced increase in levels of motor vehicle theft occurred in 1994, and the trend seems set to continue (Figure 7). South Africa has become notorious for car hijackings, a crime which is not presented statistically since police have only recently begun recording "carjackings" as a separate offence. In the first six months of 1996, 6 544 cases were reported – already close to the 7 208 cases reported for the whole of 1993 (Glanz, 1995a).

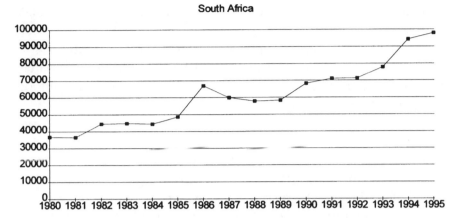

Figure 7. The number of vehicle thefts reported to police in South Africa annually from 1980-1995.

Discussion of the trends

Two salient issues are evident from the trends outlined above: the pronounced increase in crime since 1990, and the continuing high levels of crime.

Explaining the increased rates since the transition began in 1990, Shaw (1995a: 22) argued that "... the transition has led – and will perhaps continue to lead – to higher rates of criminal activity through the interlinking of two factors: the weakening of community controls, and reintegration into the world economy."

This argument builds around the transition in South Africa and its attendant changes, drawing on comparative material on Eastern Europe, the Soviet Union and Namibia which suggests that crime increases markedly in periods of political transition coupled with instability and violence. Broadly, the effects of the political transition can be understood in terms of three related dynamics: the breakdown of community bonds and weakened social control particularly in black communities; the impact of political violence; and the acceleration of political, social and economic trends which had begun before the formal political transition in 1990.

One of the explanations given by Shaw (1995a) for the decline in some types of crime in the mid-1980s was that community bonds formed in response to state aggression suppressed crime levels. Research findings on the East Rand in Gauteng supported the argument that during 1990 when the State of Emergency was lifted, state repression weakened, and as negotiations around a new government began, the process brought intra-community conflict (Shaw, 1993). Political violence further weakened social control, producing marginalised groups who, having depended on conflict for a livelihood, increasingly turned to crime (Shaw, 1994).

Another legacy of the years of political violence – and one which undoubtedly influences violent crime levels – is the abundance of firearms, most of which are illegal. Adding to this stock of illegal weapons, South Africa's permissive gun ownership laws make obtaining legal firearms easy, which increases the stock of weapons generally – and that available to criminals legally or through theft. In 1994, Market Research Africa estimated that about 1.25 million people have hand guns among metropolitan blacks, coloureds, Indians and urban whites (*Research for Action*, 1994). This figure has probably increased in conjunction with the growing crime rate and fear of crime.

The third dynamic which Shaw (1995a) links to rising crime levels is the effect of the transition on emerging political, social and economic trends in the country. Racial segregation had until the late 1980s and early 1990s largely insulated whites from crime rates which have been high for years in neighbouring black townships. This is illustrated by Marks and Andersson's (1990) review of the annual reports of the Medical Health Officer which revealed that Africans are twenty times more at risk from a homicide death than whites.

The disproportionate risk of violence for black people is also illustrated by a hospital-based survey of non-fatal injuries due to external causes in Johannesburg-Soweto between 1989 and 1990. Butchart et al. (1991) found that among victims of interpersonal violence, 22 percent were coloured (who made up 8 percent of the denominator population) and 68 percent were black (who made up 62 percent of the population). According to the authors these findings are not surprising, given the "well documented observation that interpersonal violence the world over, and in colonial societies in particular, occurs most frequently among people subject to the dual pressures of structurally entrenched economic and racial inequalities" (Butchart et al. 1991: p. 479). Despite these high crime levels, many of these incidents occurring in black areas probably went unreported due to the dysfunctional relationship between township residents and police.

Figures supplied by the Commissioner of Police in 1988 showed that whites were the victims of only 4.2 percent of rapes and 2.8 percent of murders, while crimes of property have been committed mainly against whites, reflecting patterns of wealth and ownership (Brewer, 1994b quoted in Shaw, 1995a: p. 26). With the collapse of apartheid boundaries, crime could spread into the suburbs where it is also more likely to be recorded, which could account for the escalation of crime around 1990.

Turning to the continuing high levels of crime, explanations have largely focused on the effects of apartheid and political violence, the decline in effective law enforcement and the breakdown in the criminal justice system and more recently, the growth in organised crime.

Apartheid and political violence
Some explanations for the high rates of violent crime refer to South Africa's political history, suggesting that families have been suffering from 'institutional violence' for decades through the disruption of their lives by the mass removals and migrant labour policies of apartheid (Ramsden, 1994). Political violence has compounded this disintegration of family life, not only through death and injury but also through the forcible displacement of families and destruction of homes. The resultant weakening of the family unit and thus parental control over children may prompt criminal behaviour. As Shaw (1995a) notes, these arguments remain untested, but that if this relationship exists, the situation is unlikely to be remedied soon.

"Culture of violence" theories similarly argue that the effects of apartheid coupled with years of political violence have produced a destructive culture which manifests itself in what the Nedcor Project (1996: p. 7) calls "murderous intolerance." This hypothesis should not be restricted to a particular demographic or political sector of the population according to Vogelman, who argues that "the majority of South Africans are prepared to sanction violence, especially if the victims are from another race, political group or sex" (*Financial Mail*, 2 December 1994).

Responsibility for a "culture of violence" has also been laid at the door of the liberation movements. According to Kane-Berman

(1993), the ANC's strategy of ungovernability was theoretically directed against the apartheid state, but had other destructive effects. In the process of destabilising black local government, leading campaigns against black policemen (which were often violent), and urging a people's war which involved the youth in particular, massive violence was unleashed in black communities which bred a culture of violent lawlessness and a distrust of authority.

Policing and the criminal justice process
Inherent weaknesses in South Africa's criminal justice system combined with pressures associated with the transition, have produced a situation of crisis proportions. This undoubtedly contributes to the high crime rates in the country. Shaw (1996b) identifies several blockages in the "criminal justice pipeline" – a system which encompasses, and requires close cooperation for effectiveness between, the departments of Safety and Security, Justice and Correctional Services. These blockages occur at the level of crime detection, the prosecution of offenders and the system of incarceration. The system's ability to contain crime is moreover affected throughout by poorly trained and under-equipped manpower, ineffective information technology, low wages and weak managerial expertise (*Financial Mail*, 15 December 1995).

The police represent the start of the criminal justice process, and have suffered more stresses associated with the transition than any other sectors in the pipeline. With its long history of politicised policing, the new South African Police Service (SAPS) is under extreme pressure to reform. The demands of the transition have, however, made it difficult for the police to combat crime, while high crime rates in turn frustrate the SAPS's capacity to transform (Shaw, 1996a). The police's ability to "solve" crimes – which refers to clearing crimes from their books rather than securing trial or convictions – is telling: in 1995 only one quarter of all robberies, one fifth of housebreakings, one tenth of vehicle thefts and about 50 percent of murders, were resolved (Shaw, 1996b).

The effectiveness of the SAPS is curtailed by a combination of logistical, training and management issues, and remnants of apartheid style policing. In terms of numbers, the common assumption is that South Africa is underpoliced, but comparisons with other countries suggest otherwise (Shaw, 1996a; *Financial Mail*,

2 December 1994). The problem is rather the maldistribution of police, which is a product of apartheid priorities. Not only are most police concentrated in former white residential areas – until recently about 80 percent of police were based in the suburbs and city centres, with only 8 percent in black townships – but the policing style in townships has been characterised more by crime control than prevention (Shaw, 1996a).

Reforms within the police service have focused more on visible policing (and community policing) than other activities. Detective work, for example, is a crucial part of the criminal justice process, but has been sorely neglected by policy makers (Shaw, 1996b). Detectives receive no overtime pay, have heavy workloads (each having as many as fifty dockets), and do not receive training (only about 26 percent have been on a detective course). As a result, incentives are few, and many experienced detectives leave the service for the private sector (Shaw, 1996b). Also in terms of staffing, many uniformed officers currently occupy administrative jobs: 80 percent of the 500 staff at the police's main warehouse in Pretoria for example, are trained officers. Meanwhile, Johannesburg's flying squad has no more than six of its 59 vehicles operational at any one time because there are too few policemen on duty to drive them (*Financial Mail*, 15 December 1995).

And while police administrators are aware of this situation, they cite the moratorium on police recruitment as a major inhibiting factor, especially since the Service loses more than 4 000 members through natural attrition each year (*Financial Mail*, 15 December 1995). Low morale and high levels of stress among the police since the transition also undermines performance. Between 1991 and June 1994, 29 percent of medical boardings in the Service were due to stress related disabilities. And in 1991, the incidence of suicide among police officers was twelve times higher than that for the general population (Burgers, 1994). (By 1994 the annual number of suicides in the police had doubled from 1991 levels.) Low morale is also one of the factors contributing towards corruption, which is rife in the Service. One in four officers in the Johannesburg area, for example, was under investigation for suspected crimes in 1994 (Shaw, 1996a).

Problems further along the criminal justice pipeline are signalled by the fact that while the number of crimes reported to police continues to increase, the number of convictions decreases. The conviction rate has in fact been declining steadily over the past forty years, a trend which has been associated with a declining rate of cases solved by police (Glanz, 1996). However, problems within the prosecution service abound. Lack of experience, heavy workloads, a high rate of resignations among magistrates and prosecutors, and a lack of cooperation between prosecutors and detectives take their toll. In terms of technology, prosecutors have no computer network to track and sort cases according to priority, resulting in poor management which adds to the workload (*Financial Mail*, 15 December 1995).

The cumulative impact of the breakdown in the criminal justice process is evinced by the problems with the system of incarceration in South Africa. Prisons themselves are overcrowded (presently housing about 30 percent more prisoners than their intended capacity), under-staffed (the inmate to warder ratio is almost 5 : 1 compared with Germany and Australia's 1, 5 : 1), and plagued by prisoner and warder unrest and corruption (Thinane, 1996). But many of the problems originate further back in the criminal justice pipeline. About one quarter of all the country's 118 363 inmates are awaiting trial, and as many as 55.3 percent of those currently imprisoned are repeat offenders (Prinsloo, 1996).

Some of these problems can be attributed to sentencing and parole policies. Overcrowding is partly due to the courts' inclination to favour convictions with prison terms in an effort to 'get tough' on crime. Of the convictions handed down in 1992/93, 65 percent received prison sentences. In England and Wales by comparison, 75 percent of sentenced offenders were fined and only 5 percent were sent to prison in 1994 (Thinane, 1996). South Africa's high prison population rate of 311 people per 100 000 makes it one of the most punitive societies in the world. This dubious status is likely to become entrenched by the stricter parole and release policies announced in August 1996 (Thinane, 1996). Until recently, the Commissioner of Correctional Services had the power to cut sentences by as much as three quarters of the original term (Powell, 1996), which not only meant dangerous criminals could be released in an effort to relieve pressure on the system, but also created an environment conducive to corruption (Shaw, 1996b).

Organised crime

Periods of political transition and violence provide increased opportunities for organised crime. Opportunities for these crimes emerge as legal systems of regulation are adapted to new circumstances and state resources are concentrated in certain areas of governance (Shaw, 1995a; 1996c). The former Soviet Union provides a good example, where thousands of criminal organisations emerged following the end of communist rule. The clearest evidence of this in South Africa is the targeting of the country in recent years by organised drug traffickers. These syndicates are attracted to the country by weakened border controls, lack of legislative control over money laundering and mass unemployment which presents scope for recruitment (Baynham, 1995; *Financial Mail*, 6 September 1996). The implications for the crime rate are serious, as evidence from Britain and Brazil suggests that drug use increases levels of petty theft and violent crime (Shaw, 1995a; 1996c). In addition, syndicates are often involved in more than one area of criminality.

Organised crime is a new area of focus even for the SAPS, who are currently aware of 481 well financed and armed syndicates operating in the country, almost half of which are based in the Johannesburg area (Shaw, 1996c; *Financial Mail*, 6 September 1996). Most local operations deal in a variety of goods and activities, including drugs (136 syndicates), vehicle theft (112 syndicates), commercial crime (85 syndicates), gold and diamond smuggling, arms smuggling, or a combination of these. Tentative estimates are that organised crime has doubled under the new government. Shaw (1996c) attributes this to: weakened border controls which coincided with growth of transnational criminal operations; stricter controls in North American and European countries; southern Africa's convenient position on international drug trafficking routes; its accessibility via land, sea and air; and its endless demand for illegal goods.

The operations of these syndicates have almost certainly contributed to the continuing high crime rates in the country, particularly since sources in the police suggest that the SAPS currently lacks the resources and technical expertise to respond to the problem (Shaw, 1996c). Other factors identified by Shaw (1996c) in the development

of organised crime which are important for this country in particular, are the degree to which syndicates have penetrated the state
in southern Africa, and the difficulties presented by the formation
of relationships between syndicates and gangs. Gangs have been a
feature of cities in the Western Cape (Kinnes, 1995) and Gauteng
for years, and are increasingly becoming a factor in Eastern Cape
and KwaZulu-Natal. The potential for gangs to link with syndicates
in these areas is high.

The spatial distribution of crime

An analysis of where crime occurs shows that not all areas are equally
affected and that common perceptions about which provinces are
worst off in terms of high crime rates, are not always accurate.
Rates for violent and property crimes, calculated per 100 000 head
of population, are compared for the first six months in 1994, 1995
and 1996 across the country's nine provinces. Selected crimes are
illustrated graphically. Refer to the map of South Africa for the
provincial distribution of the country's 40.7 million population.

Rates of violent crime in Northern Cape and Western Cape (the
provinces with the smallest proportion of the country's population)
are high, in some cases surpassing those in Gauteng – the province
traditionally believed to be the most crime-ridden. KwaZulu-Natal
province (which has the highest population) has also gained a reputa-
tion as one of the country's violence capitals, but the figures suggest
that compared to the three provinces already mentioned, this is not
the case.

Over the whole three year period, Gauteng, Northern Cape,
KwaZulu-Natal and Western Cape had the highest murder rates of all
the provinces (Figure 8). Importantly, the murder rate has declined
consistently since 1994 in all provinces excluding Western, Eastern
and Northern Cape. Rates are not clearly increasing in these latter
regions, with the exception of Northern Cape, where murder has
been growing steadily since 1994.

The picture for assault is quite different. By far the highest rates
of serious assault were recorded in Northern and Western Cape.
The KwaZulu-Natal and Gauteng "crime capitals" had similar or
even lower rates than even Eastern Cape and Free State provinces
(Figure 9). Also, unlike the murder figures, rates have generally

Provinces Jan-June 1994-1996

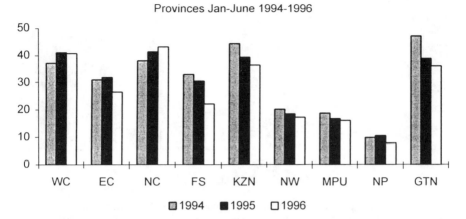

Figure 8. The murder rates per 100 000 head of population in the provinces of South Africa for the first six months of 1994, 1995 and 1996.
(Key: WC – Western Cape, EC – Eastern Cape, NC – Northern Cape, FS – Free State, KZN – KwaZulu-Natal, NW – North West, MPU – Mpumalanga, NP – Northern Province and GTN – Gauteng)

Provinces Jan-June 1994-1996

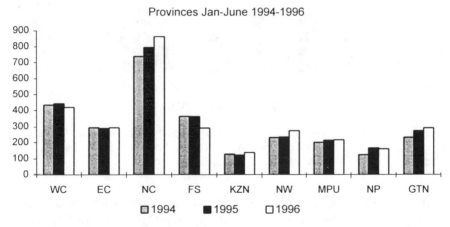

Figure 9. The serious assault rates per 100 000 head of population in the provinces of South Africa for the first six months of 1994, 1995 and 1996.

increased since 1994 throughout the country, and most steadily in Northern Cape. Common assault trends data show similar patterns. The spatial distribution of rape is similar to that of assault, with most rapes per head of population occurring in Northern Cape, Gauteng, Western Cape and Free State.

Turning to property crimes, aggravated robbery – which is also a violent crime – displays a very different trend to the other violent

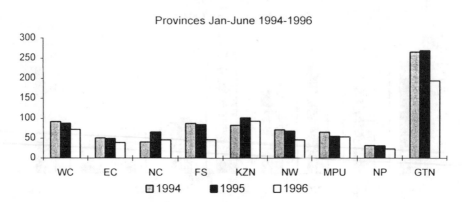

Figure 10. The aggravated robbery rates per 100 000 head of population in the provinces of South Africa for the first six months of 1994, 1995 and 1996.

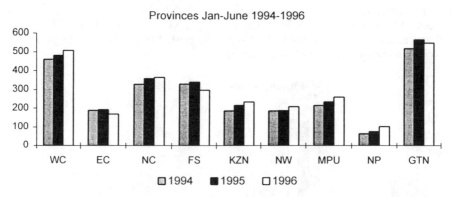

Figure 11. The housebreaking of residential property rates per 100 000 head of population in the provinces of South Africa for the first six months of 1994, 1995 and 1996.

crimes. By far the highest rates occur in Gauteng, followed at much lower levels by KwaZulu-Natal and Western Cape (Figure 10). Interestingly also, unlike the other violent crimes (except for murder), aggravated robbery is decreasing in most parts of the country except for KwaZulu-Natal and Northern Cape. Other robberies of a less violent nature also occur at a higher rate in Gauteng, although rates are higher in Western and Northern Cape than for aggravated robbery. These less serious robberies have also increased markedly in 1996, particularly in Gauteng and North West provinces.

Housebreaking is also generally increasing in most provinces. Thefts from business premises, although widespread in Gauteng, occur more frequently in Western and Northern Cape, despite the fact

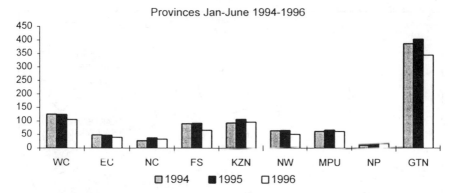

Figure 12. The vehicle theft rates per 100 000 head of population in the provinces of South Africa for the first six months of 1994, 1995 and 1996.

that most business in the country is concentrated in Gauteng. This is probably because these rates are calculated per head of population. A measure of business ownership rather than population may in fact be more accurate for comparing property crime rates. Housebreaking of residential premises clearly afflicts Gauteng more than other provinces, although rates in Western Cape are also high (Figure 11). As with other property crimes, housebreaking rates are also high in Northern Cape and Free State, while surprisingly, fewer break-ins are recorded in KwaZulu-Natal than in Free State or Mpumalanga provinces.

Theft of motor vehicles has become a concern for most South Africans, but the statistics clearly show that this property crime affects people in Gauteng far more than anywhere else in the country (Figure 12). And while carjackings are also feared throughout the country, during the first six months of 1996 this crime similarly affected people in Gauteng to a greater extent than anywhere else.

Discussion of the trends

The statistics illustrate that crime does not affect all South Africans equally as rates are not evenly spread throughout the country. Also, the high rate of violent crimes and even some property crimes in Western and Northern Cape provinces is an unexpected trend.

Theories attempting to explain the spatial distribution of crime abound, often contributing no more than informed debate, since establishing causal links between social, economic and political fac-

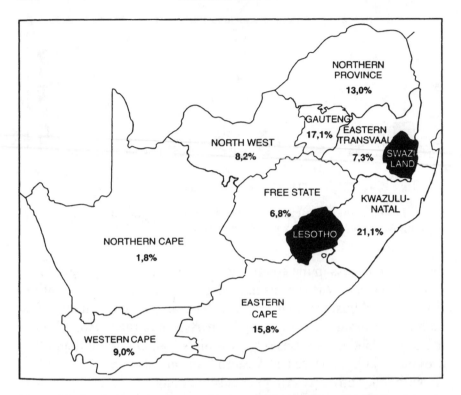

Figure 13. South Africa's nine provinces and the population distribution in each.
(KwaZulu-Natal has 21.1% of the total population of South Africa – 8.6 million
of a total population of 40.7 million. Gauteng, with a population of 6.9 million
people, has the highest population density: 369.3 people per square kilometre.)
Source: Central Statistical Services (1995) The Socio-Economic State of South
Africa as reflected by October Household Survey and the HDI.

tors and crime is difficult (Glanz, 1995b). Glanz notes nevertheless,
that world-wide, crime rates are much greater in cities than in rural
areas, with rates generally increasing according to city size. Most
factors associated with high crime rates characterise cities rather than
small towns, such as greater population density, increased opportunities for crime, urbanisation and attendant overcrowding, unemployment, gang activity and the availability of firearms. The anonymity
of cities, particularly for the perpetration of property crimes, is also
relevant.

These factors, along with the history of years of political (and
in the case of Cape Town, gang) violence, rapid urbanisation, bur-
geoning informal settlements and related dynamics associated with

the breakdown of "apartheid cities" (Hindson et al., 1993), would account for the high crime rates in Gauteng, Western Cape and KwaZulu-Natal, where the urban complexes around Johannesburg, Cape Town and Durban respectively are located. But high violent crime rates in the Northern Cape are less easy to explain, since there are no comparable urban areas in this province.

Glanz's (1995b) analysis of crime rates in 1994 in metropolitan and non-metropolitan areas of the former provinces raises further questions about the spatial occurrence of crime. Violent crime rates were found to be *higher* in the *non-metropolitan* areas of the Northern Cape, Western Cape and former Natal. (In the other provinces, crime rates generally were higher in the urban complexes than in the surrounding non-metropolitan areas). This has important implications for explaining the high violent crime rates in Northern and Western Cape, since it suggests that many of these crimes probably occur outside the urban complexes. In the case of KwaZulu-Natal, this trend is more easily explained by the spread of political violence to rural areas of the province after 1990 (Louw and Bekker, 1992).

No analyses have as yet been undertaken to explain the high crime rates in Northern and Western Cape, although tentative explanations have pointed to high levels of alcohol abuse and domestic violence in these provinces. Recently, police analysts attributed the high rates of murder and assault in Northern Cape province to "a subculture of drug and alcohol abuse . . . " (*Sunday Times*, 17 November 1996). These links have yet to be conclusively established.

A word of caution regarding the spatial distribution of crime rates represented here is necessary. Some of these trends may be the product of reporting and police recording patterns. Crime rates in provinces like Eastern Cape and Northern Province which include former independent "homelands", or KwaZulu-Natal which include former "self-governing territories" are probably an undercount. In many cases data do not exist for these regions. In areas like KwaZulu-Natal where the police were particularly politicised in the past, police-community relationships have been severely affected, which limits reporting. Conversely, the comparatively high crime rates in Northern and Western Cape and Gauteng may reflect better policing in these provinces, or greater access to resources which facilitate reporting crime, like transport and telephones.

PERCEPTIONS ABOUT CRIME, SAFETY AND SECURITY

It is not surprising, given the high levels of crime described above, that the fear of crime among South Africans is growing and that few people now feel safe in the country. Several important social and political consequences have been associated with growing fear of crime, and should be considered by policy makers. In addition, it is important to consider people's perceptions about crime in conjunction with official statistics, since the former can provide valuable information which is lost due to crime reporting and recording problems.

In Britain, the United States and Europe, the fear of crime has become as serious as crime itself (Heidensohn, 1989). This anxiety is not simply a fear of specific dangers, but should be seen as part of people's wider concept of quality of life (Williams and Dickinson, 1993). As such, these fears can change people's lifestyles by causing them to withdraw, restricting the extent to which they socialise and travel, and entrenching a form of social distance in cases where people respond by barricading themselves behind high walls, or within walled suburban complexes (Shaw, 1996a; Glanz, 1994). The fear of crime is also greatest among more vulnerable groups like women and the elderly, although they are ironically far less likely to be targeted than young males, for example.

Politically, the way that people respond to growing feelings of insecurity and lack of confidence in the government and the police, is important. This may take the form of employing private security firms for protection, undertaking self-policing, or resorting to other forms of popular justice which have been a feature of certain black communities for years (Nina, 1995; Kinnes, 1995). These measures can have both positive and negative implications for democracy and policing (Shaw, 1996a; Nina, 1996).

Most worrying are the violent vigilante responses, which in the form of people's courts have also been a feature of South African society during the transition (Minnaar, 1995). The activities of some self-defence and self-protection units, established to defend black communities against political opponents in 1990, have also raised concerns (Minnaar et al., 1993). Recently, analysts highlighted the potential threat to security posed by the activities of the militant vigilante group People Against Gangsterism and Drugs (Pagad) in

Western Cape province, which challenged state sovereignty in new and fundamental ways (Nina, 1996; Shaw, 1996d). On another level, the fear of crime and perceptions of a "crime wave" may induce responses from government and the police which are not necessarily the most appropriate.

Victimisation surveys conducted by the Human Sciences Research Council in 1992 and 1996, along with results from the Nedcor Project's survey in 1995 show that crime rather than socio-economic issues now dominates people's concerns, and that fear of crime is increasing along with feelings of helplessness. Interestingly, the surveys show that fewer people over the years report having actually been victimised.

In 1992, 52 percent of those surveyed ranked unemployment as the most pressing social problem facing the country. Housing shortages and crime, which were the next most important concerns, were each mentioned in only 11 percent of cases (Glanz, 1994). In 1995 by comparison, nearly half of all respondents identified crime as the most serious current problem, with unemployment being mentioned in only 18 percent of cases. Significantly, crime was identified by all race groups as the major concern. In earlier opinion surveys (although not as early as the 1992 survey) whites tended to identify crime as important, while other race groups mentioned socio-economic factors (Nedcor Project, 1996). A similar finding was reported in a pilot study of people's views on development in KwaZulu-Natal in 1995. Political violence and crime were identified as the most pressing problems in that province over unemployment and housing (Møller et al., 1996).

When crime is not compared with other social problems, however, the survey data show that crime has been a consistent concern among South Africans for several years. Forty five percent of those surveyed in 1995 by the Nedcor Project said they thought crime had increased during the past year in their neighbourhoods. Fifty percent had expressed a similar opinion in 1992. It is interesting that a greater proportion of respondents did not believe crime had increased in the 1995 survey, since levels of reported crime have risen substantially between 1992 and 1995.

In terms of the impact of crime and people's fear of crime, a similar trend is evident. Fifty percent of respondents in 1992, and 46 percent in 1995 thought it was likely that they would become victims of crime in the near future. However, questions about perceptions of safety and the state's control over the crime problem show that people's opinions have changed dramatically over time. Surveyed just after the 1994 elections, 73 percent of people considered themselves safe and 67 percent believed the government had the crime situation under control. By July 1996, these proportions had dropped markedly to 44 percent and 28 percent respectively (HSRC media release, 1996).

In terms of actual victimisation, however, reported incidence seems to have declined since 1992. Twenty five percent of people reported that they or a household member was victimised in the twelve months prior to the survey in 1992. This compares with 18 percent in 1995 (Nedcor Project, 1996) and only 10 percent in July 1996 (HSRC media release, 1996). In 1992, one in five households reported being the victim of property crime, while nearly one in ten experienced violent crime. The varying experiences of crime by different race groups was alluded to above in the discussion of crime trends in the 1990s.

The victimisation survey showed that overall, whites were victimised to the greatest extent, 80 percent of which was for property crimes (Glanz, 1994). A similar trend applied to Indians. However, only 62 percent of the crimes committed against blacks and 61 percent against coloureds were property crimes, which means that these groups experienced far more violence than whites and Indians. It is important to note that as further analysis showed, whether or not a person becomes a victim of crime relates to factors other than demographic variables, and could include chance, the amount of crime in the area, and exposure to risk in terms of transport mode and lifestyle. Thus, as socio-economic patterns change, so victimisation rates will change also.

Also of interest is Glanz's (1994) conclusion based on the 1992 victimisation survey, that underreporting of crime to the police was considerable. Drawing on the number of respondents who said they were victims of crime, a rate of 4 167 per 100 000 was estimated – far higher than the rate of 2 999 recorded by the police in 1991. In the July 1996 survey, however, 80 percent of respondents said that they had reported crimes committed against them in the past year to the police (HSRC media release, 1996). This finding is encouraging and may suggest that confidence in the police is improving.

CONCLUSION

Crime levels in South Africa are high and have been increasing since the 1980s, and particularly since 1990. But there have been important variations both in terms of the incidence of different crime types and in terms of the impact of crime on different areas of the country. Any attempt at explaining these trends without taking into account the effects of apartheid and the political transition on crime levels would be difficult, if not short sighted. The murder rate is most clearly associated with political violence levels, which best explains both the increase in murders in 1990 and the drop in levels in 1994. The rates of other serious crimes have varied over time and by region, but apart from attempted murder, violent crime rates show an upward trend. And while the numbers of reported property crimes are clearly on the rise, the estimated rates for these crimes show less certain trends.

Explaining changing crime trends and the spatial distribution of crime is never straight forward. In South Africa the problem is compounded by the police's failure to police crime effectively (Shaw, 1995a). Explanations here have focused mainly on political and social circumstances in the country since it is changes in these areas that have dominated the transition period. In future, as government becomes more regulated and problems in the criminal justice process and policing in particular are ironed out, the links between development, unemployment and crime will probably become the focus in the crime debate, especially in the search for long term solutions.

While it seems logical that unemployment causes crime, the connections between unemployment and rising crime are complicated, and the assumption that the unemployed are more likely to commit crimes is not consistently verified by research (Shaw, 1995b). The relationship between development and crime is also complex. Crime is thought to be one of the social consequences of development, with international surveys indicating that as development increases, so too do crimes against property (Shaw, 1995a). Development creates opportunities for crime at the same time as causing inequalities which encourage crime.

This has important implications for South Africa, where development is the key priority of the new government. Indeed, local cases like the Cato Manor Special Presidential Project in KwaZulu-Natal – the largest Reconstruction and Development Programme (RDP) project in the country, illustrate this well. Robinson and Forster (1996) report that one of the biggest obstacles to success has been the breakdown of law and order in the area during the course of the project. But evidence suggests that development over time tends to reduce crimes of violence, illustrated by the fact that less developed countries experience higher rates of violent crime than developed countries (Shaw, 1995a).

While property crime will probably continue to increase along with development, it is likely that the impact of these crimes is less for more affluent people with greater economic support than for people in poorer circumstances. The prognosis for South Africa then, is that crime levels will probably get worse before there are signs of improvement. Levels of property crimes can be expected to continue their increase well into the future. And while violent crimes should begin to decrease over the medium term, official statistics may show the opposite, as improved relations with the police and a culture of reporting crimes like rape and assault, result in more crime being recorded.

REFERENCES

Baynham, S.: 1995, 'Drugs for Africa', Indicator South Africa Crime and Conflict 3, pp. 1–4.
Bottomly, K. and K. Pease: 1986, Crime and Punishment: Interpreting the Data (Open University Press, Milton Keyes).
Brewer, J.: 1994a, Black and Blue: Policing in South Africa (Clarendon Press, Oxford).
Brewer, J.: 1994b, 'Crime and Control', J. Brewer (ed.), Restructuring South Africa (Macmillan, London).
Butchart, A., V. Nell, D. Yach, D.S.O. Brown, A. Anderson, B. Radebe and K. Johnson: 1991, 'Epidemiology of non-fatal injuries due to external causes in Johannesburg-Soweto', South African Medical Journal 79, pp.472-479.
Burgers, T.J.: 1994, 'Facing The Enemy', Indicator SA Conflict Supplement 4, pp. 5–8.
Dipenaar, M.: 1988, The History of the SAP 1913–88 (Promedia, Silverton).

Glanz, L.: 1994, Crime in South Africa: Perceptions, Fear and Victimisation (Human Sciences Research Council, Pretoria).

Glanz, L.: 1995a, 'Patterns of Crime: Deciphering the Statistics', Indicator SA Crime and Conflict 1, pp. 7–11.

Glanz, L.: 1995b, 'South African Cities Under Siege', Indicator SA Crime and Conflict 2, pp. 17–2l.

Glanz, L.: 1996, 'The not so long arm of the law', Indicator SA Crime and Conflict 5, pp. 9–14.

Heidensohn, F.: 1989, Crime and Society (Macmillan, London).

Hindson, D. and M. Morris: 1993, From Violence to Reconstruction: The Making, Disintegration and Remaking of an Apartheid City, Working Paper 10 (Centre for Social and Development Studies, Durban).

HSRC media release: 1996, 'Fear of crime could become bigger problem than crime itself', Corporate Communications 24 October (HSRC, Pretoria).

Kane-Berman, J.: 1993, Political Violence in South Africa (South African Institute of Race Relations, Johannesburg).

Kinnes, I.: 1995, 'Reclaiming the Cape Flats: A community challenge to crime and gangsterism', Indicator SA Crime and Conflict 2, pp. 5–8.

Louw, A.: 1996, Reporting Violence in KwaZulu-Natal: An assessment of selected sources for conflict research, Unpublished MA Thesis (University of Natal, Durban).

Louw, A. and S. Bekker: 1992, 'Conflict in the Natal region: A database approach', in S. Bekker (eds.), Capturing the Event: Conflict Trends in the Natal Region 1986–1992 (Indicator SA, Durban).

Marks, S. and N. Andersson : 1990, 'The epidemiology and culture of violence', in N.C. Manganyi and A. Du Toit (eds.), Political Violence and the Struggle in South Africa (Southern, Johannesburg).

Minnaar, A., T. Keith and C. Payze: 1993, "SDUs or Comtsotsis: Criminal gangs and political violence', Paper presented to the Annual Conference of the Criminological Society of South Africa 2–3 September (University of South Africa: Pretoria).

Minnaar, A.: 1995, 'Desperate Justice', Indicator SA Crime and Conflict 2, pp. 9–12.

Møller, V. et al.: 1996, Perceptions of Development in KwaZulu-Natal: A Subjective Indicator Study (Indicator Press, Durban).

Nedcor Project on Crime, Violence and Investment: 1996, Final Report (The Nedcor Project, Johannesburg).

Nina, D.: 1995, 'Going Back to the Roots: Alternative views on community justice', Indicator SA Crime and Conflict 2, pp. 2–4.

Nina, D.: 1996, 'Popular Justice of Vigilantism? Pagad, the state and the community', Indicator SA Crime and Conflict 7, pp. 1–4.

Olivier, J.: 1992, 'Political conflict in South Africa: A resource mobilisation approach', S. Bekker (ed.), Capturing The Event: Conflict Trends in the Natal Region 1986–1992 (Indicator SA, Durban).

Powell, S.: 1996, 'Reworking Parole', Indicator SA Crime and Conflict 5, pp. 18–21.

Prinsloo, J.H.: 1996, 'Coming back for more: Repeat offenders in South Africa's prisons', Indicator SA Crime and Conflict 7, pp. 24–29.

Ramsden, N.: 1994, 'Suffer Little Children', Indicator SA Conflict Supplement 3, pp. 7–10.

Research For Action: 1994, 'Hand-gun ownership and break-ins', Market Research Africa 117.

Robinson, P. and C. Forster: 1996, 'Cato Manor: Lessons from the largest RDP project', Indicator SA 13(4), pp. 32–38.

Shaw, M.: 1993, 'Crying peace where there is none? The functioning and future of local peace committees of the National Peace Accord', Research Report 31 (Centre for Policy Studies, Johannesburg).

Shaw, M.: 1994, 'Violence, development and democratic change – South Africa's East Rand, 1990–1994', paper presented to a conference on urban conflict in Africa. Ibadan, Nigeria.

Shaw, M.: 1995a, 'Partners in Crime'? Crime, political transition and changing forms of policing control, Research Report 39 (Centre for Policy Studies, Johannesburg).

Shaw, M.: 1995b, 'Exploring a decade of crime', Indicator SA Crime and Conflict 1, pp. 12–15.

Shaw, M.: 1996a, 'Crime, political transition and changing forms of policing control', in M. Shaw and L. Camerer (eds.), Policing the Transformation: New issues in South Africa's crime debate, Monograph Series 3 (Institute for Defence Policy, Johannesburg).

Shaw, M.: 1996b, 'Reforming South Africa's Criminal Justice System', Paper 8 (Institute for Defence Policy, Johannesburg).

Shaw, M.: 1996c, 'The development of organised crime in South Africa', in M. Shaw and L. Camerer (eds.), Policing the Transformation: New issues in South Africa's crime debate, Monograph Series 3 (Institute for Defence Policy, Johannesburg).

Shaw, M.: 1996d, 'Buying Time? Vigilante action, crime control and state responses', Indicator SA Crime and Conflict 7, pp. 5–8.

Steenkamp, M.: 1996, 'Rape in South Africa', Trauma Review 4(2), p. 5.

Thinane, M.: 1996, 'End of the line: South Africa's overcrowded prisons', Indicator SA Crime and Conflict 7, pp. 30–31.

Williams, P. and H. Dickinson: 1993, 'Fear of Crime: Read all about it? The relationship between newspaper crime reporting and fear of crime', British Journal of Criminology 33, pp. 33–51.

Centre For Social And Development Studies
University of Natal
Private Bag X10
Dalbridge 4014
Durban, South Africa
E-mail:louwa@mtb.und.ac.za

ROS HIRSCHOWITZ and MARK ORKIN

TRAUMA AND MENTAL HEALTH IN SOUTH AFRICA

ABSTRACT. Prior to the first democratic elections, South Africa had experienced severe political violence. In this paper, we describe the effects of this violence on mental health, concentrating mainly on post-traumatic stress disorder (PTSD), and its symptoms, including reliving aspects of the trauma, avoiding situations which remind one of the experience, and heightened irritability. As part of a nationwide survey on health inequalities covering 4 000 South African households, questions were put to 3 870 respondents aged 16 to 64 years on their mental health status, feelings of powerlessness, exposure to violence and other traumatic situations, symptoms of PTSD and access to health care for these symptoms. Weighted survey results indicate that approximately five million adults (23% of the population aged 16 to 64 years) had been exposed to one or more violent events, for example, being attacked, participating in violence and witnessing one's home being burnt. Just under four-fifths (78%) of those who had experienced at least one traumatic event had one or more symptoms of PTSD. This syndrome was found to be related to feelings of powerlessness, anxiety and depression and fair or poor self-ratings of emotional well-being. The authors concluded that healing the people of South Africa involves revealing the full extent of political violence that was committed during the apartheid era, confronting the effects of this violence, and establishing both professional and community structures to deal with it on a large scale, for example, the training of lay people to give counselling.

INTRODUCTION

South Africa has recently emerged from an era characterised by large-scale political violence. An extensive, undeclared war was fought, not only within the country itself, but also in its neighbouring states (Bridgland, 1990). Recent trials of members of security forces and evidence given at the Truth and Reconciliation Commission give an indication of how extensive torture, murder and arson were in this country during the apartheid era generally, but particularly during the 1980s and early 1990s.

In the 1980s, resistance to apartheid claimed many lives and subjected unknown numbers of people to incidents of murder, bomb blasts, "necklacing", burning of property, police brutality and other

Social Indicators Research **41**: 169–182, 1997.
© 1997 *Kluwer Academic Publishers. Printed in the Netherlands.*

forms of politically-motivated violence. Army conscripts and the police were required to fight a war in Namibia to prevent its independence. They were required to wage war against the vast majority of citizens of South Africa to prevent the advent of democracy, and to attack the neighbouring countries in order to uphold the policies of apartheid. In the early 1990s, orchestrated political violence also was wide-ranging (Everatt and Orkin, 1993; Everatt, Jennings and Orkin, 1994). Train violence in which commuters were brutally assassinated, the burning of homes and shacks, attacks by hostel dwellers on township residents, shootings of taxi-commuters, demonstrators and marchers were commonplace events.

The possible effects of exposure to violence on the mental health status of South Africans have previously been described (Hirschowitz, Milner and Everatt, 1994), but these effects have not been estimated by means of quantitative survey research methods.

In this paper, we investigate the extent of exposure to these events, and the possible impact of such exposure on mental health.

The research on which this paper is based is part of a much wider study on health inequalities in South Africa (Hirschowitz and Orkin, 1995). A nationwide survey among 4 000 households was conducted to measure perceptions among the general public regarding their own and their family's health status, access to health-care and utilisation of health services. Information was obtained by face-to-face interviews. The questionnaire was available in English and four other languages spoken in the country. The training of field workers stressed the way in which the various questions should be interpreted.

The survey was wide-ranging, covering a variety of health-related topics. But, during each interview, a series of questions were posed on mental health, including exposure to violence, emotional problems experienced as a result of this type of exposure, feelings of powerlessness, and perceived mental health status. The answers given to these questions form the basis of this description of mental health in South Africa.

RATIONALE

In this paper, we focus on the effects of an oppressive political system generally, and political violence in particular, on the mental health of the people of South Africa.

In the survey, we concentrated mainly on the subjective indications of mental disorders such as anxiety and depression, and on subjective experiences of stress in relation to exposure to violence, manifested as post-traumatic stress disorder (PTSD), and its three groups of symptoms – reliving aspects of the trauma, avoiding situations which remind the individual of the trauma, and symptoms of heightened irritability (Gersons and Carlier, 1992).

The literature on war-related stress indicates that PTSD may have long been an unrecognised consequence of exposure to war. In the past, this syndrome could have been known under a variety of names. For example, symptoms of shell-shock suffered in the First World War have much in common with PTSD (Gersons and Carlier, 1992).

In addition, Eitinger and Strom (1973), in a longitudinal study among survivors of Nazi concentration camps, found that these survivors maintained higher than expected morbidity and mortality rates, compared to controls. They had significantly more tuberculosis, neurosis, alcohol and drug abuse. They also had less successful work lives, more time on sick leave, and more and longer hospital admissions. These are symptoms which are typical of PTSD.

It is therefore important to realise that PTSD may be a well-known condition, even if it has only recently been clearly defined and distinguished from other syndromes. It is one possible set of consequences that can result from living through traumatic, violent and highly stressful war situations.

Even though it is highly likely that PTSD has a long history, it was only recently documented as a clearly distinguishable syndrome of severe mental stress in studies of the psychological effects in relation to relatively new conflicts such as the Vietnam war (Green et al., 1990; Bremner et al., 1992) and the conflict in Iraq in 1990 (Engel et al., 1993).

PTSD can be caused, not only through exposure to war, but also through exposure to other traumatic events. Evidence of this syndrome has been found, not only among war veterans, but also among civilians exposed to disasters, for example the collapse of a dam at

Buffalo Creek (Green et al., 1992) . It has also been identified as a response to a variety of other violent situations. For example, victims of bombings in public places in France between 1982 and 1987, in relation to the Middle-East conflict, showed symptoms of PTSD (Abenhaim et al., 1992). It has also been found as a syndrome related to squalid urban situations, where the risk of being exposed to violent situations is high. For example, among urban populations living in "black ghettos" of the United States, 40% of males aged 21 to 30 years were exposed to violence, and 25% of those who were exposed experienced symptoms of PTSD. (Breslau et al., 1991).

In spite of the evidence cited above pointing to a syndrome of PTSD, the existence of this condition has been disputed. For example, Summerfield (1996) states that the definition of PTSD is too "narrowly deterministic and pathologized" (p. 376). It ignores the culture in which these events occur. He argues that the vast majority of people suffering from trauma seek to rebuild their lives, and "all over the world, huge numbers of ordinary, unremarkable people demonstrate a capacity to endure, adapt and transcend" traumatic events (Summerfield, 1996, p. 376).

In this paper, we will present findings which support PTSD as a stress-related condition which develops in relation to violent and other traumatic experiences. Even though people may attempt to rebuild their lives, to cope at work and socially, the scars left by negative experiences through the development of PTSD is a reality.

METHODOLOGY

We first describe the general methodology used for the national household survey on health requirements, since the data given here form part of this general study. Afterwards, we focus on the mental health questions that were asked in the survey, how they were tested and modified, and the group of respondents who answered these questions. Finally, we describe how the sample was weighted.

Drawing a sample for the household survey

A nationwide probability sample of 4 000 households, stratified by race, province, and metropolitan, urban and rural components was drawn for the study of health in South Africa, of which mental health formed a sub-set. A thousand different sampling points or areas were selected for interviews to be conducted throughout the country, and four households were visited at each sampling point or area, making a total of 4 000 households where interviews were conducted.

General information in the questionnaire

In the questionnaire, information was obtained on the household in general, for example, number of people in the household, number of rooms, access to clean water and sanitation and access to health-care services. These facts were provided by a senior person in the household who assumes responsibility for the health of its members. In 90% of cases, this respondent was a woman.

Information was also obtained on randomly selected individuals in the household in different age categories – 0 to 5 years, 6 to 15, 16 to 64 and 65 years or older (one individual was selected per age category). Ninety five percent of the 4 000 households where interviews were conducted contained at least one individual in the age category 16 to 64 years. These people were interviewed separately from the person responsible for the health of the household.

Mental health questions

The mental health questions discussed in this paper were put to the 3 870 respondents in the age category 16 to 64 years. They focused on a subjective rating of the individual's mental health status, feelings of powerlessness and alienation, exposure to violence and other traumatic situations, symptoms of PTSD and access to health care for these symptoms.

Some of the questions used in the section on mental health in the questionnaire were based on those developed for the *National Survey of Health and Stress* in the United States (Kessler, 1994), and the Lao version of the *Harvard Trauma Questionnaire* (Blendon, 1994).

The use of focus groups and a pilot study

To determine ways in which to formulate or adapt questions to reflect local circumstances, qualitative methodology was used. A series of 10 focus group discussions were held in different parts of the country, using a discussion guide to facilitate the process. Due to lack of funds, only one group was directed specifically to discuss mental health issues. The nine people selected for this group were African male shack dwellers aged 16 to 30 years who had lived through severe forms of pre-election violence. They described their experiences and the effects of these experiences on their present life. We adapted the mental health questions on the basis of this discussion.

In addition, the questionnaire was tested out and modified after the researchers observed face-to-face interviews conducted by field workers. Use was made of one-way viewing facilities to observe the interviews.

Field workers also conducted a pilot survey of 100 interviews, based on area probability sampling, among all population groups in all parts of the country before the main survey took place.

Weighting the sample

Data concerning households were weighted back to the estimated number of households in the country in the various provinces in 1994, according to the proportions found in urban and non-urban areas, and by the race of the head of the household. Data on individuals within households were weighted by age, race and gender, according to 1994 estimates of population size in urban and non-urban areas in the nine provinces.

LIMITATIONS OF THIS ANALYSIS

Since the study cited here is based on survey research methodology, the limitations of this type of research need to be borne in mind. Surveys are descriptive in nature. They are snapshots of the life situation of people at a given point in time, and they rely on perceptions in relation to attitudinal questions, and on memory when questions are posed in relation to past events.

When surveys are used to ask individuals to recall what happened to them in the past, they are examples of *ex post facto* research. In this type of research, one looks for correlations between variables indicative of the present life situation of the individual and variables indicative of the past. One assumes that there is a causal relationship between these correlations – the past determines the present. These assumptions remain hypothetical (Kerlinger, 1973), but if they are supported by other research findings on the same topic, using similar methodology, but with different respondents in alternative settings, for example, war veterans in other countries, they are strengthened and gain credibility.

Although this research is *ex post facto* in nature, other international studies identifying this syndrome in similar situations lend credence to this one.

RESULTS OF THE SURVEY

We now discuss the research findings by first focusing on traumatic events which individuals in South Africa have experienced, and their effects on mental health, particularly the experience of symptoms of PTSD. Then we examine some general results related to mental health, namely ratings of mental health, feelings of being in control of ones life and symptoms of anxiety and depression and how these are related to PTSD.

Traumatic events

The survey showed that exposure to political violence among South Africans aged between 16 and 64 years was indeed widespread, comparable to a war situation (Bremner et al., 1992). We asked respondents to indicate whether or not they had experienced one or more traumatic event related to political violence, including fighting a war, living through a life-threatening incident, being attacked or witnessing an attack, being raped, participating in violence, being tortured, witnessing one's home being burnt or being evicted from one's home.

We found that large numbers of people across all race groups have experienced extreme forms of violence. Altogether approximately five million adults (23% of the population aged 16 to 64 years) had been exposed to one or more of the events listed above. Although a smaller proportion of Africans (20%) and Indians (19%) had experienced at least one traumatic event compared to whites (32%) and coloureds (33%), in actual numbers, the picture looks different. Approximately 3.3 million Africans, 0.6 million coloureds,

0.1 million Indians and 1.0 million whites had these negative experiences.

Males (28%) were more likely than females (19%) to have experienced at least one traumatic event. Among the male respondents, whites (41%) and coloureds (41%) were most likely to have had these experiences, rather than Africans (24%) or Indians (24%). The large proportion of white males being exposed to traumatic events can probably be ascribed to compulsory conscription during the apartheid era (those aged between 25 and 34 years having experienced more traumatic events than older or younger respondents). The large proportion of coloured males subjected to traumatic events can probably be explained, at least in part, by the large numbers of gangs and of gangsterism in coloured townships.

People in all population groups living in metropolitan areas (35%) were more likely to have experienced at least one traumatic event than those living in smaller urban (26%) or rural (12%) areas.

Psychological effects of a traumatic experience

Table I indicates that nearly four-fifths (78%) of those who had experienced at least one traumatic event had suffered from one or more of the following effects: ongoing, unwanted remembrance of the event, ongoing dreams and nightmares about it, suddenly acting as if the event was happening all over again, becoming extremely upset in a similar situation, inability to feel love and warmth towards others, extreme behaviour to avoid situations that remind one of the event and blocking it out by forgetting the details. All these are symptoms of PTSD. Africans in particular (85%) displayed at least one symptom of PTSD.

Table I also shows that Africans were more likely to have recurring, unwanted memories of the event (66%) than coloureds (43%), Indians (41%) or whites (32%). Overall, Africans were less likely to react by blocking out the details of the event (16%), or to avoid similar events (37%), perhaps because their life circumstances made it difficult to do so.

Relationship between PTSD and other aspects of mental health

Bearing in mind the extent of exposure to political violence in South Africa, and the large proportion of people exposed to violence and

TABLE I
Psychological effects of a traumatic experience

Symptoms of post-traumatic stress	Total %*	Africans %*	Coloureds %*	Indians% *	White%*
Unwanted memory of event	56	66	43	41	32
Recurring nightmares	22	23	23	27	16
Sudden actions	24	26	29	29	16
Extreme upset in a similar situation	42	46	43	52	31
Lost feelings of warmth	13	14	10	12	11
Avoidance of similar situations	39	37	53	51	34
Block out of details	19	16	31	23	20
Any of above	78	85	74	71	60

*The balance of each percent in the table adds up to 100.

other traumatic events who have experienced at least one symptom of
PTSD, we now examine how this syndrome relates to other aspects
of mental health covered in the survey.

Ratings of mental health status

Respondents were asked to rate their perceived emotional state on
a five point scale, ranging from excellent to poor. Altogether, 26%
of respondents considered their emotional state to be excellent, 32%
very good, 31% good, 9% fair and 2% poor.

Rating one's emotional state as being fair or poor was related
to life circumstances. For example, respondents who were unable
to work due to illness or disability were more likely to rate their
emotional state as poor (10% rated their emotional state as poor) than
the average respondent (2%). Respondents with a level of education
of Standard three or lower, if any, were more likely to rate their emotional state as fair or poor (16%), compared to those with Standard
10 or higher (9%). Those living in shacks were more likely to rate
their emotional state as fair or poor (15%), compared to those living
in formal housing (12%) or in traditional dwellings (8%). Poverty
and low mental health ratings were correlated. For example, 11% of
respondents living in households where the inhabitants frequently
went hungry rated their emotional health as poor, as against 2%
of those in households where the inhabitants sometimes, seldom or
never went hungry.

However, what is significant in relation to the past history of
apartheid, is that proportionately more people living in those
provinces containing former "bantustans" rated their emotional state
as being fair or poor than those living in other provinces. For
example, 24% of those living in the North West province rated their
emotional state as being fair or poor, compared to 11% overall.

What is most important in relation to this paper is that 17% of
those who had experienced a disturbing or traumatic event described
their emotional state as poor, compared to 2% overall. Experiencing
traumatic events is therefore related to the subjective perception of
being in poor mental health.

Feeling in control of one's life

To assess the extent to which respondents felt powerful and in control
of their lives, we asked them to indicate whether or not they felt
powerless to solve major worries, and whether they found it difficult
to understand why major events that disturb or affect their lives are
happening.

We found that just over one quarter of respondents (27%) felt
powerless to solve major worries. In addition, 21% of respondents
had difficulty in understanding why major events affecting their
lives were occurring. These two alienation measures (powerlessness
and bewilderment) were highly correlated ($r = 0.60$; $p < 0.001$),
indicating that they measure closely related variables.

Adverse life circumstances were directly related both to feeling
powerless and to bewilderment. For example, those living in shacks
(41%) were more likely to feel powerless, compared with those living
in formal housing (27%) or traditional dwellings (20%); while 54%
of those living in households that frequently went hungry were likely
to feel powerless, as against 19% of those living in households that
never went hungry.

Feelings of powerlessness ($r = 0.56$; $p < 0.001$) and bewilderment
($r = 0.61$, $p < 0.001$) were highly correlated with having at least one
of the symptoms of PTSD in the total sample.

Symptoms of anxiety and depression

To examine the extent of symptoms of anxiety and depression among
adults aged 16 to 64 years in South Africa, we asked respondents to
indicate whether or not, in the past few months or so, they (a) frequently felt isolated, (b) found little point thinking about the future,
(c) lost interest in things, (d) had trouble concentrating, (e) were
unusually irritable, (f) had trouble sleeping, and (g) were sweating
or trembling or feeling that their heart was beating fast.

Altogether, 34% of respondents (36% of females and 32% of
males) experienced at least one of these symptoms of anxiety or
depression. The most frequent symptom was losing interest in things
(14%), followed by feeling isolated (13%), trouble sleeping (12%),
feeling irritable, (12%), feeling that the future is hopeless (11%),
sweating, trembling and palpitations (10%) and difficulty concen-

trating (9%). These symptoms are more likely to be found among those living in metropolitan (41%) rather than in rural (21%) areas.

There was a high correlation between these symptoms and having at least one symptom of PTSD: 60% who had experienced at least one disturbing event experienced symptoms of anxiety and depression, as against just over a quarter (26%) of those who had not experienced a disturbing event.

CONCLUSIONS

The undeclared war that was fought against the people of South Africa during the apartheid era has taken its toll. Approximately five million adults aged between 16 and 64 years have lived through violent and other traumatic events related to the apartheid regime forcibly imposing an unjust system on the population, and resistance to this system.

Exposure to violence in South Africa has resulted in a large proportion of the population suffering from one or more effects of PTSD. Other symptoms of mental ill-health, including fair or poor ratings on self-rating scales, feelings of powerlessness and bewilderment, and symptoms of anxiety and depression were found to be correlated with exposure to traumatic events and PTSD.

The concept of PTSD developing as a syndrome in relation to traumatic events has therefore found clear and strong support in this paper. Being exposed to violence was closely related to experiencing symptoms of distress. While the symptoms may not necessarily be so severe as to prevent the vast majority of people from rebuilding their lives, they are nevertheless related to other symptoms of poor mental health such as anxiety and depression.

It is clear from this paper that it is inappropriate to view PTSD as an illness affecting only a few individuals. Large numbers of people exhibit at least one symptom of this condition. Healing the nation involves revealing the full extent of political violence that was committed during the apartheid era, confronting the effects of this violence, and setting in place both professional and community structures to deal with it on a large scale, for example, the training of lay people to give counselling and community support programmes.

The research has indicated structural variation in the extent of exposure to traumatic events and reactions to them. For example, proportionately fewer of those living in rural areas were exposed to traumatic situations (12%) as against those living in metropolitan areas (35%); symptoms of PTSD were different when comparing the life circumstances of the various race groups. Our analysis has hitherto been descriptive. The interplay of individual manifestations and wider contextual causes requires further research.

ACKNOWLEDGEMENTS

The authors wish to thank Dr David Everatt and Dr Avy Hirschowitz for their intellectual contribution.

The research was commissioned by the American-based philanthropic trust, the Henry J Kaiser Family Foundation, which is dedicated to improving the health and life chances of the disadvantaged. It was conducted by the Community Agency for Social Enquiry, who, in turn, sub-contracted the field work to Market Research Africa.

REFERENCES

Abenhaim, L., W. Dab and L.R. Salmi: 1992, 'Study of civilian victims of terrorist attacks (France 1982–1987)', Journal of Clinical Epidemiology 45, pp. 103–109.

Blendon, R.: 1994, Lao version of the Harvard Trauma Questionnaire (unpublished).

Breslau, N., G.C. Davis, P. Andreski and E. Peterson: 1991, 'Traumatic events and posttraumatic stress disorder in an urban population of young adults', Archives of General Psychiatry 48, pp. 216–222.

Bridgland, F.: 1990, The war for Africa: Twelve months that transformed a continent (Ashanti Publishing, Gibraltar).

Bremner, J.D., S. Southwick, E. Brett, A. Fontana, R. Rosenheck and D.S. Charney: 1992, 'Dissociation and posttraumatic stress disorder in Vietnam combat veterans', American Journal of Psychiatry 149, pp. 328–332.

Eitinger, L. and A. Strom: 1973, Mortality and morbidity after excessive stress: A follow-up investigation of Norwegian concentration camp survivors (Humanities, New York).

Engel, C.C. Jr., A.L. Engel, S.J. Campell, M.E. McFall, J. Russo and W. Katon: 1993, 'Posttraumatic stress disorder symptoms and precombat sexual and physical abuse in desert storm veterans', Journal of Nervous and Mental Disease 181, pp. 683–688.

Everatt, D. and M. Orkin: 1993, "Growing up tough": A national survey of South African Youth (Community Agency for Social Enquiry (CASE), Johannesburg).

Everatt, D., R. Jennings and M. Orkin: 1994, The reef violence: The election endgame (Community Agency for Social Enquiry (CASE), Johannesburg).

Gersons, B.P.R. and I.V.E. Carlier: 1992, 'Post-traumatic stress disorder: The history of a recent concept', British Journal of Psychiatry 161, pp. 742–748.

Green B.L., M.C. Grace, J.D. Lindy, G.C. Gleser and A.C. Leonard: 1990, 'Risk factors for PTSD and other diagnoses in a general sample of Vietnam veterans, American Journal of Psychiatry 147, pp. 729–733.

Green, B.L., J.D. Lindy, M.C. Grace and A.C. Leonard: 1992, Chronic posttraumatic stress disorder and diagnostic comorbidity in a disaster sample, Journal of Nervous and Mental Disease 180, pp. 760–776.

Hirschowitz, R., S. Milner and D. Everatt: 1994, Growing up in a violent society, in D. Everatt (ed.), Creating a future youth policy for South Africa (Ravan Press, Johannesburg).

Hirschowitz, R. and M. Orkin: 1995, A national household survey of health inequalities in South Africa (Henry J. Kaiser Family Foundation, Washington, DC).

Kerlinger, F.: 1973, Foundations of behavioural research (Holt, Rinehart and Winston, New York).

Kessler, R.: 1994, University of Michigan: Questionnaire for the National Survey of Health and Stress (unpublished).

Summerfield, D.: 1996, 'The psychological legacy of war and atrocity: The question of long-term and transgenerational effects and the need for a broad view', Journal of Nervous and Mental Disease 184, pp. 375–377.

Central Statistical Service
Private Bag X44
Pretoria 0001
South Africa

CLIVE K. CORDER

THE RECONSTRUCTION AND DEVELOPMENT PROGRAMME: SUCCESS OR FAILURE?*

ABSTRACT. The Reconstruction and Development Programme (RDP) of the Government of National Unity (GNU) represents a major initiative to redress the imbalances of the past. The RDP consists of six principles and five key programmes which are outlined in this paper. It addresses, to a degree, the position of youth and women. It also stresses the importance of education and training. Various research studies that provide measurements of poverty against which the RDP can be evaluated have already been completed. They show the gross disparities in quality of life, before the April 1994 election, between people of different racial groups and urban and rural dwellers. The RDP can be assessed in both physical and psychological terms; and results of a longitudinal study measuring awareness, perceived delivery and expectations of the RDP among urban adults are given. A successful outcome for the RDP is seen as essential, if a stable South African society is to materialise. This paper sets out to examine whether this is feasible.

KEY WORDS: Gini Coefficient, Human Development Index, living standard, Mandela, poverty, reconstruction

INTRODUCTION

Development priorities in South Africa over the next decade will be driven, to a large extent, by the Reconstruction and Development Programme. This ambitious plan, mooted by the African National Congress (ANC) in its Policy Framework document (ANC, 1994), and taken up in the Government of National Unity's RDP White Paper – Discussion Document (GNU, 1994) encompasses virtually the total range of business and social activity.

The spirit of the RDP was expressed by President Nelson Mandela in his opening address to a Joint Sitting of Parliament, 24 May 1994 (GNU, 1994, p. 1).

"My Government's commitment to create a people-centred society of liberty binds us to the pursuit of the goals of freedom from want, freedom from hunger, freedom from deprivation, freedom from ignorance, freedom from suppression and freedom from fear. These freedoms are fundamental to the guarantee of human dignity. They

Social Indicators Research **41**: 183–203, 1997.
© 1997 *Kluwer Academic Publishers. Printed in the Netherlands.*

*will therefore constitute part of the centrepiece of what this Government will seek
to achieve, the focal point on which our attention will be continuously focused. The
things we have said constitute the true meaning, the justification and the purpose
of the Reconstruction and Development Programme, without which it would lose
all legitimacy."*

The aim behind this paper is to provide an outline of the RDP
and the reasons for its existence. Then to describe some benchmark
studies against which the success of the RDP can be measured.
The results of a survey representing South African urban adults
undertaken at three different periods after the commencement of the
programme are provided. This study examines the extent to which
publicity for the RDP has developed awareness and the degree to
which people believe the RDP has already been of benefit to them.
Expectations for the future are also examined. An assessment is
made of the effectiveness of the programme and the implications, if
it does not succeed in reducing the gross disparity in living standards
that exist in South Africa.

What is the RDP?

"The Reconstruction and Development Programme (RDP) is an integrated, coherent socio-economic policy framework" which "seeks
to mobilise all our people and our country's resources toward a final
eradication of the results of apartheid and the building of a democratic, non-racial and non-sexist future" (Ibid., p. 4).

The RDP incorporates ideas of democracy, prosperity and sustainable growth that are environmentally friendly. It seeks to address
both the moral and ethical development of South African society
(Ibid.).

In the first year of operation "22 Lead Programmes were identified, planned and budgeted to kickstart the delivery" of the RDP.
These covered a broad range of activities, for example: land reform,
redistribution and restitution; health care, in particular the provision
that "no child under 6 years of age and no pregnant women may be
turned away from a hospital or clinic"; electricity; primary school
nutrition, under which "5,4 million children are being fed a basic
snack every morning" and the provision of rural water (Ministry in
the Office of the President, 1995, pp. 5–16).

The Six Basic Principles of the RDP

It is the six basic principles of the RDP that in combination will ensure a coherent programme (GNU, 1994, p. 5).

What is envisaged in the RDP White Paper is "an integrated and sustainable programme" that "must become a people-driven process" which is "closely bound with peace and security for all." Once "peace and security are established" it will be possible "to embark upon nation-building" which in turn "links reconstruction and development." All of which "depend on thorough going democratisation of South Africa" (Ibid., pp. 6–7).

The Five Key Programmes

To achieve these basic principles, five key programmes are envisaged (Ibid., pp. 7–10).

Meeting basic needs

First on the agenda of the RDP key programmes is meeting basic needs, which are: "jobs, land, housing, water, electricity, telecommunications, transport, a clean and healthy environment, nutrition, health care and social welfare" (ANC, 1994, p. 7).

A fundamental principle of the RDP is that the people should be consulted and "become part of the decision-making process" (GNU, 1994, p. 8). Van Zyl Slabbert (HSRC, 1995, p. 61) has focused on a dilemma in this process. "There is a tension in terms of popular accountability, between technical competence and popular ignorance." Van Zyl Slabbert is questioning the ability of the person in the street to fully comprehend the complexity of the issues involved, particularly when it comes to decisions related to scientific matters. A possible response to this criticism is that each community could elect well-informed people to represent it. What is inevitable is that such a procedure, though morally highly praiseworthy, given the feudal approach of the past, will take an inordinate amount of time. Needs can change quite quickly in an open modern economy and the response to initial requirements, if long delayed, could be inappropriate. Bernie Fanaroff, as RDP deputy director general, quoted in the Sunday Times, regarding delays in the Katorus project, a township on the East Rand, identified a further problem, "We've got so many interest groups in the area that it is hard to know when (*sic*) you have consulted" (Sunday Times, 1995, p. 2).

Developing human resources

It is conceived that people will not only gain higher rewards for latent, unrecognised, and existing skills, but that this will also empower them for management and government. This can only be achieved with extensive education and training across the full spectrum of society, both in the educational system and at places of work. Removal of barriers to entry and obstacles to promotion would clearly be beneficial in achieving this goal.

Art and culture are given recognition "in unlocking the creativity of our people, allowing for cultural diversity within the project of developing a unifying national culture" (GNU, 1994, p. 9). Sport and recreation, including access to facilities, are seen as means of redressing the ravages of apartheid that denied the majority of people such benefits.

Building the economy

Essentially a conservative financial approach is planned, with constraints on government spending, "appropriate tax reforms and a review of exchange controls" (Ibid.). Tax equality for men and women was addressed in the 1995 March Budget. The abolition of the Financial Rand in the same month was an initial step in the normalisation of currency controls.

A prime motive behind changes in the economy is to benefit the previously disadvantaged; and the rights of labour "to organise and strike will be entrenched" (Ibid.).

The position of South Africa in world trade is also given consideration, as is the importance of our interdependence with our southern neighbours.

Democratising the state and society

A major problem facing the GNU is also recognised in the formation of a unified Public Service, with conditions of equality. A trimmed down Civil Service with greater productivity and efficiency is seen as essential to the successful implementation of the RDP; together with a restructured Public Service that "is representative of all the people of South Africa, in racial, gender and geographical terms" (Ibid.,

p. 42). Guidelines for achieving this have been outlined (Ministry for the Public Service and Administration, 1995).

Implementing the RDP

The RDP is not the province of government only and the emergence of a wide range of new players involved in its implementation, which was not part of the apartheid administration, is regarded as a matter of some complexity.

A fundamental aspect of the RDP is that the poor should not only participate in the process but also be empowered. The aim is "that they progressively take more control over their own development, thus ensuring that the RDP is a people driven program." The poor should "plan, implement, supervise and help fund projects in which they are involved" (World Bank, 1995).

Funding the RDP

A wide range of resources is available for the RDP Fund: from money appropriated from parliament; international aid; interest on amounts invested; taxation, especially on gambling and lotteries; the sale of state assets and local government (GNU, 1994, pp. 16–17).

Potentially a major source of funds would be the sale of state enterprises. There is a natural reluctance to go ahead with this on a major scale, not only because such assets could be regarded as the property of the people, but also because for the most part the potential buyers would be the existing wealthy, thus perpetuating the dominance of the ownership of the economy in the hands of the white minority, international companies and overseas investors. Then finance minister, Chris Liebenberg, was quoted in Business Times (1995, p. 1) in response to ANC concern regarding the sale of state assets, "I just want to state that this government is not on a road of an ideology of privatisation."

Science and Technology and the Role of Research

While the scientist may believe that his or her actions have been in the best interest of their profession, and the pursuit of knowledge is in itself a worthwhile endeavour, the RDP, though appreciating the role that these disciplines can play, takes a somewhat different view.

"Science and technology have served the interests of the minority and the political goals of apartheid" (GNU, 1994, p. 35).

Christie (1994, p. 3) poses the question, "Can our human sciences be said to have discovered, and told us, how to rid society of racism, how to reconstruct and develop the country?" He foresees that "natural science and technology, joined to human science and the arts, together may solve the problems."

Youth

Everatt (1994 and 1995) believes that "the RDP has little of substance to say about the youth, beyond citing them as one particularly needy category alongside rural dwellers, women, the disabled and others." He draws attention to the large number of black children who left school before completing their studies, mainly because of poverty, but also pregnancy and family pressures. The problem, however, relates to "all youth – but particularly those who were unable to attain high educational levels" (Everatt, 1995).

Women's Rights

"A key focus throughout the RDP is on ensuring a full and equal role for women in every aspect of our economy and society" (ANC, 1994, p. 9).

The results of a study on women's rights (WNC, 1994) conducted to provide input for the new constitution, carried out in February and March 1994 among urban adults, showed that the RDP will be hard put to achieve this praiseworthy goal. Though there was a broad level of agreement that "women should get the same rates of pay as men, if they are doing the same work" (93%) and that "women should get the same promotions at work that men do" (90%), there was less enthusiasm for giving a woman "the right to say no to sex even to her husband" (76%) and even less support for changing traditional culture to allow women the same rights as men (66%). In this regard "women face specific disabilities in obtaining land" (ANC, 1994, p. 21). One person in every three felt that women should not be allowed to decide for themselves how many children to have, nor to decide whether to have an abortion. One person in every ten also condoned a man beating a woman, even if she is his wife!

Subsequent to the survey, on 5 November 1996, the Choice on Termination of Pregnancy Bill was approved by the Senate by 49 votes to 21 (Business Day, 1996, p. 1).

Education and Training

Perhaps the greatest challenge for the RDP is in the areas of education and training. One can readily support the declaration that "the democratic government must enable all children to go to school for at least 10 years" (ANC, 1994, p. 64). It is, however, one thing to use the limited means of the state in favour of a minority group, but quite another to allocate those resources for all the people.

It is estimated that there is a shortfall of 473 000 teachers and trainers in South Africa (National Training Board, 1994, p. 47). However, only 1,084 million (3,7%) of the RSA's population had a qualification of Standard 9 and diploma or higher and "one can deduce that it would not be possible to supply these demands from the present pool of high level people" (Ibid.).

A major dilemma has been whether to allocate funds to school children, or to adults, in view of the estimated 2,5 million people between the age of 20–64 in South Africa who have no schooling (Ibid., p. 46).

In 1994, 48,210 unemployed people were given formal sector training and 65,044 were trained for the informal sector, of these it is known that 6,564 and 14,168 respectively, found employment of some kind, though the numbers could well have been higher (Department of Labour, 1995, pp. 18–19). The cost of this training, which was over R70 million, highlights the sums needed for providing people with the requisite skills to earn a living.

Measuring Poverty and Living Standards

South Africa is a country with dramatic differences in living standards. "The Reconstruction and Development Programme was formulated in response to this situation and aims to alleviate poverty and reduce inequality among races and between rich and poor" (Whiteford, Posel, and Kelatwang, 1995, p. 1).

But how does one define and measure poverty? This is a crucial issue, since if we cannot identify who is poor, why they are poor and where they are located, there is really no way to logically start

TABLE I
Gini Coefficient for developing countries

Developing Country	Gini
South Africa	0,65
Brazil	0,61
Cote d'Ivoire	0,55
Turkey	0,51
India	0,42
Pakistan	0,36
Taiwan	0,27

Source: Whiteford, Posel, and Kelatwang, 1995. A profile of poverty, inequality and human development in South Africa.

to address the problem. Nor can any progress be evaluated without some acceptable ongoing measurement of poverty.

The Gini coefficient
South Africa's level of income inequality can be compared with that of other countries by the Gini coefficient that ranges from 0, where all households have the same income, to 1, showing absolute inequality, where one household earns all the income (Ibid., p. 44).

South Africa has a Gini coefficient of 0,65, higher than that of other developing countries (see Table I).

A feature of poverty in South Africa is that "the within-race Gini coefficients are also very high suggesting that inequality within races is contributing to overall inequality" (Ibid., p. 19), (see Table II).

Human development index
South Africa rates 86 out of 173 countries on a Human Development Index (HDI), (Central Statistical Service (CSS), 1995, p. iii). The HDI is made up of three key components, longevity, knowledge and income and "is best seen as a measure of people's ability to live a long and healthy life, to communicate, to participate in the community and to have sufficient means to be able to afford a decent living" (Ibid., p. i).

South Africa has improved its HDI during the period 1980 to 1991. There are however extensive variations between different communities and racial groups (see Table III). South African blacks,

TABLE II

Gini Coefficient for South Africa, within race

Race	Gini
Black	0,53
Indian	0,47
White	0,45
Coloured	0,44

Source: Whiteford, Posel, and Kelatwang 1995. A profile of poverty, inequality and human development in South Africa.

TABLE III

Human Development Indices, by community and race

	1980	1991
Community		
Urban	0,639	0,807
Non-Urban	0,379	0,466
Race		
Black	0,394	0,500
Coloured	0,532	0,663
Indian	0,655	0,836
White	0,739	0,901
Total	0,557	0,677

Source: Central Statistical Service 1995. Human Development Index (HDI).

based on their rating in 1991, had a similar HDI to Swaziland (ranked 117), coloureds to Cuba and Sri Lanka (ranked 90 and 91), Indians to Singapore (ranked 43) and whites to Israel, which was ranked 19th of the countries assessed (Ibid., pp. 6–9).

All Media and Products Survey (AMPS)
The annual All Media and Product Survey that was started in 1975 and is conducted for the South African Advertising Research Foundation (SAARF) provides a good before and after measure of cer-

tain aspects of the RDP, including poverty. The AMPS universe is defined as "adults aged 16 years or older resident in private households, or hostels, residential hotels and similar accommodation in the Republic of South Africa" (SAARF, 1996, vol. 1, p. 6). In 1996 an area-stratified, probability sample of 15,833 covering both urban and rural dwellers in all the nine new provinces, representing 25,7 million adults, was used.

The Living Standard Measure (LSM), developed by the South African Advertising Research Foundation (SAARF) is based on 13 variables, covering durables ownership, shopping behaviour, size and type of community, availability of water and electricity in the home and domestic help. It provides a means of evaluating the total adult population of South Africa in terms of a common denominator. As such, it is an ideal measure of the progress of the RDP, particularly as results prior to the first fully democratic elections held in April 1994 are available.

A comparison of the percentages of people falling into the eight Living Standard Measures (LSMs) in 1993 and 1996, showed that there had been considerable material progress among blacks in the post election period, but not in the two top groups (see Table IV).

Method

There are other criteria that are important in evaluating the success of the RDP. These relate to the extent to which people are aware of the programme and believe it has been successful. A further consideration is the level of expectation built up for the future. In order to measure these aspects a longitudinal study was conducted (Market Research Africa, 1995). Fieldwork was done during three periods, 7th December 1994–15th January 1995, 16th May–20th June 1995 and 9th November–21st December 1995.

Sample and procedure
The coverage of the survey was urban adults, aged 16 years and over, representing 13,5 million people. Samples of 2740, 2508 and 2506 were taken for the three periods. Households were selected from a census of dwelling units, and in each house either all male, or female, adults were listed and one chosen using a random selection grid. Three calls were made at different time periods, before a substitute of the same gender was taken from a neighbouring household.

TABLE IV
South African living standards, by racial group

LSM Group	Total 93 %	Total 96 %	Black 93 %	Black 96 %	Coloured 93 %	Coloured 96 %	Indian 93 %	Indian 96 %	White 93 %	White 96 %
1 – The Traditional Have-Nots	16	12	22	17	1	*	*	–	1	–
2 – Self-centred Non-earners	14	12	18	16	4	2	*	*	*	–
3 – Transitional Rurals	14	13	17	17	12	6	1	*	*	*
4 – Urbanised Singles	13	14	16	18	14	12	6	4	*	*
5 – The Young Aspirers	13	16	14	18	19	23	18	15	2	2
6 – Emerging Market	13	15	10	13	27	32	28	33	14	12
7 – Established Affluents	13	12	2	2	20	20	34	35	52	50
8 – Influential Affluents	6	7	*	*	3	5	14	14	32	36

* Less than 0,5%

Source: South African Advertising Research Foundation. 1993 and 1996 AMPS.

Measures

The questionnaire formed part of an omnibus study (Ibid.). Respondents were asked a series of questions designed to measure their awareness of the Government of National Unity's Reconstruction and Development Programme, whether they felt they had benefitted from the programme, and in what way. Future expectations were also gauged.

Comprehensive demographics, including: race, gender, age, household income, province and community were obtained. Access to television was also measured.

RESULTS

Awareness of the RDP

By November 1995 over four out of every five urban adults were aware of the RDP. In response to the question "Have you heard of the RDP, the Government of National Unity's Reconstruction and Development Programme?", 87% of blacks, 86% of whites, 83% of coloureds and 74% of Indians answered in the affirmative. It is unusual to find higher levels of awareness among blacks than other racial groups, because of their relatively lower level of media consumption. It therefore seems probable that word of mouth, stimulated by political activity, played an important part in spreading knowledge of the RDP among the black population.

Overall awareness of the RDP showed further increases over the period December 1994/January '95, to October/November 1995, particularly among coloureds (see Figure 1).

The odds of the RDP being known was estimated using logistic regression (Agresti, 1990, p. 85). This is expressed by the formula:

O = odds of RDP known

$$O = \mu \times race \times income \times age \times province \times access\ to\ TV$$

Where $\mu = 1.53189$.

The odds varied extensively according to a person's access to television and their demographics. The likelihood of being aware of the RDP was higher if you were: black, in the A household income group (R6,000+ per month), aged 25–34, male, living in the Eastern Cape and with access to television. It was particularly low for those

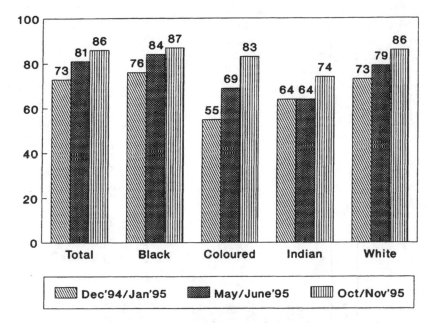

Figure 1. Awareness of the RDP (Source: RDP Index, MRA, 1995).

who were: coloured, with D household income (R500— per month), aged 50 and over, female, living in the Northern Province or Eastern Transvaal, without access to television (see Table V).

Benefitted so far
One in every five urban blacks believed that they had already benefitted from the RDP. A far lower proportion of coloureds (6%), Indians (6%) and whites (2%), at that stage, regarded themselves as beneficiaries (see Figure 2).

Perceived benefits
The major areas where the RDP was perceived to have had a beneficial effect were: installation of electricity (3%), access to water (2%), education facilities (2%), housing (2%), better environment (2%) and improved health facilities (2%).

It is impossible to relate activities resulting from the RDP with claims to have been advantaged by such actions, which was confined almost exclusively to blacks. It is likely that many people would have enjoyed improved facilities and services following from normal business and government activity. However, the perception may be

TABLE V
Awareness indices

Variable	Categories						
MEAN (μ)	1.53189						
RACE	Black	Coloured	Indian	White			
	2.71896	0.51805	0.76523	0.92775			
MONTHLY HOUSEHOLD INCOME	R6000+	R2500– R5999	R500– R2499	R1– R499			
	2.22288	1.27384	0.84720	0.41685			
AGE	16–24	25–34	35–49	50+			
	0.83263	1.13828	1.10092	0.95839			
SEX	Male	Female					
	1.52754	0.65465					
PROVINCE	W/Cape	OFS	E/Cape	N.W. & N/Cape	N/Prov & E/Tvl	Gauteng	KwaZulu /Natal
	1.42261	0.90025	1.40634	1.08791	0.45769	0.82835	1.34614
ACCESS TO TV	Access to TV	No TV access					
	1,41453	0.70695					

Source: Corder, 1995. Statomet analysis of unweighted RDP Index data.

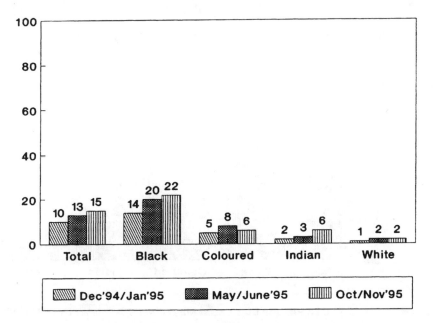

Figure 2. Already benefitted from the RDP (Source: RDP Index, MRA, 1995).

more important than actuality in ensuring a peaceful transition to democracy in a country with such a wide diversity of wealth.

Future expectations

Despite an increase in awareness of the RDP, the expectations that the RDP will be of assistance in the future declined. Among blacks just under one person in every two was anticipating that the RDP would be helpful to them; which contrasts with only one in every four coloureds and one in every seven Indians. Very few whites expected the RDP would be to their advantage (see Figure 3).

Perceived future benefits

The major areas where blacks expected the RDP would be of assistance were in employment (52%), housing (46%), job training (35%), education facilities (29%), better environment (28%) and health facilities (23%). Expectations for employment were found to be increasing, whereas those for education showed a decline (see Figure 4).

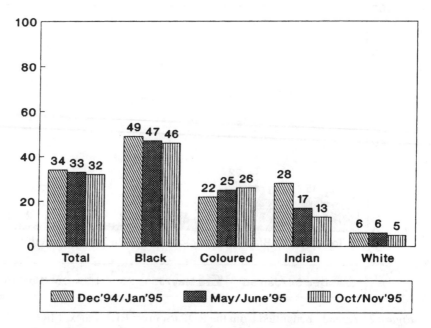

Figure 3. Expected benefits from the RDP (Source: RDP Index, MRA, 1995).

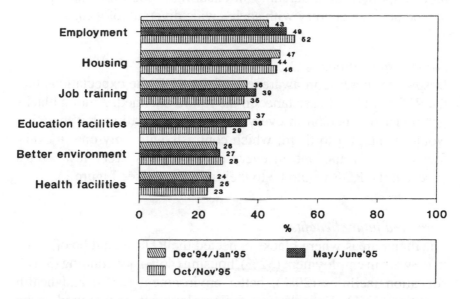

Figure 4. Expected benefits from the RDP – Urban blacks (Source: RDP Index, MRA, 1995).

DISCUSSION

Private Sector
The backlash from a failure of the RDP to deliver could threaten the future of free enterprise in South Africa. When deprived of what people regard as their due, the temptation is to demand compensation and redress from those who are comparatively well-off. Major corporations are already conscious of the need to get behind the RDP to ensure its success and many are taking an active part in its fulfilment. However, faced with the massive differences in living standards that exist, it is unlikely that such efforts will be able to satisfy the needs of those who are outside the capitalist system.

After a long period of isolation and sanctions, business needs to invest in technology to improve its international competitiveness; but Benjamin (1994, p. 262) warns that "South Africa cannot afford a further increase in the capital intensity of the economy if it is to get on top of the job creation problem."

Public Sector
The policies of the democratically elected Government of National Unity (GNU) entail a major metamorphosis of the public service. This is described in the Draft White Paper on the Transformation of the Public Service and Administration as "a complex and potentially controversial process" (Ministry for the Public Service and Administration, 1995, p. 5). What is envisaged is a far greater focus, than hitherto, on meeting the basic requirements of all the people of South Africa, but especially the "40 per cent or more South African citizens living below the poverty line" (Ibid.). What is also conceived is that the people employed by the Public Service will move rapidly towards a close match of South Africa's race and gender proportions, certainly as far as recruitment and training are concerned. "The main beneficiaries of (such) affirmative action programmes will be black people, women and people with disabilities" (Ibid., p. 13). It is unlikely that in the short term such goals could be met. This is recognised in the White Paper that questions the RDP idea of "defined quotas" and proposes that "it might be more practical to work on the basis of measurable and achievable departmental targets" (Ibid.).

While it is easy to understand the motives and objectives of this transformation process, it seems that too much is being attempted within a limited budget and time period.

What is evident is that a large proportion of the national income is going to be redirected in favour of those who were previously disadvantaged. However, the scope "for increased public spending on social services would be severely limited" (Government policy document, 1996, p. 3) and government is now seeking the cooperation of business and its social partners "to catapult the economy to the higher levels of growth, development and employment needed to provide a better life for all South Africans" (Ibid., p. 2).

CONCLUSIONS

The Financial Mail (1995, p. 24) considered that "it would be a mistake to dismiss the RDP because it has so far failed to match the politicians' extravagant promises." Moreover, awareness of the RDP has been remarkably high so soon after its introduction, especially when it is considered that "only 45% of the monies available to the RDP fund" had been disbursed by April 1995 (Business Day, 1995a, p. 8). Awareness among blacks was particularly high, suggesting that word of mouth played an important role, besides above the line media.

Fifteen percent of the urban adult population – in particular blacks – believed they had already benefitted from the RDP. This was despite the opinion of Business Day (Ibid.) "that it is still too early to begin measuring the success of the reconstruction and development programme whether by the amount of money spent or by the units of homes or dams built, children taught, improvements in life expectancy or any other of a number of yardsticks." Clearly, some positive perceptions may have been due to improvements in living conditions that would have occurred during general economic activity.

The RDP could become the victim of its own success in communicating so effectively to a deprived populace promises of a better life to come. Levels of expectation clearly cannot be met in the short term, if at all; and there is considerable danger that disillusionment will occur, if rapid and tangible progress is not evident. Cyril

Ramaphosa, when ANC secretary general, was all too aware of this risk, "unless there is substantive improvement in the standard of living of South Africans in the foreseeable future, we could see a level of unrest and popular dissent far greater than that of the mid-'80s" (Business Day, 1995b, p. 14). There could also be a reaction from other racial groups, especially those who are less well off, if they find that the RDP is not to their personal advantage.

A further danger looms. Unless there is a sustainable upliftment in the subsistence living conditions of rural dwellers, urbanisation will accelerate from its already high levels. This will lead to an intolerable situation in the main metropolitan areas, which are already unable to cope with the demand for services, education, housing and the maintenance of law and order.

If it is going to make a meaningful contribution to the creation of an egalitarian society, the RDP will need a massive injection of funds and commitment from both private and public sectors. However, in an attempt to reduce the government deficit, the focus has been on cutting funds allocated to the RDP, and it would appear that the programme has been down graded. A manifestation of this was the closure of the RDP office in March 1996 and the relocation of the RDP fund within the Ministry of Finance (BBC Monitoring Service, 1996). Though, Trevor Manual, shortly after his appointment as Finance Minister, argued that "effectively what is happening to the RDP is that it is shifting from 7,5 billion rand to 173,7 billion rand", as it is now part of the budget as a whole (Loxton, 1996).

The future stability of South Africa depends on a more equitable allocation of resources and opportunities. The RDP has been a bold and imaginative attempt to achieve this, but its success at this stage is perhaps more in the mind than in the reality.

NOTE

* This is an updated and revised version of a paper titled "RDP or RIP?" which was presented at the 17th Southern African Marketing Research Association (SAMRA) Convention, Swaziland, September 1995.

REFERENCES

African National Congress (ANC): 1994, The Reconstruction and Development Programme: A policy framework (Umanyano, Johannesburg), pp. 1–147.

Agresti, A.: 1990, Categorical data analysis (Wiley-Interscience, United States), pp. 85–91.

BBC Monitoring Service: 1996, South African Broadcasting Corporation (SABC) SAfm radio in Johannesburg, 28 March, 1536 gmt.

Benjamin, R.W.: 1994, 'Reconstruction and development in South Africa', South African Journal of Economics, Pretoria: 62(3), pp. 281–305.

Business Day, Johannesburg, 12 April, 1995a, p. 8.

Business Day, Johannesburg, 4 May, 1995b, p. 14.

Business Day, Johannesburg, 5 November, 1996, p. 1.

Business Times, (Sunday Times, supplement), Johannesburg, 2 April, 1995, p. 1.

Central Statistical Service (CSS): 1995, Human Development Index (HDI) (May, Pretoria).

Christie, R.: 1994, 'The need for balance in human and natural science: Research funding in South Africa: Do we need an RDP research council?' University of the Western Cape. Unpublished manuscript, Human Sciences Research Council (HSRC), Pretoria.

Corder, C.K.: 1995, 'RDP or RIP?' Proceedings of the Southern African Marketing Research Association 17th Conference, Swaziland, pp. 1–29.

Department of Labour: 1995, Annual report 1994, Pretoria.

Everatt, D.: 1994, Youth and the reconstruction and development of the 'new South Africa' (Community Agency for Social Enquiry, Johannesburg).

Everatt, D. (in press): 1995, 'School reject or eject?' Contextualising 'out-of-school youth' in the new South Africa (Community Agency for Social Enquiry, Johannesburg).

Financial Mail, Johannesburg, 6 April, 1995, p. 24.

Government of National Unity (GNU): 1994, RDP White Paper: Discussion document, Government Printer, pp. 1–60.

Government policy document: 1996, Growth, employment and redistribution (Department of Finance, Pretoria), pp. 1–37.

Human Sciences Research Council (HSRC): 1995, 'Reconstruction and development – the challenge for social research', Focus 2(12), pp. 61–68.

Loxton, L.: 1996, 'South Africa: End of S.African RDP shows clearer vision by depts', Reuter News Service. 28 March.

Market Research Africa (MRA): 1995, Reconstruction and development programme (RDP) index, Johannesburg.

Ministry in the Office of the President: 1995, The RDP (Ministry in the Office of the President, Cape Town), pp. 1–20.

Ministry for the Public Service and Administration: 1995, Draft white paper on the transformation of the Public Service, May (Government Gazette, Pretoria).

National Training Board: 1994, A discussion document on a national training strategy initiative.

South African Advertising and Research Foundation (SAARF): 1993 (5 vol.) and 1996 (7 vol.), All Media and Product Survey (AMPS) (Market Research Africa (MRA) and SAARF, Johannesburg).

Sunday Times, Johannesburg, 23 July, 1995, p. 2.

Whiteford, A., Posel, D. and Kelatwang, T.: 1995, A profile of poverty, inequality and human development (Human Sciences Research Council (HSRC), Pretoria).

Woman's National Coalition (WNC): 1994, Woman's issues study (WNC and Market Research Africa (MRA), Johannesburg)

World Bank: 1995, 'Monitoring poverty and the progress of the RDP', Manuscript materials (RDP monitoring and social indicators workshop, Midrand).

Department of Business Economics
University of the Witwatersrand
Johannesburg
Private Bag 3
Wits 2050
South Africa

ROBERT MATTES and JENNIFER CHRISTIE

PERSONAL VERSUS COLLECTIVE QUALITY OF LIFE AND SOUTH AFRICANS' EVALUATIONS OF DEMOCRATIC GOVERNMENT[1]

ABSTRACT. In this paper, we examine the political consequences of quality of life, focusing on the link between perceived well-being and people's support for democratic government. We make two key distinctions. First of all, with regard to quality of life, we distinguish between assessments of personal, or household, quality of life, and assessments of collective (national, community) quality of life. Secondly, we follow David Easton in distinguishing between specific support (attitudes about specific leaders, parties and policies) and diffuse support (attitudes toward the political system in general). We find that personal quality of life is only weakly and inconsistently connected to specific or diffuse support. Perceptions of collective quality of life, however, are strongly related to both specific and diffuse support. Thus, South Africans are holding their government accountable to their perceptions of national well-being. Of greater concern, however, is that they also appear to be holding the democratic system accountable to such developments. Teaching people to distinguish between their evaluations of a specific government and their evaluations of the larger system of democratic government appears to be a key challenge confronting the development of a democratic political culture in South Africa.

KEY WORDS: democracy, diffuse support, political culture, quality of life, South Africa

Past research has investigated the components of South Africans' evaluations of their quality of life (see Møller, 1992a, 1996). However, so far as we can determine, the political *consequences* of quality of life have remained largely unexplored. Of specific concern to us are the possible consequences of quality of life for the consolidation of democracy in South Africa. The consolidation of a new democracy is intimately tied to citizens' support for and commitment to the democratic process, and these factors may be linked to their quality of life.

We assume that it is citizens' *perceptions* of well-being which ultimately matter politically and, thus, focus on *subjective* quality of life. Our first research question concerns the extent to which

Social Indicators Research **41**: 205–228, 1997.
© 1997 *Kluwer Academic Publishers. Printed in the Netherlands.*

popular support for South Africa's fledgling democratic system is tied to the new government's ability to deliver material improvements which will improve perceived quality of life. With one of the highest GINI coefficients in the world, quality of life in South Africa is highly unequal.[2] Unsurprisingly, the new government, led by the African National Congress, has made development, growth and redistribution its principal focus. Its 1994 campaign was a positive, issue-oriented and forward-looking one centered around the slogan of "A Better Life For All" and focused largely on the benefits of its proposed Reconstruction and Development Programme. Thus, material improvements to quality of life and redressing inequality have become the centrepiece of the democratic government's political agenda. It is possible, therefore, that evolving citizens' evaluations of quality of life could play an especially important role in shaping their attitudes about the new government. More importantly, they could shape their evaluations of democracy in general.

If perceptions of quality of life do indeed shape evaluations of leaders, government and democracy, a second important research question concerns the relevant criteria which people use to form those evaluations. Do they link them to their own, immediate circumstances, and thus tie the personal directly to the political? Or, do they tend to look beyond their immediate circumstances and focus on broader social conditions? Thus, we distinguish between perceptions of *personal* quality of life (based on assessments of personal and household well-being) and *collective* quality of life (based on assessments of community and national life).

This article represents a preliminary investigation into the political consequences of subjective perceptions of quality of life. Using data from the South African version of the 1995 World Values Study (conducted by the Centres for International and Comparative Politics, and Interdisciplinary Studies, both at the University of Stellenbosch), we examine the political consequences of peoples' subjective perceptions of personal quality of life. Then, making use of data from a separate 1995 study conducted by the Institute for Democracy In South Africa, we examine the political impact of collective quality of life and compare it with that of personal quality of life (see Appendix 1 for a discussion of these surveys).

Quality of Life and Democracy

Why should there be a connection between perceived quality of life and popular support for democracy? Typically, perceptions of quality of life are seen to be linked to evaluations of the government, but not of the democratic system. In other words, one would expect citizens to hold government incumbents (leaders and political parties) responsible for their own and, or the nations' well-being. Citizens' longer-term commitment to, and support for the democratic system, however, should preferably not be linked to their short-term performance evaluations of leaders, governments or parties.

This distinction forms the core of David Easton's well-known theory of the stability and maintenance of political systems. Stability is based on *political support,* a key part of which is evident in the attitudes of the mass public.[3] Such support is decomposed into two basic types (Easton, 1965). *Specific* support is based on short-term satisfaction with government performance and policy output. It "flows from the favourable attitudes and predispositions stimulated by outputs that are perceived by members to meet their demands as they arise or in anticipation" (Easton, 1965: p.273). On the other hand, political support can be *diffuse,* based largely on longer-term, affective attachments to authority learned in childhood, attachments which are unrelated to cost-benefit calculations. Easton saw diffuse support as the crucial "reserve of support that enables a system to weather the many storms when outputs cannot be balanced off against inputs of demands. It is a kind of support that a system does not have to buy with more or less direct benefits ... " (Easton, 1965: p. 273).

Diffuse support is seen to arise from perceptions of *legitimacy.* Legitimacy "endows governmental decisions with moral oughtness" (Eldridge, 1977: p. 8). It is the sense that rule-makers have the right to make laws, and that those laws ought to be obeyed (Tyler, 1990: p. 27–28). Legitimacy is thought to contribute to political stability, if only because it is seen to lead to cooperative behaviour on the part of citizens (Mezey, 1995: p. 4). People will be more likely to obey the law and refrain from anti-system behaviour if they view the sources of those laws as legitimate.[4] Thus, acting as a buffer to cushion the system against any shocks from short-term policy dissatisfaction, diffuse support is seen to be key to the long-term maintenance and stability of a political system (Easton, 1965).

The practical distinction between specific and diffuse support, however, needs to be closely examined. In any political system, diffuse support for democracy is almost certainly connected to policy performance over the long-term. It is difficult to imagine that people (no matter how much an initial "cushion" of support for authority exists) will indefinitely support political institutions that fail to deliver. Furthermore, there are a number of reasons why short-term material improvements may be tightly connected to overall evaluations of the political system in South Africa.

First of all, vast sections of South Africa's population face an unacceptable quality of life. People concerned with meeting basic needs on a daily basis may be expected to have less time to devote to democratic participation, and less reason to care about the survival of democracy. Secondly, not only does widespread poverty exist, but it does so alongside pockets of significant wealth. The continuation of such vast economic inequality may lead many people to question the usefulness or relevance of the political equality of democracy. Thus, the political equality of citizenship may be insufficient to legitimate a political system which fails to deliver the economic equality desired by so many.

Thirdly, because the vast majority of South Africans have little experience with formal, institutionalised democracy, most citizens may not have yet learned to differentiate between the incumbents, the institutions, and the overall democratic system. At first glance, this would appear to suggest that black South Africans would be more likely than whites to tie short-term performance evaluations to their beliefs about democracy in general. Such racial distinctions seem even more likely when one looks to a final factor relevant to the specific versus diffuse support distinction. That is, given the repressive history of apartheid, the majority of South Africans have had little reason to develop positive attachments to authority. Thus, it is likely that no initial "buffer" of support for formal political authority exists among black South Africans.

However, things may not be so clear as they first seem. To begin with, while the white minority does have a comparatively longer history of experience with competitive multi-party elections (since

1910), the value of such an experience for building a strong democratic culture must be severely limited by the racial definition of that democracy, as well as the heavy doses of authoritarianism and repression that were necessary to sustain apartheid. Furthermore, it is also likely that white South Africans have not yet developed any positive attachment to the new democratic system which is heavily identified with the liberation struggle generally and the African National Congress specifically, a political party which until only six years ago was portrayed to whites as a terrorist, communist organisation.

Thus, it seems that the absence of ready-made support for democratic authority is characteristic of the larger population, rather than any specific racial group (though clearly, for different reasons). It also seems likely that, for the entire population, the new democratic regime may be heavily identified with the ANC (positively so for blacks – or at least for Africans, and negatively so for whites).

Taken together, all these reasons suggest that the analytic distinction between diffuse support for democratic authority on one hand, and specific support for government output on the other, may not exist in practice for most South Africans. If true, it is reasonable to suspect that support for the democratic system may be heavily dependent on South Africans' short-term performance evaluations and their perceptions of how government policy and performance have materially affected quality of life. Because there may be no enduring "cushion" of affective support for democracy among most South Africans if the incumbents fail to perform, policy failures may come to undermine popular support for the larger system as much as for the specific leaders or political party in power.

Subjective Personal Versus Collective Quality of Life

To restate, because it is citizens' *perceptions* of well-being which ultimately matter politically, we focus on measures of subjective, rather than objective quality of life. We further differentiate between peoples' assessments of personal versus collective well-being.[5] Previous research suggests that perceptions of personal and collective well-being have differential consequences.

Evidence suggests that people do not connect clearly personal circumstances to political factors. They do, however, tend to draw a more direct link between their perceptions of larger conditions and political factors. For example, research on electoral behaviour demonstrates that, when forming their partisan preferences, voters place a great deal of weight on their evaluations of evolving economic conditions. However, in contrast to the widely-believed "pocketbook effect" (voting on the basis of the perceived consequences of government performance for personal finances), voters look beyond their personal circumstances to larger scale developments at the community, provincial or national level (what have been called "sociotropic" conditions) (Kinder and Kiewet, 1981).

This phenomenon was clearly evident in South Africa's 1994 election. Voters' partisan identification was strongly related to their retrospective evaluations of national political and economic conditions, as well as of the performance of the National Party government of F.W. de Klerk. However, partisanship was unrelated to retrospective assessments of changes in personal finances (Mattes, 1995: pp. 66–77).

Research also seems to indicate that this phenomenon is a function of the amount and type of information which people possess. Experimental studies on electoral behaviour demonstrate that when given information which clearly links personal conditions to larger political policies or decisions, people will vote accordingly. Lee Sigelman and his colleagues (1991) concluded that the natural propensity to reward and punish incumbents according to personal conditions was "overridden by the very complexity and interrelatedness of the electoral setting in the real world" (1991, p. 143) where voters often receive mixed information about economic conditions and conflicting arguments about the corresponding responsibility of government.

MEASURING SUBJECTIVE QUALITY OF LIFE

Personal Quality of Life

Using items from the South African version of the 1995 World Values Study, we developed a reliable scale to measure Personal Quality of Life (PQL) which taps different aspects of personal satisfaction and well-being (Table I). The scale contains one item assessing people's perceptions of their poverty status, and three items assessing general

TABLE I
Personal Quality of Life

Item	Mean	Std Dev	Factor Loading
Personal Happiness	3.16	0.86	0.52
Household Financial Satisfaction	4.81	3.01	0.81
Overall Life Satisfaction	6.10	2.76	0.80
Self-Described Poverty	1.94	0.84	0.52

N = 2927
Eigenvalue = 1.84
46% of common variance explained by factor
Reliability (Standardized Kronbach's Alpha) = 0.76

The items read:
Q2 "Taking all things together, would you say you are . . . " (very happy/happy)
Q18 "How satisfied are you with the financial situation of your household?" (satisfied)
Q19 "All things considered, how satisfied are you with your life as a whole these days?" (satisfied)
QA1 "Taking all things into consideration, where would you put yourself on the following scale: poor, on the borderline, not poor, don't know." (not poor)
(Note: An item measuring satisfaction with personal health loaded very weakly (0.32) on this factor.)

satisfaction (household financial situation, personal happiness, and overall life satisfaction).

Collective Quality of Life

Unfortunately, the World Values Study does not contain evaluations of collective well-being. Thus, we turn to data from the 1995 Institute for Democracy In South Africa (IDASA) Local Elections Study. We used several items to develop a reliable scale to measure Collective Quality of Life (CQL) (Table II). Tapping different aspects of community and national well-being, this scale contains four items measuring retrospective evaluations of overall national conditions, the overall conditions of the respondents' group, the national economy, and respondents' local economy. It also contains one item which assesses people's expectations concerning overall national conditions.[6]

TABLE II
Collective Quality of Life

Item	Mean	Std Dev	Factor Loading
Local Community Economic Conditions	3.36	1.04	0.82
National Economic Conditions	3.15	1.15	0.89
Expectations of National Conditions In Next Year	2.52	1.26	0.75
Overall Group Conditions	3.18	1.03	0.70
Overall National Conditions	3.22	1.19	0.89

N = 2275
Eigenvalue of 3.31
Factor explains 66% of the common variance
Reliability (Standardized Kronbach's Alpha) = 0.87

The items read:
Q6 "Would you tell me whether over the past 12 months, the following have got worse, stayed the same or got better?"
Economic conditions in your local economy (much better/somewhat better)
State of the economy in the country (much better/somewhat better)
Expectations of national conditions in the next year (much better/somewhat better)
Overall conditions in South Africa (much better/somewhat better)
Q62 "Since the election of the last year do you think the conditions of (self-described community) have improved, stayed the same or got worse" (improved)

MEASURING POLITICAL SUPPORT

The various measures of political support in the two studies differ from each other (see Appendix 2). From the World Values Study (WVS), we use as measures of *specific support* items which tap satisfaction with the overall performance of the government, as well as approval of its performance with regard to poverty reduction. From the IDASA survey, we use a scale of three items which tap job performance of the government, approval of the president, national government, and national parliament.

As measures of *diffuse support*, from the WVS we use a single item measuring satisfaction with the nation's political system; a scale of three individual items measuring confidence in representative institutions (government, political parties and national parliament);[7] a scale of three items measuring negative attitudes about democracy (it tends toward disorder, a bad economy, and indecisiveness); a scale measuring support for non-democratic forms of government (rule by strong leader, by technocrats, and by the military), and an additive index consisting of two items measuring commitment to democracy (democracy is always best, and support for democratic rule).

From the IDASA survey, we assess diffuse support with a scale of three items measuring trust in government (national, provincial government, and local), a single item assessing satisfaction with the way democracy works in South Africa, and a single item measuring people's commitment to democracy.

CONNECTING QUALITY OF LIFE AND POLITICAL SUPPORT

Personal Quality of Life

Is there an empirical connection between measures of subjective well-being and measures of specific and diffuse support for democratic politics? We begin by assessing bivariate relationships between Personal Quality of Life (PQL) and political support. Table III displays the bivariate Pearson's r product-moment correlation coefficients between PQL and various measures of political support.

For the entire sample, the correlations are generally non-existent-to-low in strength. With regard to two separate measures of specific support, PQL is very weakly related to evaluations of government performance on poverty ($r = -0.13$), and not related to evaluations of overall government performance ($r = -0.03$, and not significant at the 0.95 confidence level).

A slightly stronger relationship exists between PQL and various measures of diffuse support: satisfaction with the overall political system (-0.17); confidence in institutions (-0.24); negative attitudes toward democracy (0.22); support for non-democratic decision-making (0.14); and commitment to democracy (-0.25).

These findings appear to be counterintuitive. It would appear from the overall sample that the greater South Africans' sense of personal well-being, the weaker their support for their new democratic system. However, considering what is obvious about the history of apartheid, it could well be that these results are an artefact of a high correlation between race and PQL: that is, well-off whites satisfied with their personal conditions but generally pessimistic about the

TABLE III
Correlates of Personal Quality of Life

	Total (n = 2935)	African (n = 1618)	White (n = 729)	Coloured (n = 392)	Indian (n = 196)
Specific Support					
Evaluations of Government Performance					
Satisfaction With Overall Government Performance	-0.03	0.17***	0.08	0.13	0.07
Satisfaction With Government Performance On Poverty	-0.13***	0.17***	0.08	0.05	0.09
Diffuse Support					
Evaluations of South Africa's Political System					
Satisfaction With South Africa's Political System Today	-0.17***	0.05	0.10*	-0.01	-0.05
Confidence In South Africa Political Institutions					
Representative Institutions	-0.24***	0.07	0.08	-0.08	-0.09
Views of Democratic Rule					
Negative Views Toward Democracy	0.22***	-0.10**	0.10*	-0.15*	-0.20*
Support for Non-Democratic Rule	0.14***	0.18***	0.04	0.09	-0.02
Commitment to Democracy	-0.25***	-0.18***	-0.07	-0.06	-0.17

***: significant at 0.001
**: significant at 0.01
*: significant at 0.05

TABLE IV
ANOVA Subjective Quality of Life and Race

	Total	African	White	Coloured	Indian
Mean	0.00	−0.37	0.63	0.21	0.32
Std Dev	1.00	0.86	0.63	0.82	0.75

$Eta^2 = 0.23***$

new political dispensation, and poor Africans dissatisfied with their personal conditions but who are generally optimistic about politics, with coloureds and Indians somewhere in between on both counts.

As might be expected, an analysis of variance conducted on our PQL scale indicates significant differences in mean subjective quality of life across the four classificatory race groups imposed by apartheid (Table IV). Examining the comparisons between these groups, African PQL is significantly different from all other groups, as is white PQL. Coloured and Indian differences, however, were not significant. Eta^2, a measure of the overall degree of association between group and PQL indicates that 23% of the variance in well-being can be explained by race group membership.

In fact, once we control for race group, the bivariate correlation coefficients between PQL and political evaluations generally reduce sharply, and usually become insignificant (see Table III). This is especially true for whites, coloureds and Indians. The only exceptions appear to be among coloured respondents where there emerges a small, positive association between PQL and overall government performance, and among coloured and Indian respondents where there remains a modest relationship between PQL and negative attitudes toward democracy.

Interesting patterns emerge among Africans. Compared to the overall population, the size of the coefficients between PQL and specific support *increase* to moderate strength and actually *change direction* and become positive. Thus, the greater Africans' well-being, the greater their satisfaction with and approval of government performance. On measures of diffuse support, the relationship between PQL and overall evaluations of the system and confidence in institutions becomes insignificant for Africans. However, the positive relationship between PQL and support for non-democratic rule observed in the overall sample remains positive and increases slightly (0.18). The moderate negative relationship between PQL and commitment to democracy also remains (–0.18). Thus, the greater Africans' sense of personal well-being, the more they positively evaluate non-democratic means of decision-making, and the lower their commitment to democracy.

Broadly speaking, however, the political consequences of personal perceptions of subjective Personal Quality of Life, as measured at the bivariate level, are generally weak and vary by race. PQL has some political impact among Africans' evaluations of government performance and their beliefs about democracy as a system of government. The greater their subjective well-being, the *more positive* their evaluations of specific government performance, but also the *greater* their support for non-democratic rule and the *less* their commitment to democracy. In general, however, PQL appears to have little to do with South Africans' assessments of their political system or their confidence in their political institutions.

Collective Quality of Life

While subjective measures of *personal* or household well-being correlate only weakly and inconsistently with measures of political support for the democratic government and system, the bivariate associations between perceptions of Collective Quality of Life (CQL) and political support are broadly more consistent, much stronger and in the opposite direction (Table V).

The strongest association of CQL was with a measure of specific support – job approval of various institutions of government (r = 0.55). As might be expected, the more positive South Africans' evaluations of community and national conditions, the more positive their performance evaluations of government.

However, CQL is also quite strongly related to two indicators of diffuse support: trust in institutions (0.44) and satisfaction with democracy (0.43). Thus, the more positive their evaluations of conditions, the more South Africans trust government and are satisfied with the way democracy works. Or, perhaps more importantly, the more negative their evaluations of evolving conditions, the less diffuse support they exhibit for the democratic system. At the same time, while collective quality of life is strongly related to satisfac-

TABLE V

Correlates of Collective Quality of Life

	Total (n=2674)	African (n=1699)	White (n=547)	Coloured (n=378)	Indian (n=50)
Specific Support					
Approval of Institutional Performance	0.55***	0.41***	0.45***	0.50***	0.45
Diffuse Support					
Institutional Trust	0.44***	0.28***	0.36***	0.52***	0.13
Satisfaction With Democracy	0.43***	0.28***	0.43***	0.46***	0.57*
Commitment to Democracy	–0.07*	–0.03	–0.22***	–0.16	–0.02

***: significant at 0.001
**: significant at 0.01
*: significant at 0.05

tion and trust, it does not yet seem to be related to South Africans' long-term commitment to sticking with democracy even if it does not appear to be "working." Responses to this item are only weakly related to assessments of collective well-being (–0.07).

Furthermore, and in contrast to Personal Quality of Life, controlling for race does not have a consistently clear impact on these relationships. Relationships between CQL and specific support stay relatively the same within the same race group. With regard to diffuse support, the coefficients for Africans are weaker, but still significant and important. For whites, coloureds and Indians, they remain strong and positive.

The only real change appears to be with regard to commitment to democracy, where a moderate and negative relationship with collective evaluations emerges among white respondents where a very weak one existed among the entire public. Those whites who believe things in the country are going well are also the ones who are less likely to express an enduring commitment if it seemed to be the case that democracy was not delivering the goods.

Implications

It appears that South Africans' perceptions of quality of life may be an important factor in developing long-term popular support for democracy. Using the Eastonian distinction between specific and diffuse support, we find that perceptions of personal well-being are, at best, weakly related to diffuse and specific support among the larger sample. Among Africans, there is a moderate connection between greater personal well-being and greater support for non-democratic forms of government, as well as with weaker long-term commitment to democracy. Among coloureds and Indians, there is a moderate relationship between greater well-being and greater negative views about democracy. Among whites there seems to be little connection between a sense of personal well-being and attitudes about government or democracy.

However, perceptions of collective well-being are quite strongly connected to evaluations of government performance. Thus, all South Africans seem to be holding their new government accountable by hinging their approval of government on perceptions of collective developments. What is more worrying, however, is that they also seem to be holding democracy itself accountable. Easton saw diffuse support for a political system as largely unrelated to short-term outputs. However, among our sample of South Africans, measures of diffuse support (eg. trust in government, satisfaction with democracy) are also strongly related to their perceived quality of collective life. Thus, popular evaluations of well-being not only affect their evaluations of the performance of the incumbents of government, but of the very democratic system. This suggests that people have not as yet learned to distinguish between the incumbents of democratic government (leaders and political parties) and the system of democratic government.

Furthermore, this also appears to be true for all South Africans, not only blacks (with relatively little experience with competitive multi-party democracy), but also of whites (with a longer history of experience with democratic practices such as competitive elections (albeit racially defined elections). This suggests that the problem of building support for the democratic system in South Africa may not be so much a function of experience with democratic practices, as a function of experience with apartheid and the struggle against it. Before 1994, Africans had little reason to develop any positive attitudes toward formal political authority, but plenty of reason to develop positive attitudes toward the African National Congress and

Nelson Mandela. Whites, on the other hand, are now confronted with a democratic system heavily identified with a political organisation of which they were told for years used terrorism and was bent on one-party domination.

Clearly the challenge seems to be one of finding ways to develop an identity for the new democratic constitution, its institutions and practices: an identity separate from the current incumbents of those institutions. Such a task is not made any easier by the probability that the ANC will remain in power for the foreseeable future, thus blurring the desired distinction. However, if citizens do not learn to make such a distinction, the results presented in this article suggest serious consequences for the popular legitimacy of democracy if the new government is not seen to deliver growth, development and redistribution.

Even at this early date, South Africans' are not enamoured with their new democracy. Just 41% of respondents in the IDASA survey (polled only sixteen months after the first universal franchise election) indicated that they were satisfied with the way democracy worked in South Africa. Trust in government was also low – only 48% of respondents indicated that they felt they could trust government "always" or "most of the time." Furthermore, as Valerie Møller has demonstrated in her research, with the exception of a brief bout of post-election euphoria, South Africans' perceived quality of life has been steadily declining throughout the past decade.[8] Our results suggest, therefore, that these relatively low levels of support for democracy may erode even further if the government is not able to reverse this trend.

At the same time, it is also important to remember that while South Africans seem to be holding government and the democratic system accountable for quality of life, support for democracy is much more strongly related to perceptions of Collective, rather than Personal Quality of Life. Thus, people appear to be tying beliefs about democracy, not to their satisfaction with their personal circumstances, but to their perceptions of the well-being of society at large.

One explanation for this may be that, in Robert Lane's words, people "morselize" their own personal experiences and are unable to see them as part of a greater whole (cited in Kinder and Kiewet,

1981: p. 161). Another may be that South Africans are highly altru-istic, and base their evaluations of government on how government performance affects the greater good, rather then their own personal self-interest (Kinder and Kiewet, 1981: p. 129). If true, this could indicate that South Africans are willing to forego short-term personal gains in the future as long as they believe that the nation as a whole is benefitting.

However, a more likely explanation is that it is simply more rational for people to base their evaluations of government on larger community and national conditions. Government and party spokes-people, parliamentary debate, and political commentators in the news media all provide information which help people make connections between larger conditions and government policy. In contrast, peo-ple lack good information with which to connect their individual circumstances to the decisions and policies of democratic govern-ment. It may be difficult for citizens to connect clearly their personal circumstances to government policy, given the myriad of other things which may account for their conditions: such as the quality of, or whether they even have, a house, job or income. In many cases this may appear to have nothing to do with government policy. People, therefore look to larger trends as the next most reasonable set of criteria to forecast their own likely prospects.

Using collective conditions as a criteria of evaluation may not only be more rational from the standpoint of citizens, it may also be more reasonable from the standpoint of those in government. In com-parison to their limited, and largely unsystematic and unpredictable ability to influence people's personal situations, governments may have at least some form of systematic and predictable influence over collective conditions via macro-economic policy.

At the same time, perceptions of collective quality of life – even if accurate – may lag behind objective economic developments.[9] People know whether they have, and the conditions of their house, job and income. They are less certain, however, about the larger community, regional or national picture of housing, employment and inflation. This may present a government with a range of opportuni-ties (not all of which are wholly positive, at least from the standpoint of democratic accountability).

Governing and opposition parties, the news media and civil society all compete to persuade people to their version of larger collective developments, as well as who is responsible for them. In this contest, however, governments often have a built-in advantage, especially to the extent that the state has a monopoly over, or dominates the production of economic statistics, or controls or dominates the news media. They are also often able to create impressions of economic improvement through short-term, "pump priming," economic stimulation actions, such as temporarily increasing the money flow through massive state expenditure, or highly visible labour-intensive projects (eg. dams, highways, community centres) which create short-term employment.

Thus, the challenge to building enduring support for democracy in South Africa appears to be clear. South Africans appear to be holding both government and the democratic system accountable to collective developments. Furthermore, trust in government and satisfaction with democracy are already quite low. Those involved in education for democracy must direct themselves towards building support for the enduring institutions of democratic government (eg. the Constitution, Parliament, Presidency, and Constitutional Court). It would also be useful if the governing party could find ways to build some distance between itself – as a party – and the institutions of government.[10] In the short term, however, it seems as if South Africa's new government must find ways to deliver national and community-wide economic improvement in a visible way, or in lieu thereof, convince people that such improvements are at least around the corner.[11]

APPENDIX 1:

South African World Values Study 1995

Fieldwork
Fieldwork was conducted during October 1995. Interviews were conducted by Markinor in Northern Province, North West, Mpumalanga and KwaZulu-Natal, and by Market and Opinion Surveys in the remaining provinces.

Universe
All adult South Africans, 16 years and older.

Sample size
2935 interviews were conducted.

Sampling method
A probability sample, stratified by province, population group and community size was drawn. Within each stratum, sampling points were selected at random. From each sampling point, 10 interviews were determined according to a random selection procedure, marked on maps. Within each household which qualified, all males/females 16 years and older were listed and the qualifying respondent selected according to a random selection procedure. If the selected person could not be interviewed (after three calls were made), the person was substituted in a prescribed way. A minimum of 20% back-checks was administered on each interviewer's work.

Weighting and projection
The sample was weighted according to population group, province, region, age, gender, income and language and projected onto the universe. It is therefore representative of the universe from which it was drawn.

Interviewing procedure
All interviewers were briefed by their field manager or field supervisor. Interviews were conducted on a personal, face-to-face basis. The questionnaire was available in all the major languages and the interview was conducted in the language preferred by the respondent.

Idasa Local Government Election Study 1995

Fieldwork
The survey was designed by Idasa's Public Opinion Service. Fieldwork was conducted by Market and Opinion Surveys between late September and November 1995.

Universe
All South Africans, 18 years and older.

Sample size
2674 interviews were conducted.

Sampling method
Respondents were randomly selected from a list of panel respondents which was compiled from Idasa's National Election Study in October 1994. The original probability sample was stratified according to province, population group and community size. As there was particular interest in specific subgroups ie. rural Zulus in KwaZulu-Natal and coloured people in the Western

Cape, a disproportionate sample was drawn in order to obtain a significant number in those sub-groups. Within each stratum, sampling points were selected at random. Five interviews which were randomly determined, were conducted at each sampling point.

If the selected person could not be interviewed (after two call backs were made), the person was substituted in a prescribed way. A minimum of 10% back-checks were made on each interviewer.

Weighting

Due to the disproportionate sample, it was necessary to weight the data up to the universe ie. the South African voting public (estimated to be 24,32 million). The sample was weighted to reflect the distribution of the different culture/language groups in each of the nine provinces. Results based on the total national sample have a margin of error of plus/minus three percentage points. Results based on smaller sub-samples will obviously have greater margins of error depending upon the number of interviews in that group.

Interviewing procedure

The questionnaire was designed by Idasa's Public Opinion Service. All interviewers were briefed by their field supervisors. Interviews were semi-structured and conducted on a personal basis. Each interview lasted between 45 and 60 minutes. The questionnaires were available in all the major languages and the interview was conducted in the language preferred by the respondent.

APPENDIX 2: MEASURES OF POLITICAL SUPPORT

Measures of Specific Support

Overall Government Performance (WVS)
The item read:
Q60 "How satisfied are you with the way that the people now in national government are handling the country's affairs?" (satisfied)

Government Performance on Poverty (WVS)
The item read:
Q67 "Do you think that what the government is doing for people in poverty in this country is too much, about the right amount, or too little?" (right amount)

Institutional Performance (Idasa)

Item	Mean	Std Dev	Factor Loading
President Nelson Mandela	1.84	1.00	0.85
Government of National Unity	2.28	0.97	0.93
National Parliament	2.33	0.96	0.92

N = 2331
Eigenvalue is 2.4
Factor explains 81% of the common variance
Reliability (Standardized Kronbach's Alpha) = 0.88

The item read:
Q7 "We would like to know whether you approve or disapprove of the way each of the following has performed its job over the past year." (strongly approve)

Measures of Diffuse Support

Evaluations of South Africa's Political System (WVS)
The item read:
Q54.2 "People have different views about the system for governing this country. Here is a scale of how well things are going .... Where on this scale would you put the political system as it is today?" (very good)

Confidence In Representative Institutions (WVS)

Item	Mean	Std Dev	Factor Loading
Government In Pretoria	2.77	0.96	0.78
Political Parties	2.36	0.96	0.58
Parliament	2.74	0.96	0.92

N=2550
Eigenvalue = 1.80
Factor explains 60% of common variance
Reliability (Kronbach's Alpha) = 0.80

The item read:
Q53. "For each (organisation) could you tell me how much confidence you have in them?" (a great deal)

    Government In Pretoria
    Political Parties
    Parliament

Negative Attitudes Toward Democracy (WVS)

Item	Mean	Std Dev	Factor Loading
Economic System Runs Badly	3.40	1.54	0.75
Indecisive and Squabbling	3.24	1.60	0.83
Can't Maintain Order	3.31	1.53	0.80

N = 2935
Eigenvalue = 1.91
Factor explains 64% of the common variance
Reliability (Standardized Kronbach's Alpha) = 0.84
Items read:
"I'm going to read off some things that people sometimes say about a democratic political system."

Q58.1 "In a democracy, the economic system runs badly." (disagree)
Q58.2 "Democracies are indecisive and have too much squabbling." (disagree)
Q58.3 "Democracies aren't good at maintaining order." (disagree)

Support for Non-Democratic Decision-Making (WVS)

Item	Mean	Std Dev	Factor Loading
Rule by Strong Leader	2.11	1.14	0.72
Rule by Expert	2.44	1.03	0.51
Rule by Army	1.75	0.98	0.54

N = 2331
Eigenvalue = 1.08
Factor explains 36% of common variance
Reliability (Standardized Kronbach's Alpha) = 0.61
Items read:
"I'm going to describe various types of political systems and ask what you think about each as a way of governing this country."

Q55.1 "Having a strong leader who does not have to bother with parliament and elections" (very good)
Q55.2 "Having experts, not government, make decisions according to what they think is best for the country." (very good)
Q55.3 "Having the army rule." (very good)

Commitment to Democracy (WVS)

Item	Mean	Std Dev
Rule by Democratic System	3.36	0.79
Democracy Always Best	3.25	0.74

Reliability (Standardized Kronbach's Alpha) = 0.61
Items read:
Q55.4 "Having a democratic political system" (very good)
Q58.4 "Democracy may have problems but it's better than any other form of government" (agree)

Institutional Trust (Idasa)

Item	Mean	Std Dev	Factor Loading
National Government	2.39	0.94	0.87
The Government of this Province	2.63	0.93	0.84
New Town Councils	2.52	0.91	0.86

N = 1816
Eigenvalue is 2.2
Factor explains 74% of the common variance
Reliability (Standardized Kronbach's Alpha) = 0.82

Q34 "About how much of the time do you think you can trust each of the following types of government to do what is right?" (just about always/most of the time)

> National Government
> Government of this Province
> New Town Council

Satisfaction with Democracy (Idasa)
Q11 "On the whole are you ... with the way democracy works in South Africa?" (satisfied)

Commitment to Democracy (Idasa)
Q16 "Sometimes democracy does not work. When this happens, some people say we need a strong leader that does not have to bother with elections. Others say that even when things don't work, democracy is always best." (democracy is always best)

NOTES

[1] We want to thank Marlene Roefs and Cherrel Africa for their advice, comments and criticisms on this paper.

[2] In 1991, South Africa's coefficient was 0.676 and was higher than the 36 developing countries for which data is available. The top 10% of households received 51.2% of income, while the poorest 40% received 3.9% (McGrath and Whiteford, 1994).

[3] We are aware that political support emanates from many other important sources. In South Africa, democracy should be heavily dependant on the support of political activists (eg. mid-level party members), and upper-level elites in key sectors like party leadership, news media, business, religion and the security forces.

[4] Research supports a link between feelings about authority and anti-system behaviour. Those who see political and legal authority as legitimate (measured as trust) are more likely to obey the law, though the relationship is only a moderate one. However, illegal protest is much more strongly influenced by perceptions of legitimacy. Thus, political discontent is clearly linked to unconventional behaviour. This literature is reviewed by Tyler (1990: p. 30–33).

[5] This distinction has also previously been made by Møller (1992b: p. 102). However, she focuses on the determinants of personal and national well-being, rather than their consequences.

[6] Wording differences may limit the direct comparability of the two measures. The PQL scale measures individual satisfaction with economic developments, while the CQL tapes more cognitive evaluations of those developments.

[7] The World Values Study measures confidence in a much larger series of political, economic and social institutions. However, this combination of three-items produced the strongest and most reliable scale.

[8] Perceived quality of life has been marked by a clear racial hierarchy, with whites the most happy and satisfied and Africans the least. However, there has been a steady and significant decline in personal happiness and satisfaction since 1983 among coloureds and Indians, while Africans' levels remained largely the same. In 1994, whites, coloureds and Indians remained the same whereas Africans' perceptions increased greatly and surpassed those of whites. However, the hierarchy re-emerged in 1995, though at a flatter slope. Møller does note that more specific socio-political domain measures of satisfaction did show increases from 1983 to 1995 (see Møller, 1996).

[9] This seems to have been at least one factor behind the defeat of George Bush in November 1992, where voter perceptions had not yet caught up with the recent upturn in economic indicators which promised the end of the recession.

[10] The ANC's recent replacement of the Free State provincial cabinet, and the "redeployment" of people between provincial and national institutions, however, is a step in the exact opposite direction.

[11] This last point may indicate the irony of opposition politics in South Africa at this moment. Opposition gains popular support by convincing people that things are not going well, that the government is responsible, and that they can realistically offer a better solution. However, in a situation where people may not have

yet learned to distinguish the government from the larger system, such criticism (if believed) may decrease support for the democratic system, as much as for the party in power.

REFERENCES

Easton, D.: 1965, A Systems Analysis of Political Life (Chicago University Press, New York).

Eldridge, A.: 1977, 'Introduction: On Legislatures In Plural Societies', in Eldridge, A. (ed.), Legislatures In Plural, (University Press, Durham, NC, Duke).

Kinder, D. and B. Kiewet: 1981, 'Sociotropic Politics: The American Case', British Journal of Political Science 11, pp. 129–61.

Mattes, R.: 1995, The Election Book: Judgement and Choice In South Africa's 1994 Election (IDASA, Cape Town).

McGrath, M. and A. Whiteford: 1994, 'Disparate Circumstances', Indicator South Africa 11(3), pp. 47–50.

Mezey, M.: 1995, Legislatures and the Creation of Consensus in Divided Societies, Paper presented to the Colloquium on Reconciliation and Reconstruction in Ethnically Divided Societies of the International Political Science Association Research Committee on Politics and Ethnicity, Johannesburg, South Africa, 10 July.

Møller, V.: 1992a, Applications of Subjective Well-Being Measures In Quality of Life Surveys, CSDS Working Paper No. 5, Durban, CSDS University of Natal.

Møller, V.: 1992b, 'A Place In the Sun: Quality of Life In South Africa', Indicator South Africa 9(4), pp. 101–108.

Møller, V.: 1996, Quality of Life In South Africa: Post Apartheid Trends, Paper Presented to Symposium on Subjective Well-Being, International Congress of Psychology, Montreal, 22–25 August.

Sigelman, L., C. Sigelman and D. Bullock: 1991, 'Reconsidering Pocketbook Voting: An Experimental Approach', Political Behavior 13(2).

Tyler, T.: 1990, Why People Obey the Law (Chicago University Press, New Haven).

Public Opinion Service
Institute for Democracy In South Africa
8 Spin Street, Church Square
Cape Town 8001
South Africa
E-mail: rbmat@pic.iaccess.za

ELWIL BEUKES and ANNA VAN DER COLFF*

ASPECTS OF THE QUALITY OF LIFE IN BLACK TOWNSHIPS IN A SOUTH AFRICAN CITY: IMPLICATIONS FOR HUMAN DEVELOPMENT

ABSTRACT. This article explores the use of quality of life studies for the analysis of development potential from a human development perspective. For this purpose, an empirical study was made of the assessment of quality of life in the black community in Bloemfontein, a medium-sized South African city. This was done by way of a questionnaire survey of a sample selected from poorer people living in areas formerly demarcated for black people by the apartheid policies of the previous government. The findings of the survey were analysed in such a way that conclusions could be drawn about the potential for human development in these communities. The conclusions show that quality of life studies seem to lend themselves for use as the analytic base for development policy-making from a human development perspective. It must be acknowledged, though, that this kind of application still needs much refinement, further analysis and experimentation before it can be said to finally pass the test which was attempted in this study.

INTRODUCTION

Development is not about the delivery of goods and services to a passive citizenry. It is about active involvement and growing empowerment. (ANC, 1994, p. 5)

Quality of life studies have emerged since the late 1960's as an extension of the set of measuring instruments to gauge the impact of development policies and efforts. Recognition of the multidimensional nature of the development process gave rise to a growing dissatisfaction with the narrow and truncated contribution of GDP per capita as a measuring instrument. This led to the search for a wider range of social and economic indicators reflecting a more holistic picture of how well people live.

Despite the problems, measuring social indicators is recognised as capable of illuminating something of the human, social and cultural contexts of poverty in addition to its economic side. While the GDP measure implicitly points to a "race" between rich and poor and

Social Indicators Research **41**: 229–250, 1997.

"catching up" as the way ahead, social indicators point to common values and problems and opportunities for learning from and cooperating with each other (Khan, 1991: pp. 158-159).

The new dispensation in South Africa since 1994, and the national agenda of reconstruction and accelerated development as embodied in the Reconstruction and Development Programme (RDP), has made it necessary to look at all possible and appropriate ways to contribute to improving life-chances and options for the poor majority of its people. The RDP also recognises that development is a 'people-driven process' (ANC, 1994: p. 5) and it wants to break decisively with the idea that development is a deduction from economic growth (ANC, 1994: p. 6).

The sentiments about and understanding of development in South Africa, as expressed in the RDP and all manner of public announcements since 1994, have undergone a major turn towards becoming more in line with recent ideas of people-centredness and increased life-chances for the ordinary person. There is a much greater acceptance today among decision-makers that development is in essence human development and that most concrete measurements of development have to say something about the manifestation of human development. But sentiments alone are clearly insufficient to improve actual conditions in our country. In particular, it is decisive that the development policies and actions of government at all levels should be informed by and reflect the new understanding of development as human development.

It is in this latter regard that the enhanced measurement of development via 'social indicators' can make a substantial contribution to the still widely prevalent use of economic measurements. While social indicator studies can serve at least the dual purposes of public information and policy analysis, this contribution attempts to use its results for drawing some conclusions about the possibilities for human development among the residents of the black townships of Bloemfontein.

QUALITY OF LIFE AND HUMAN DEVELOPMENT

The "social indicators" approach refers to the various attempts to measure the contribution to general well-being of health, nutrition, housing, income distribution, some 'economic' indicators (like transport and communications) and other aspects of social and cultural development in combination (Khan, 1991: pp. 153–158). It is generally acknowledged that this approach is beset with many conceptual and statistical problems. In addition, it has not yet acquired a clear purpose: is it an alternative to GDP or a supplement? (Khan, 1991: p. 158). It is not the purpose of this contribution to enter the debate about these issues. Instead, it will be assumed that measurements of how people experience and perceive their own lives, does add to our understanding of the challenge that has to be overcome.

It must be granted that the concept of quality of life is a complex yet seemingly superficial concept when used for scientific purposes although much work has been done in fields like psychology to make this a more rigorous and tested area of inquiry. In South Africa, this concept is more commonly used by journalists, politicians and the person in the street. Regarding definitions, the situation is still roughly that admitted by Møller and Schlemmer in 1983 when they said that "... a more precise definition is impossible at this stage ..." (1983: p. 225). Their continued work since then has nonetheless provided a measuring instrument for South African conditions with a sufficient degree of standardisation to allow time and inter-group comparisons. A slightly simplified and amended version of this instrument has been used in the study done for this contribution.

The essence of this form of measurement is that it tries to appraise in a consistent way what people themselves feel about their living conditions. Ordinary people are given the opportunity of making and communicating their own judgements about their social, economic and political condition. The scientific precondition for this process is that the appraisal must be done in a way that corresponds with scientific measurement procedure and that the inferences drawn from this technique must be made with the necessary circumspection.

A particularly fruitful aspect of quality of life studies stems directly from its attempt to record subjective feelings and opinions about what people think and feel about their conditions. This refers to the fact that the steadily growing view of development as essentially human development is predicated on what the ordinary person in a situation of poverty or deprivation sees as his/her own life-chances and what can be done by the individual to change this for the better. Griffin and Knight expressed this as follows: "The process of economic development can be seen as a process of expanding the capabilities of people. ... That is, we are ultimately concerned with what people are capable of doing or being" (1992: p. 576). The enhancement of capabilities requires changes which lead to the unblocking of the creativity within human beings.

A shorthand way of describing human development is an adaptation of Lincoln's definition of democracy: it is development *of* people, *for* people, *by* people. *Of* people implies adequate income generation through jobs and production activity, *for* people implies supportive collective services, and *by* people means participation and self-reliance. The movement in understanding of development since the middle of this century has gone from income to welfare, to chosen bundles of goods and services, to the characteristics of these goods and services, to the needs that they meet, and finally to the enlargement of people's choices and the enhancement of their ability to do more for themselves (Streeten, 1994: p. 6).

Understanding development as human-centered has been given particular meaning through the work of Amartya Sen (1982, 1984, 1987, 1992). In a series of papers and books, Sen developed a set of concepts and measures of well-being which contributes much to a richer understanding of what human development means. First, he draws a distinction between a commodity and its set of characteristics or desirable properties. Second, he argues that these characteristics must be distinguished from the "functionings" of persons – that which a particular person can achieve or succeed in doing with the set of specific commodities at his/her command. The set of functionings which persons can choose – their freedom of "choice" of functionings – he calls their "capabilities." Functionings and capabilities are in turn distinguished from the final state of mind of the specific person, such as happiness or desire-fulfilment. Thus Sen constructs an analysis of consumption and welfare which is richer in meaning for the measurement of development than that which flows from orthodox economics and which can be summed up as follows:

Commodities ⇒ Characteristics ⇒ Capabilities/Functionings ⇒ Mental states

Human development is determined in this frame of thinking by the complex variety of functionings and capabilities of people in the everyday course of their lives in which commodities and access to these can play an enabling role but does not in itself establish living standards and the quality of life (Doyal and Gough, 1991).

If we are interested in the progress of human development, it is thus necessary that appraisals are made of whether the capabilities of people and their use of these abilities are improving. This places considerable emphasis on local resource availability and mobilisation as a way of allowing people to do more for themselves. For both these purposes – the availability and the use of local resources – the study of quality of life indicators can make a very useful contribution. It not only tells us what resources are available, but also how people evaluate the use they can make of these resources and whether they are experiencing progress in improving their lives. Instead of bland measurements of what resources – public or private – are put at people's disposal, this form of investigation gives indications of whether these resources are actually what people can and want to make use of.

APPLYING THE ANALYSIS OF QUALITY OF LIFE STUDIES TO ESTIMATING DEVELOPMENT POTENTIAL

In the second quarter of 1996, an empirical quality of life study was made in Bloemfontein, a fairly typical middle-sized city in South Africa[1] and also regarded as one of the most telling examples of apartheid-based urban development. An attempt was made to analyse the findings from the vantage point of determing the potential for human development in a community which had just recently become free of the bonds of a repressive societal system and its accompanying patterns of living. The hypothesis investigated was whether the findings could throw light on the way in which people experienced the resources at their disposal and whether deductions could be made about their willingness to use them constructively.

The elementary device used, was to ascertain whether gaps existed between what people have at their disposal – as appraised by themselves – and how they experience the usefulness of these resources for improving their lives. These "tensions" were interpreted as possible "windows of opportunity" through which people have to improve matters for themselves. This can then be taken as an indicator of the potential for human development. To ascertain the subjective willingness to use these opportunities to improve functionings, questions were put from which inferences could be drawn about the likelihood of a positive or negative use of the observed "tensions."

The first dimension investigated was the relation between what people consider their objective resources to be and how they evaluate the sufficiency of these resources. The second dimension explored was the relationship between the public and private spheres of people's lives and the satisfaction they derive from both of these. From the "tensions" discovered in these two dimensions, a first set of conclusions can be drawn about opportunities for improvement. The third set of impressions concerned who people thought should carry the responsibility for improvement in their conditions. The temptation exists to view this as a direct measurement of their willingness to assume responsibility for their own improvement or not. It must be granted though, that more information is needed on what the concept of "responsibility" means in the popular view, before definitive conclusions can be drawn from this measurement. If this probe provides positive indication of the acceptance of own responsibility, it does, however, provide grounds for the possibility that everything is not expected to be delivered from elsewhere.

The last dimension investigated, concerns the change in people's view of the general state of affairs – which can be considered a measurement of the change in their degree of optimism or pessimism about how things were changing.

Taking all of the above together, a set of conclusions are drawn about the potential for human development in a historically disadvantaged community of a middle-sized city.

ANALYSIS OF THE BLOEMFONTEIN STUDY

Some general characteristics of the survey

A stratified random sample of 348 was selected from a total universum consisting of 39739 households (274138 inhabitants) of the black township and surrounding informal settlements and squatter areas in Bloemfontein. The sample was stratified according to the socio-economic status of different areas and sections of these communities, the type and quality of housing (including the size of erven), and the quality of public services. This gave rise to four main geographic groupings: Mangaung (the main township), Heidedal (a former coloured group area), Freedom Square (upgraded informal settlement) and the rest of the squatter settlements (not upgraded).[2]

Subjects were interviewed on the basis of a standardised questionnaire in the second quarter of 1996. The field workers who conducted the interviews, were well-trained and their work was regularly checked. The questionnaire contained both objective and subjective measures. Satisfaction and happiness were assessed in terms of 5-point scales with categories ranging from *very satisfied* to *very dissatisfied*. For the purpose of the further analysis in this paper, the categories were condensed to *satisfied, neutral* and *dissatisfied*. The following results were obtained.

Objective and subjective evaluations of the standard of living

The first set of results deals with some objective measures of the standard of living, as indicated by the respondents themselves. This was followed in the questionnaire with indications of how these same conditions were subjectively evaluated by respondents as satisfactory or not. From this, observations can be made about what degree of "tension" exists between what means people have at their disposal to better their lives, and how positive/helpful they consider these means.

It is argued that if this "tension" is substantial, it may give rise to the release of energy to improve matters, i.e. it indicates potential for human development. If this energy is not channelled constructively but translates into a pent-up demand for matters to be improved by outside institutions, this potential is wasted as a spark for human development.

The argument is that most of the dimensions of access to services and opportunities investigated, can be seen as satisfiers for human needs. Therefore peoples' access to these "means", form part of what can be considered basic preconditions for human development. At issue here are dimensions like housing, health services, educational achievement, income and general public services. In what follows, the respondents' own description of elements of their standard of living is compared with their evaluation (or level of satisfaction) of the same. From this it follows whether "tension" exists or not.

Housing

Of the dwellings found in the research area, 37% are of a western type,[3] 33% are of a traditional type[4] and 30% are shacks.[5] In addition, 78% of the dwellings are owned by the inhabitants and 22% rented. The occupation densities found in the more established areas like Mangaung and Heidedal were one or two persons per room in about 75% of cases. In the squatter areas, 70% of people live in homes with three or more persons per room.

As far as the size of dwelling is concerned, only those in Heidedal were 50% satisfied. Those in other areas were distinctly dissatisfied, with 90% of people in Freedom Square indicating dissatisfaction. The percentage of those dissatisfied with size decreased systematically from 68% among the young to 45% among the 64+ age group. Based on educational level, only among those with no education or those with a degree, more satisfaction than dissatisfaction was expressed. In summary, people expressed definite dissatisfaction with their size of dwelling.

A surprising finding was that 52% of the total sample indicated feeling satisfied with the present *location* of their dwellings, despite the size, while 39% indicated dissatisfaction. The inhabitants of "old" Mangaung were more dissatisfied than satisfied (49% vs. 46%), with Heidedal and the squatters more satisfied than dissatisfied. The most interesting finding here was that 95% of the inhabitants of the upgraded informal settlement of Freedom Square indicated satisfaction. This means that Freedom Square's people are highly satisfied with where they stay but not with the size of their homes.

Educational level

The level of school education found among the total sample indicate a literacy rate of at least 80% among the people of Bloemfontein's townships, with 46% obtaining std. 8 or higher. The highest figures were obtained by the inhabitants of Heidedal and the lowest among those living in the squatter areas and Freedom Square. When age groups are considered, it was found that people below 40 years of age had far higher educational achievements than people over 40. Of people with no schooling, 71% were older than 40 and of those with achievement between std. 8 and 10, 76% were under 40.

Almost no differentiation between male and female respondents was found as far as the spread of different levels of education obtained is concerned.

Another important objective indicator concerning education is the willingness to improve own standard of education. It was found that 58% of the total sample were willing and 42% unwilling to consider improvement. The highest percentage of those willing (71%) was found among people living in Freedom Square and the lowest among those in Heidedal – the latter which relates to the already attained level of schooling and the current involvement in schooling in the area.

As far as age group is concerned, those in the 30–39 year bracket were found to be most eager to improve their education. This group corresponds with those who were in their teens during the Soweto uprising of 1976 and who are likely to have missed out on account of the general climate of revolt at the time.

The *evaluation* of own level of education indicates that only 25% of the sample were satisfied and 42% dissatisfied, with 22% indifferent. The highest levels of dissatisfaction were found in Freedom Square (90%) and Mangaung (70%) with the rest substantially lower.

The level of satisfaction with education among age groups indicates that only the aged are no longer worried about this. As far as the gender split is concerned, it was found that 70% of females were dissatisfied, compared to 57% of males, indicating a higher realisation among women that education today is a basic necessity for improving ones own condition in society.

Income
The distribution of income in different categories for the four main areas under investigation is shown in Table I. Table I shows that if R 900 is taken as the poverty line (Whiteford et al., 1995) for a household of 5 persons, about 65% of the households in Heidedal receive a higher figure, and so do 50% of the households in Mangaung. In Freedom Square, only about 33% receive more than a poverty line income and the squatter settlements are worst off with only 16% of households receiving above a poverty line income.

The levels of dissatisfaction expressed per residential area with salary or wage, is the highest among those with the lowest monthly income, but with a surprising 58% of Mangaung's respondents also

TABLE I
Monthly household income distribution per area

Area	less than R800	R801–R1000	R1001–R2000	R2001–R4000	R4000+
Mangaung	36%	15%	24%	16%	9%
Heidedal	29%	7%	12%	32%	20%
Squatters	72%	14%	11%	3%	0
Freedom Square	56%	15%	23%	7%	0

indicating dissatisfaction although they have a meaningfully higher income level. In gender terms, 59% of females and 55% of males expressed dissatisfaction with their salary or wage, while only 8% of females and 16% of males were satisfied.

The generally high level of dissatisfaction with salaries and wages is also reflected in the age group and education level breakdown, with satisfaction levels reaching 20% in only one category in each of these levels of disaggregation (old age and those with a degree). With the exception of Heidedal, respondents also indicated that they did not expect this situation to improve as they grow older.

Health services

The sample showed that 85% of the total population lives within a distance of 5 km or less from the nearest medical care facility. The time required to reach this facility is 30 min. or less for 74% of the population of the area. The level of satisfaction with the health situation of families in the total sample area was 60%, with 29% indicating dissatisfaction. In general, higher levels of satisfaction than dissatisfaction occur at all further disaggregations of the data, with the exception of people living in squatter areas and in Freedom Square. Both these areas are located the furthest from treatment centres.

The figures indicate that the objective provision of health care facilities as well as the subjective experience of the effectiveness of service provided by them, as experienced in family health, is viewed in a more positive light than any other indicator of social service level and performance.

Public services

In a comparative perspective, the level of service provision regarding water, sanitation, refuse removal and energy is quite good. The main source of household water for 89% of people in Mangaung are taps in dwelling or on site. In Heidedal 98% of households have taps in the dwelling or on site. In Freedom Square, the corresponding figure is 100%, while 70% of squatters have to make use of a communal tap which is less than 100 m from the dwelling.

The main source of household energy is electricity, even in the upgraded informal settlement, where 60% of households have this service. It is only in the squatter settlements that paraffin provides 89% of households with energy. Flush toilets are used by an amazing 100% of the people of Freedom Square, 98% of those in Heidedal and 77% of Mangaung. Only the squatters use mainly buckets (53%) and 56% reported that these are removed weekly. Refuse is removed at least once a week in more than 90% of all households outside the squatter settlements, where weekly removal was indicated in 73% of cases.

Despite the fact that access to all of the abovementioned services is comparatively good (ESKOM, 1996), the expressed levels of satisfaction of people in all areas, all age groups, across gender, different educational levels all indicate a higher level of dissatisfaction than satisfaction with public services in general, with squatters expressing the highest figure (70%).

The general conclusion that can be drawn from the data in this section is that a surprisingly high level of "tension" exists between what the inhabitants of Bloemfontein's black residential areas have at their disposal as public services and how satisfied they are with it. While this "tension" can be seen as a possible source of energy for development, the problem in this situation is that the comparative level of facilities in Bloemfontein's black townships is very high when seen in provincial or national perspective. It is therefore not clear what more is expected immediately, particularly in view of very low or no contributions to local government revenue by a large segment of the population included in this survey.

TABLE II

Levels of satisfaction and dissatisfaction with public spheres of life (total sample)

	Dissatisfied	Satisfied
Education	65%	
Public services	58%	
Availability of housing	58%	
Job opportunities	70%	
Own life compared with other race groups	72%	
Possibilities for cooperation with others to improve matters	30%	45%
Getting on with other races	39%	42%
Respect shown by other race groups	42%	40%

Comparison between levels of satisfaction with public and private spheres of life

A second form of tension which can be investigated is that between people's levels of satisfaction with their private (personal) and public spheres of life. What constitutes the two spheres, is something of an *ex-post* categorisation of questions put. Some validation for the categorisation is provided by the fairly stark bifurcation of responses to the two kinds of issues.

The hypothesis made in connection with this form of tension is that a substantial disparity between people's satisfaction in private (or personal) versus public spheres of life is an indication of a creative tension that can lead to action to improve the situation in the area where less satisfaction occurs. If a fairly resilient and large measure of satisfaction occurs in one sphere, this is assumed to be a positive energy that can provide the impetus for attempting to improve matters in the less satisfactory sphere.

With regard to the levels of satisfaction with the public spheres of life, the findings are given in Table II. The breakdown of opinions in these matters in terms of area, gender, age group and education level showed little deviation from the general pattern in the sample as a whole.

The findings show that the sample population are in general fairly dissatisfied with what they have at their disposal in terms of public goods and services. This dissatisfaction in the public realm is some-

TABLE III
Level of satisfaction with private spheres of life (total sample)

Health of own family	60%
Family happiness	72%
Time spent with family and friends	81%
Loyalty of friends	73%
Most intimate relationship	70%
Self as a person	80%

what softened by opinions on the possibilities for cooperation with others to improve conditions and options – a more positive indication of the potential for greater self-reliance. The opinions of the sample on relations with other races shows a slightly more positive than negative evaluation – something which suggests that this does not represent a major obstacle for human development.

In stark contrast to the degree of satisfaction with elements of public life given in Table II, stand the findings on the satisfaction expressed by respondents with the private (personal) spheres of existence in Bloemfontein's townships. Figures in Table III indicate a very high and consistent level of satisfaction with a series of elements in the private sphere. The picture drawn from the overall numbers do not differ to any significant degree from those gained from a breakdown into categories such as area, etc. The very high level of satisfaction expressed with the internal family or friendship cohesion, is a testimony to the resilience and staying power of these relationships in African community life despite the extreme pressure it was exposed to under the previous political regime (or maybe partially because of it). This cohesion is a powerful factor to regard as a positive building block for human development in the poorer communities of Bloemfontein and it should be seen by community leaders as a powerful resource which can and should be harnessed for further improvement.

Responsibility for improvement of conditions

In order to ascertain what the likely "use" will be of the creative tension which was identified in both the previous two subdivisions of the data, the question was asked where respondents thought the

TABLE IV

Main responsibility for improving the overall quality of life

Yourself	51%
Your family	14%
The local government	14%
The provincial government	3%
The national government	17%

TABLE V

Responsibility for improving conditions, per age group

Responsibility	18–29 years	30–39 years	40–49 years	50–64 years	64+
Self	51%	47%	65%	43%	45%
Family	16%	16%	6%	14%	14%
Government	32%	35%	27%	39%	41%
Other	1%	3%	2%	5%	0

main responsibility lay for improving their overall quality of life. The response of the sample population as a whole is given in Table IV.

The overall result is heartening for the RDP-idea that development is a people-centred process in which ordinary citizens become less rather than more dependent on outside institutions or powers. A majority of people (51%) in the total sample indicated that they themselves are the main determinants of their future life quality, while 34% holds the government (at various levels) responsible, and 14% look to their families for improving things (Table V).

The inference which can be made from the above is that the gaps and resulting tension that exist between Bloemfontein township people's description of the conditions in which they live and their evaluation of the same, as well as the tension between how satisfied they are with the more private (personal) compared to how dissatisfied they are with the public spheres of their lives, harbour distinct possibilities for creative and constructive application of people's energy and resourcefulness to change their lives for the better.

The disaggregation of the data on this point shows a very resilient and consistent reinforcing of the overall result. The gender breakdown of the data shows that male and female respondents are almost identically resolved to take own responsibility rather than expecting others to improve their lives for them (and therefore the pattern is almost identical to that of the sample).

The breakdown of the response according to household income level provides the result that willingness to accept more responsibility for self-improvement rises consistently with growing size of household income, from 26% at the lowest to 82% at an income level between R 4000 and R 6000. This is in line with expectations, showing that the higher people's income, the less they have need of others to bring about further increases in their conditions. The same result is obtained if education level is used as a basis for distinction. The percentage of people willing to take own responsibility increases consistently from 21% among people with no education to 85% among those with a post-secondary diploma or degree.

When distinguishing on the basis of the nature of occupation of the respondent, it is only among manual workers that less than half (48%) regard themselves as responsible for self-improvement. Even among the self-employed (which include hawkers and street vendors), 56% accept responsibility for improvement, as is the case with 86% of professional people and 95% of office workers.

This set of responses in the survey gives an unambiguous and strong underpinning to the conclusion that the people of the black townships in Bloemfontein are willing to make the major input into the improvement of their life-chances and that they are not going to sit and wait for other institutions (including different levels of government) to do this for them. Despite the association and interdependence between individual and collective inputs and effort in development processes, it is a positive finding that the people of the area surveyed have a clearly expressed inclination towards self-reliance – one of the main dimensions of human development.

Past and future projections of well-being/satisfaction

A dimension of people's experience of their situation which can have a distinct role in their willingness and inclination to tackle development challenges and to deal with issues in a resourceful and self-reliant way, is their feeling of optimism or pessimism. Put differently, if people experience the general tide of events as going against them or that overall conditions are degenerating, the chances

TABLE VI
Feelings about overall satisfaction with life *five years* ago

Satisfied	31%
Neutral	12%
Dissatisfied	58%

TABLE VII
Direction of change since the April 1994 election

Improving	57%
Unchanging	26%
Worsening	17%

increase that they will either become apathetic or increasingly restive and demanding in their relations towards government. The survey gave rise to the following results as indicated in Tables VI–VIII.

Table VI shows that people were highly dissatisfied with life five years ago – shortly after the lifting of the ban on normal political activity. If this result for the sample is broken down into subcategories, the expressed opinion remains the same. The general feeling about what the political changes in 1994 have led to, is indicated in Table VII. This indicates a distinct change in sentiment from that of five years ago. The majority of respondents expressed a positive sentiment about what the 1994 elections have brought about in their own lives. This picture is even more optimistic if indications are given about what the case will be five years into the future. This is presented in Table VIII.

This table shows that the expectation among Bloemfontein's township dwellers about which way development will go during the rest of this decade, is decidedly positive. Further disaggregation of the data shows that this opinion exists in almost the same quantitative extent across all the cross-sections of the data.

There is thus a general tendency for increased optimism as this community looks back five years into the past, and then looks ahead for the next five years. An increase in optimism can act as a powerful stimulus for this community to channel their energy and effort in a constructive and useful way rather than the other way round. This is

TABLE VIII
Expected satisfaction with life *five years* into the future

Better	71%
Same	9%
Worse	20%

TABLE IX
Appreciating present life

Rewarding	31%
Frustrating	20%
In between	45%
Don't know	4%

another indication of a positive potential for human development and a willingness of people in Bloemfontein to do more for themselves.

Overall happiness and contentment

To gain a general assessment of the quality of life of the inhabitants of the survey area, questions were asked about their general mood when thinking about their life. This inquiry provided results that were much in line with the indications given of people's general optimism or pessimism. Table IX shows that people's minds are to a large degree still open about what the changes in the recent past mean for them. The largest segment (45%) indicated that their appreciation of life now in their vicinity was undecided, while 31% found it rewarding. This finding does at least show that decision makers and public administrators do not have to deal with a solid block of frustrated people who are more likely than not to make the government the focus of their demands for improvement.

Table X supports the finding of Table IX and gives further foundation to the interpretation of its findings. It also indicates a sizeable component of people who are undecided on where things are developing to, but the majority this time have a positive appreciation of this issue.

The global summary of people's feeling about their general well-being, which would include private and public concerns, once more shows that matters are finely balanced. An identical percentage

TABLE X
Present direction of change

Deteriorating	15%
Improving	46%
Unchanging	31%
Don't know	7%

TABLE XI
Overall happiness

Very happy	12%
Fairly happy	27%
In between	22%
Fairly unhappy	22%
Very unhappy	17%

(39%) indicate both happiness and unhappiness, with 22% in between (Table XI).

This result lends further support to the interpretation of the general situation among the residents of Bloemfontein's poorer areas as balanced in a "window of opportunity." The public mood is readily capable of going into a positive or a negative direction. At this stage there are strong indications, however, that the basis for it going into a positive direction is stronger than the opposite. What the situation will be in five years time, will thus depend decisively on whether people in the area realise the opportunities for human development and whether they are supported in this by public authorities and other support structures.

GENERAL CONCLUSIONS

The foregoing study and its initial analysis has been done as an investigation into the merging of two fields of investigation. The first is the well-established one of quality of life studies. Although the study under consideration has been closely linked with and largely based on the methodology and instruments of quality of life studies, its intention and analysis is not to contribute mainly to that. The main intention of this study is to use quality of life findings to investigate the opportunities and options for human-centred development policy in an urban community.

Based on this general analytic thrust and the exploratory nature of such a merging of fields, the results lead to a first basic conclusion. It seems as if quality of life studies can be used and their results interpreted in a way that provides grounds for assessing the potential for human development in a surveyed area. The results are still mainly exploratory and will have to be tested in additional ways. But it can at least be said that they do not provide reasons for a negative outcome to the experiment. The analytic device used to come to this finding, was that of identifying the elements in people's quality of life assessments which indicate positive and creative tensions between their current and their desired future condition. These can then be seen as the priority areas in which policy interventions (or improved provisioning) may have the largest chance of enhancing people's capacity to become more self-reliant and to improve their own life-chances and standard of living.

A second conclusion is that if the findings are interpreted on the basis of the method proposed above, the general result obtained is that there does exist a definite potential for human development (as understood in the current theoretical debate) among the people in the survey area. The potential may even be larger than is recognised from a first scan of the situation and expressions of public opinion from the area. This is an almost counter-factual result when the extremely low levels of provisioning in most of the survey areas are taken into account.

The third finding is that a surprisingly strong opinion was expressed by the respondents that people in their situation carry own responsibility for improvement in their general situation, rather than actors like the government or others outside the community. This is a very positive indication for positive change in the surveyed area along the lines of a more people-centred and a less commodity/service oriented view of development. Although this study did not attempt to assess the exact understanding of "responsibility" which underpins this finding, it does provide reason for stating that it would be wrong to assume that the poorer part of our population expects all improvement in their lives from sources other than themselves. At least a clear handle exists to which initiatives can be linked which would support greater self-reliance and less dependence. This finding must be qualified by the high degree of satisfaction expressed with the self – which may be seen as detracting somewhat from the willingness to provide effort for improvement. Closer investigation may give reasons for this high level of self-satisfaction that do not detract from such a willingness. The high level of discontent expressed with elements of public service provision, which are comparatively seen not all that bad, may still refer to the experience under the previous political regime when public services for the non-enfranchised were of a very inferior quality and nature.

This last possibility is strengthened by the finding that the perceptions about development held by ordinary people in Bloemfontein's townships consist of a mix of true self-reliance and a feeling that previously disadvantaged people are now entitled to much better service and provision from public sources than they already have. The task ahead for public policy-makers and authorities therefore includes helping ordinary poor South Africans realise more of their inherent potential to do more for themselves by providing those kinds of services and assistance that can be afforded and sustained in the foreseeable future and which do not create or recreate the dependency and helplessness which characterise so many urban situations in Africa.

NOTES

* Elwil Beukes was Professor of Economics at the University of the Orange Free State in Bloemfontein and Anna van der Colff was Lecturer in Economics at Vista University's Bloemfontein campus while carrying out the research reported in this paper.
[1] Bloemfontein is the capital of the Free State province, a small province with about 2.8 million inhabitants (7% of the SA total). It harbours about 400 000 people of whom more than 55% can be regarded as poor. The comparative level of per capita production and income in Bloemfontein ranks it as a medium-income city in the South African context.
[2] The socio-economic characteristics of the four areas are as follows: (1) Mangaung is the largest and oldest settlement of blacks in the city with a history of over 100 years. It contains the more settled and relatively well-off sections of the poor in the sample. (2) Heidedal is a relatively small area, adjacent to Mangaung, formerly set apart as residential area exclusively for mixed-race (Coloured) people. Its community is the most well-off and educationally advanced of the four areas. (3) Freedom Square, contained in the larger Mangaung, originated as a squatter

settlement in 1990 and was upgraded during the course of the 1990's. Although still very poor, its community is settling down and have gained access to public services. (4) The rest of the squatter settlements also form part of Mangaung, but are scattered throughout. They harbour the poorest people and have very limited public services.

[3] Built with solid material, steel doorframes and windows and not in need of repair.

[4] Of a semi-permanent nature and in need of repair.

[5] Of a non permanent nature and constructed of removable and non-conventional material.

REFERENCES

African National Congress (ANC): 1994, The Reconstruction and Development Programme (Umanyano Publications, Johannesburg).

Botes, L., S. Krige and J. Wessels: 1991, Informal Settlements in Bloemfontein (Bloemfontein, Urban Foundation).

Clarke, J.G.L.: 1993, Human scale Development: A South African Perspective (Ecumenical Foundation of Southern Africa, Bellville).

Doyal, L. and Gough I.: 1991, A theory of human need (Macmillan, London).

ESKOM: 1996, The Decision Maker's Encyclopaedia of the South African Consumer Market: 1996 edition (Johannesburg).

Gasper, D.: 1996, Needs and basic needs: A clarification of meanings, levels and different streams of work, Working Paper Series No. 210 (Institute of Social Studies, The Hague).

Goulet, D.: 1992, 'Development . . . or Liberation', in C.K. Wilber and K.P. Jameson (eds.), The Political Economy of Development and Underdevelopment, 5th edition (McGraw-Hill, New York).

Griffin, K and J. Knight: 1992, 'Human development: The case for renewed emphasis', in C.K. Wilber and K.P. Jameson (eds.), The Political Economy of Development and Underdevelopment, 5th Edition (McGraw-Hill, New York).

Kallman, K.: 1996, An Introduction to Social Indicators and Social Reporting: A Digest of the Literature (Centre for Social and Development Studies, Durban).

Khan, H.: 1991, 'Measurement and determinants of socio-economic development: a critical conspectus', Social Indicators Research 24, pp. 153–175.

Møller, V. and L. Schlemmer: 1983, 'Quality of life in South Africa: Towards an instrument for the assessment of quality of life and basic needs', Social Indicators Research 12, pp. 255-279.

RSA: 1995, Key Indicators of Poverty in South Africa (Ministry in the Office of the President – RDP, Pretoria).

Rothenbacher, F.: 1993, 'National and international approaches in social reporting', Social Indicators Research 29, pp. 1–62.

Sen, A.: 1982, Choice, Welfare and Measurement (Blackwell, Oxford).

Sen, A.: 1984, Resources, Values and Development (Blackwell, Oxford).

Sen, A.: 1987, The Standard of Living (Cambridge University Press, Cambridge).

Sen, A.: 1992, 'Development: Which way now?', in C.K. Wilber and K.P. Jameson (eds.), The political economy of development and underdevelopment, 5th edition (McGraw-Hill, New York).

Streeten, P.P.: 1994, Human development means and ends, Paper delivered at the UNDP Stockholm Roundtable on Global Change, Stockholm, 22–24 July.

United Nations Development Programme: 1990, Human Development Report (Oxford University Press, New York).

Van Zijl, J.C.: 1995, Needs–based development strategy and the RDP: Some broad issues, Occasional paper No. 47 (Development Bank of Southern Africa, Midrand).

Whiteford, A., D. Posel and T. Kelatwang: 1995, A profile of poverty, inequality and human development (Human Sciences Research Council, Pretoria).

Wilber, C.K. and K.P. Jameson (eds.): 1992, The political economy of development and underdevelopment, 5th edition (McGraw-Hill, New York).

The Kings University College
9125 – 50th Street
Edmonton
Alberta T6B 2H3
Canada

PETER GILL[1] and PETER HALL[1]

PLAYING NUMBERS OR POLITICS? APPROACHES TO THE PRIORITISATION OF DEVELOPMENT NEEDS IN SOUTH AFRICA

ABSTRACT. This paper uses a case study to highlight the implicit political and developmental assumptions which underpin an indicator and index based prioritisation of developmental needs. A key issue for the successful implementation of development objectives in South Africa is the identification and prioritisation of development needs. Indicators could play an important role in terms of informing the decisions made by various levels of government. An indicator based index supported by a computerised system called the Development Indicators Monitoring System (DIMS) has been used to prioritise housing and service provision need within the province of Gauteng. The article shows that the prioritisation of areas in terms of service need is sensitive to the index construction method employed. It is argued that various choices around the index construction method depend on certain developmental assumptions which are fundamentally political choices. In particular, the choice between absolute and relative indicators of need has a considerable impact on the prioritisation of areas. However, this is not a total rejection of the use of indicators in the planning process. Rather, it is a call for the appropriate use of the tools that are available.

KEY WORDS: development, housing, indicators, indices, prioritisation ranking, resource allocation, service provision

1. INTRODUCTION

Until recently, South African development choices have reflected the political system of Apartheid. With the transition to democracy in South Africa, there needs to be more transparency and accountability with regard to how development decisions are made. The implementation of sustainable development policies and strategies requires the allocation of scarce resources through delivery programmes and projects. In most cases, the development gap between different areas is so large that it is difficult to know where to begin.

This paper seeks to present a conceptual approach towards the use of indicators and development indices to identify and prioritise between different areas of need. The research focuses on one

Social Indicators Research **41**: 251–278, 1997.

of the six basic principles of the Reconstruction and Development Programme (RDP) (African National Congress, 1994), namely "Meeting Basic Needs" and within that context it only addresses housing and engineering services. Nevertheless, the basic principles outlined here can be applied to many other development areas. The RDP documentation clearly spells out the goals and objectives with regard to housing and engineering services, namely:

- Housing: "At a minimum, one million low cost houses should be built over 5 years" (p. 22).

- Water and Sanitation: ". . . to provide all households with clean, safe water supply of 20–30 litres per capita per day within 200 metres and an adequate/safe sanitation facility per site . . . " (p. 29).

- Electricity: ". . . must provide access to electricity for an additional 2.5 million households by the year 2000 to about 72 per cent of all households . . . " (p. 33).

The RDP document identifies the promised minimum housing and services levels, but does not state on which basis resources will be allocated. One of the fundamental problems with the initial implementation of RDP programmes was that the emphasis was on highlighting political hot spots or only allocating funds to those who were sufficiently organised and motivated to apply for funding. While this approach could be defended from the perspective of kick-starting the RDP, it did not represent an equitable or rationally sustainable development approach towards the distribution of development funds. A more practical and less politically reactive approach would have been to clearly identify those areas which had the highest priority in terms of development need and potential.

The key issue therefore is how does one identify and prioritise areas of development need and potential? What are the weights and variables that need to be considered? How do such rankings operate within a policy framework? In an attempt to address these issues, the Development Indicators Monitoring System (DIMS) was developed.

The initial research philosophy underlying the development of DIMS was that decisions relating to the allocation of development funds could be assisted by a more objective assessment of needs, rather than being based purely on political criteria. A series of indicators were identified which could be used to compare areas of different geographical extent, location and population. DIMS was developed as a first attempt to use a basic set of indicators and a composite indicator index which would allow decision makers within the development process in South Africa to identify priority areas for development.

The work outlined in this paper represents one of many possible conceptual approaches to the use of indicators and the development of composite indices to guide the allocation of development funds. It would be wrong to assume that the more objective empirical analysis of data can be divorced from the political process, but it is hoped that the process of decision making can be better informed by the use of empirical data in the development of indicators and composite indices. The essential argument presented in this paper is that decisions based on index construction depend on a set of developmental assumptions which represent fundamentally political choices, but that there is scope for the decision making process to be more transparent and better informed.

The paper briefly assesses both the international and local research on the topic (Section 2) and discusses the role of indicators within the South African development environment (Section 3). The paper then investigates the methodological issues associated with the index construction method (Section 4), and reviews the impacts of index construction method and the different development philosophies within the context of the province of Gauteng, most notably the impacts of relative and absolute indicators (Section 5). The paper concludes with some recommendations for further research work in the use of indicators and indices to guide development planning decisions (Section 6).

2. THE RESEARCH CONTEXT

The allocation of public resources for development is complex and has provoked extensive debate. As governments increasingly come under pressure to justify why some communities benefit and others do not, there has been an increase in activity both nationally and internationally around establishing quantitative measures of development.

In South Africa, soon after the 1976 Soweto uprising, the idea of being able to measure the "quality of life" or "well-being" became an issue of national concern (Møller, Schlemmer and Du Toit, 1987). There was a need for measures to assess the existing conditions of communities so that efforts could be made to improve such conditions. On one hand, the objectives of the then national government were focused towards attaining political stability, while on the other hand researchers were establishing a framework within which development priorities of communities could be more clearly identified and prioritised. Much of the research focused on establishing a set of "quality of life" indicators that considered a combination of both "objective" and "subjective" influences. Regrettably, this valuable research did not have a medium through which to make a meaningful contribution to development, and research in this area remained dormant until the political context was more conducive.

While research efforts in South Africa stagnated, research was being undertaken in different parts of the world that looked at constructing indicators and using multi-variate analysis techniques to rank different places based on the combined scores of different measures. For example, in the United Kingdom extensive research was done into how "quality of life" indicators could be used to establish a local prosperity index for cities (Rogerson, Findlay, Morris and Coombes, 1989). Others used indicators to measure local economic performance to identify so-called "booming" towns in Britain (Green and Champion, 1988; Green and Champion, 1991). In Israel researchers used quantitative research techniques to identify the socio-economic differences between cities and used such information to determine differential development policies for different parts of the country (Lipshitz and Raveh, 1994). One issue which seems to have characterised most of these research initiatives is that there is no consensus on the types of indicators used or the ranking criteria to be incorporated (Rogerson, Findlay, Morris and Coombes, 1989).

Within the international context, the World Bank and the United Nations established the Housing Indicator Programme and subsequently, the Indicator Programme (linked with the Habitat II initiative), in a bid to develop a conceptual, analytical and institutional framework for dealing with sustainable development (Housing

Indicator Programme, 1993). The United Nations has also used indicators more broadly by establishing the Human Development Report. The report uses indicators, measuring numerous aspects of development, to compare and rank countries (United Nations Development Programme, 1994).

3. INDICATORS

In this paper, an indicator is taken as a measure or evaluation of the level (or progress) of development that allows for comparison across time and space. Indicators are used to make information meaningful and accessible. In this regard, indicators represent the best possible manner for presenting information for managerial or decision-making processes.

While there is acceptance that indicators can be used as the basis for the planning and the monitoring of development, thus making government more transparent and accountable, there is significant confusion surrounding the use and definition of indicators. This creates the conditions for the abuse of indicators to misinform the public by, for example, obscuring the failure of government to implement development programmes in an appropriate fashion.

The use of indicators as measures of development and as tools for planning and monitoring development activities has been driven by major development agencies such as the World Bank and the United Nations. The value of this international work is that it established a framework whereby a range of indicators could be used to normalise comparisons across different countries. Similarly, in South Africa, there is a need to normalise comparisons at provincial, regional and local levels so that more effective planning, resource allocation and monitoring can take place.

There is a need to develop indicators which reflect the dynamics of the South African situation. Clearly, the debate around the use of indicators is extensive and cannot be fully explored within the scope of this paper. South Africa has not had a well established statistical function that provides data for the development planning process. This results in one not having data to support the desired key indicators that have been identified. There is often the need to identify proxy indicators to measure a particular dimension of the development environment. In some instances one indicator may be used with different intentions by different sectors. This raises the issue of indicator terminology and definition, which is especially problematic when one considers the use of quantitative versus subjective indicators.

In contrast with the international recommendations, this paper advocates the use of indicators based on both *absolute* numbers of people in need, as well as the *relative* proportion of people in need.[2] This is based on the pragmatic view that in the allocation of resources, decision makers may need to consider both the scale of the problem as well as its relative dimensions. The implications of this decision are discussed in more detail below.

Furthermore, the researchers have had to make subjective choices in the formulation of their indicators. The issue of housing backlogs illustrates the impact that such subjectivity can have. A housing backlog can be defined in many ways and highlights the fact that decision makers have to determine what they consider to be acceptable forms of housing. There are at least two ways of looking at housing backlogs. The first is to regard the number of informal housing units as the clearest manifestation of a housing backlog. This indicator, however, does not address what may be called the hidden backlog, or overcrowding. An alternative way of looking at the housing backlog is to determine the desired number of housing units required based on assumptions regarding household size and to derive the backlog based on the shortage of such housing units. While there could be extensive debate around this issue, the focus of this study is not on the standard per se, but rather on identifying the impact of such a standard on a prioritisation index once different standards have been established.

The indicators used in this paper address the following issues, namely housing backlog, access to electricity supply, access to different standards of water supply, and access to different standards of sanitation supply[3]

4. METHODOLOGICAL ISSUES OF INDEX CONSTRUCTION

In this section three methodological issues are explored. Firstly, data sources and data quality are discussed recognising that an index is only as good as the data from which it has been calculated. Secondly, the implications of choosing a particular index construction method are examined. Thirdly, we explore issues relating to the use of index based prioritisation within the development context.

4.1 Data Sources and Data Quality

One of the key problems with any planning initiative is access to a commonly accepted and reliable core database. In principle, the quality of the output of a prioritisation index is largely dependent on the quality of the data used. In the absence of resources to establish a national database and in anticipation of the results of the strongly developmental 1996 population census, it was decided that for the purposes of our research to use a database developed by the electricity utility company ESKOM for the National Electrification Forum (NELF).[4] While this supplied a readily available source of information that could be used for the project, it was recognised that the database was problematic in terms of the quality of the information and the coverage of the database. This is especially true for the former homelands[5], which are often poorly represented in the available statistics. Those areas for which statistics are not available cannot be included in any prioritisation index. Furthermore, it is probably inadvisable to include areas for which information on one or more service need category is missing, since an index calculation based on incomplete data may be inaccurate. Available data is also subject to the problem of out-datedness, especially in terms of areas which have experienced rapid influx of population. Such areas are likely to be ranked favourably, while those which have enjoyed recent, yet unrecorded, service provision are likely to be ranked unfavourably.

4.2 The Index-Construction Method

DIMS constructs an index of need using a linear scale transformation (LST). This is based on the same index construction method as the United Nations Human Development Index (HDI) (see Anand and Sen, 1994).[6] The main advantage of the LST or HDI method is its simplicity, since it ranks variables and areas on a scale from 0 to 1. However, we must ask whether the LST index construction method provides a sufficiently 'accurate' (consistent and rational) final ranking of areas.

One highly rigorous test is that of 'transitivity'. If an index was completely transitive, then the index would be able to rank all areas consistently relative to all other areas. Transitivity posits that if area A is better-off than B, and B is better-off than C, then A must be better-off than C. Within the context of the LST, an index constructed from one single indicator will be transitive since all areas are scored relative to the maximum and minimum value within a range. However, when three or more indicators are combined across three or more areas, the ranking of an area cannot be consistently determined.[7]

A simpler intuitive test of the 'accuracy' of an index method could be an assessment of the extent to which the final ranking of areas concurs with the distribution of the underlying data which contribute towards the final index scores. The variation in a final index score can be thought of as consisting of two components, intra-variable and inter-variable variation. In terms of intra-variable variation, if one variable is highly skewed, we would expect the final index to reflect this skewness. The linear scale transformation method does reflect such intra-variable variation since the variables are allocated on the scale according to size. However, inter-variable variation is inadequately reflected in that all variables are reflected on the same scale, that being 0 to 1. Consequently, the LST index method does not reflect absolute variations in the underlying data. This raises questions about the comparability of index results; for example, an area in which no household has a safe water supply will get the same index value as an area with 50% electrification which happens to be the least electrified.

However, this may not be such a major problem. The fact that the LST does not reflect absolute variations in the underlying data may actually be regarded as a desirable property of the index, if the objective of the index is to compare entities in terms of a range of factors which cannot be regarded as having a common scaling. For example, life expectancy is not scaled on the same basis as literacy. Even in the case of service provision levels, this may or may not be the case. For example, 50% water provision is an arguably worse developmental situation than 50% electrification. At the very least, such a decision requires a prior judgement as to the relative value of different services.

This discussion does however highlight the fact that the index of need constructed here can only be taken as a method for ranking areas relative to each other. Furthermore, precisely because indices summarise several items of data into one score, they only represent a partial reflection of the real situation.

4.3 Limitations of Index Construction Within the Development Context

The index of development need also faces certain other methodological problems, especially when we consider the development context within which the index construction methodology needs to operate. We discuss three aspects of this below.

Firstly, the comparison of need in different development contexts, especially between rural and urban areas, is problematic, since the need for certain basic services and facilities has a different meaning across different contexts. For example, the developmental importance that one attaches to the lack of water-borne sewerage (for example, relative to electrification) might be greater in an urban area because of the problems of population density and public health. For this reason, it may be desirable to construct separate indices for different spatial/developmental zones, but such data rarely exist.

This relates to the problem that the available data is often not organised or disaggregated in such a way that reflects different functional settlement types. For example, the NELF data does not distinguish informal from other settlement types. Numerous studies have highlighted informal areas as being particularly in need of basic services (for an example of KwaZulu-Natal, see Morris, 1995). This has particularly problematic implications for the delivery of services which may take place in a sectoral or highly targeted fashion. In fact, most spatial units of analysis for this study contain a variety of spatial-developmental contexts (for example, magisterial districts in rural areas may contain a small rural service centre, a dense informal settlement, and a commercial and subsistence agricultural sector). On the other hand, it could be argued that certain services and facilities are a basic right, irrespective of the developmental context.

The second point relates closely to the first. Indices of need are sensitive to the spatial scale of analysis, and changes in the spatial scale of reporting can have considerable impact on the resulting prioritisation of areas. Obviously, larger areas will score higher than smaller areas on an index based on absolute need, given the same proportion of service need. In South Africa, redrawing of administrative boundaries has more subtle implications with respect to this issue. A prioritisation of historically (well-serviced) white suburbs and (poorly-serviced) black townships will look very different to a prioritisation of new administrative areas which have been constructed to include both formerly white and black areas with redistributive goals in mind.

In theory, the spatial unit of analysis should co-coincide with functional and administrative units. There seems little point in constructing an index of service need which takes no account of the administrative entities through which services are delivered, since it is at this level which budgetary allocations are made. However, administrative units for different services seldom coincide. This is often for good reasons; the service areas of health facilities and schools differ according to the nature of the facility and its place within the service hierarchy (for example, the catchment areas of a primary and secondary schools could differ greatly). Similarly, water provision entities tend to follow natural catchment areas. This is not always an intractable problem, and provided that the basic spatial unit of analysis is sufficiently small, a planner can combine areas according to planning and administrative requirements.

The third problem leads us into the application of the need index in planning activities. The DIMS index construction method does not take into account the relative costs (and benefits) of service provision. In other words, it does not take account of the developmental impact, sustainability considerations and interconnections resulting from the delivery of a particular service. For example, provision of electricity may create new employment opportunities which result in improved housing conditions. However, in an index, electricity and housing provision may be weighted equally. This point highlights the fact that the purely technocratic application of an index ignores crucial underlying questions, such as, for example, whether services should be applied where they are most needed, where they cost the least to deliver, or where they have the greatest potential to be a growth catalyst. In other words, we cannot see indicator based indices as separate from a series of underlying developmental questions.

5. DEVELOPMENT PHILOSOPHIES

To date, the development of DIMS has been limited to consideration of development needs thereby implicitly supporting a basic needs approach to development. This is not to say that the researchers necessarily advocate the basic needs approach to development. DIMS, as presently constituted, has been devised as a tool to aid decision-making within the context of the RDP, where the meeting of basic needs is viewed as having an important role in addressing the overall developmental issues facing South Africa.

Albeit that DIMS is currently limited to a broadly basic needs approach, certain developmental issues need to be considered in the construction of the index. We have identified four such issues: firstly, whether one regards relative or absolute need as more important, secondly what standard of service-delivery is regarded as basic, thirdly what dimensions of need are included, and fourthly, how much importance one attaches to each dimension of need. The main strength of DIMS is that it allows one to manipulate the index which is constructed according to one's *a priori* answer to each of these questions.

We discuss each of these issues in greater detail below. In order to illustrate the effect of different index constructions on the final ranking of development need, we have taken the Gauteng Province as a case study. Gauteng is an almost completely urbanised province (which overcomes some of the problems of urban and rural comparisons), and is regarded as the economic heartland of South Africa (Hall et al, 1993). However, there are considerable inequalities in the distribution of services and facilities throughout the province. The paper concentrates on the relative rankings of eight of Gauteng's 23 magisterial districts on different indices (see Figure 1). The eight, Vanderbijlpark, Heidelberg, Johannesburg, Westonaria, Brakpan, Cullinan, Wonderboom and Pretoria, reflect the diversity within the province, and will guide readers in understanding the impact of various developmental assumptions on the prioritisation of service need. A brief description of each of these is provided as an appendix.[8]

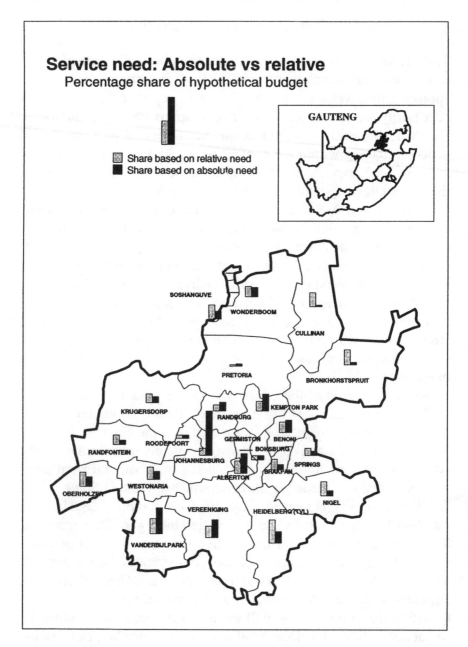

Figure 1.

5.1 Absolute versus Relative Service Need

There is no objective way of determining whether absolute or relative
need is more important in the construction of the index of service

need. The question arises because units of analysis, and of policy-making and service delivery, vary in size. For example, is a 50% electrification rate in a pool of 1000 households (thus 500 households without electricity) worse than a 90% electrification rate in a pool of 10000 households (thus 1000 households without electricity)?

It could be argued that in terms of the allocation of funds, absolute need is the correct criterion, since this indicates the gross dimensions of meeting current needs. However, policy decision-making processes around the meeting of needs are generally not a simple case of providing funds to scale at one moment in time. Firstly, available resources are simply too small in relation to needs, and secondly budget allocations are made to administrative and functional entities which differ markedly in scale and extent. The usage of the absolute measure provides a potentially distorted interpretation of which areas deserve greatest priority in the allocation of scarce resources. However, to simply assume that intensity is more important than scale (or vice versa) presupposes a crucial development decision. The choice of relative versus absolute need (or the relative weighting of the two) is thus a development policy choice which has to be addressed before the index is constructed.

To illustrate this point, we compared the final development need ranking of the Gauteng magisterial districts in two scenarios:

- **Absolute service need:** – which included the number of housing units without electricity (25% weighting), the number of housing units without access to adequate sanitation (25% weighting), the number of housing units without access to on-site water (25% weighting), and the absolute shortage of housing units (25% weighting).

- **Relative service need:** – which included the percentage of households without electricity (25% weighting), the percentage of housing units without access to adequate sanitation (25% weighting), the percentage of housing units without on-site water (25% weighting), and the relative shortage of housing units (25% weighting).

The results are shown in Table I, while full details regarding the calculation of each these two indices may be found in the Appendix in Tables A1 and A2.[9] There are marked differences between the rank-

TABLE I

Absolute versus Relative Need for Services

Range	Magisterial District	Relative Service Need Index	Rank		Magisterial District	Absolute Service Need Index	Rank
0.00	HEIDELBERG (TVL)	0.	1		JOHANNESBURG	0.	1
0.25							
	VANDERBIJLPARK	0.35	2				
	BRONKHORSTSPRUIT	0.353	3				
	CULLINAN	0.381	4				
	SOSHANGUVE	0.383	5				
	OBERHOLZER	0.4	6		VANDERBIJLPARK	0.424	2
	NIGEL	0.401	7				
	ALBERTON	0.448	8				
	WESTONARIA	0.481	9				
0.50	VEREENIGING	0.517	10				
	BRAKPAN	0.541	11		ALBERTON	0.548	3
	BENONI	0.551	12				
	WONDERBOOM	0.553	13		VEREENIGING	0.593	4
	KEMPTON PARK	0.574	14				
	RANDFONTEIN	0.576	15		KEMPTON PARK	0.621	5
	KRUGERSDORP	0.611	16				
	JOHANNESBURG	0.697	17				
	SPRINGS	0.706	18		BENONI	0.726	6
	RANDBURG	0.749	19		HEIDELBERG (TVL)	0.737	7
0.75					WONDERBOOM	0.77	8
					OBERHOLZER	0.777	9
	BOKSBURG	0.806	20		RANDBURG	0.802	10
					SOSHANGUVE	0.812	11
					WESTONARIA	0.817	12
					KRUGERSDORP	0.85	13
					BRAKPAN	0.871	14
	ROODEPOORT	0.832	21		NIGEL	0.882	15
					SPRINGS	0.895	16
					RANDFONTEIN	0.899	17
					BOKSBURG	0.905	18
					ROODEPOORT	0.91	19
	PRETORIA	0.94	22		PRETORIA	0.933	20
					BRONKHORSTSPRUIT	0.94	21
					CULLINAN	0.951	22
1.00	GERMISTON	1.	23		GERMISTON	1.	23

ordering obtained from the absolute and relative indices.[10] Worst off in relative terms is Heidelberg, where 56% of households are without electricity, 27% have inadequate sanitation, and 67% are without on-site water. However, in absolute terms, Heidelberg is 7th worst, since only around 16 500 households are without on-site water. Johannesburg, which is 17th worst in relative terms, is worst off in absolute terms, with around 91 600 households without on-site water.

Another important difference between the absolute and relative indices, is the distribution of need across the index. The average final index score for the relative index is 0,559, while for the absolute index it is 0,768. Certainly the index scores for the relative index are more normally distributed than for the absolute index (for the relative index, 9 districts have scores of less than 0,5 and 6 have scores of more than 0,7, while for the absolute index, only 2 have scores of less than 0,5 and 18 have scores of greater than 0,7). This may be regarded as a correct reflection of the fact that relative need variables across the districts are less positively skewed than absolute need variables across the districts (for three out of four variables this is the case). The absolute index thus suggests a higher degree of spatial selectivity in the allocation of funds than the relative index.

One question which arises at this stage is whether we can expect any systematic bias to result from the usage of absolute rather than relative need indicators. Given that one would normally expect absolute need indicators to be more variable than relative need indicators (since relative need indicators are normalised), we might expect the relative need index to suggest a lower degree of variability in the underlying pattern of need. This would be an important finding for policy-making based on indices, since it suggests that there would be an inherent bias in spatial (or some other) selectivity towards larger areas in the absolute index. However, this was found not to be the case, since the linear scale transformation eliminates variability.[11]

However, indicators which are positively skewed give rise to index values which are positively skewed, thus implying a higher degree of spatial selectivity when the index is used to allocate development resources. This has relevance to the issue of the size/scale of the unit of analysis. Given that certain socio-economic variables tend to be more skewed for smaller rather than larger areas, it can thus be argued that smaller units of analysis may have an in-built bias towards spatial selectivity. However, this need not be an undesirable property of the index, rather that users should be aware of the implications of this feature of the index.

The shift from relative to absolute indicators of need also has important implications for the allocation of development funding. To illustrate this, we allocated a hypothetical budget of 100% in proportion to the final index score.[12] A shift from absolute to relative indicators of need implies a huge budget loss for larger areas (in terms of population) such as Johannesburg, which moved from almost 19% of the budget to about 3%. This represents a 527% decrease in the hypothetical budget allocation (see Figure 1 and, in the Appendix, Table A3[13].) Smaller areas gain considerably; Cullinan's budget rises by almost 85% (with its share increasing from 1% to 6%).

It is also interesting to note that contradictory effects of the absolute and relative scale cancel each other in a combined index. A combined index (which includes both absolute and relative indicators) ranked Johannesburg and Heidelberg 1st and 3rd most needy respectively. Here the average index score was 0,445. This implies a far lower degree of spatial selectivity. However, this may simply be a feature of the underlying data, and not reflect any bias inherent in the index-construction method.

Since the decision about whether to use absolute or relative indicators of need is so fundamental to development planning, both absolute and relative indices have been constructed in the illustrative examples below.

5.2 Different Services Need Dimensions/Levels

The range of services which are regarded as constituting basic needs is also a prior developmental decision. DIMS allows us to select from water, sanitation, electricity, and housing, but with additional data, the list could include police services, postal and telecommunications, waste removal services, health and educational facilities, employment opportunities, and so on. This index construction issue is underpinned by the developmental question of what is regarded as a basic service need. For example, under a site-and-service conception of urban development, housing would be excluded as a need dimension.

Using relative indicators and then absolute indicators, we compared the final development need ranking of the Gauteng magisterial districts in the following two scenarios:

- **Basic range of services:** – including housing units without water on site (50% weighting) and with inadequate sanitation (50% weighting) only.

- **Intermediate range of services:** – including housing units without water on site (34% weighting), with inadequate sanitation (33% weighting) and without electricity (33% weighting).

The introduction of different need dimensions appears to cause most movement in the rank-ordering of need in the middle levels. In terms of the relative indicators of need, Heidelberg, Soshanguve, Bronkhorstspruit, Cullinan and Vanderbijlpark are the five most needy areas in both scenarios, while Germiston and Pretoria are the two least needy. However, Westonaria, Brakpan and Oberholzer are relatively more needy when electricity is introduced.

Westonaria is an example of an area whose relative position shifts considerably when different need dimensions are included. On the most basic level, it performs second best, because only 3.7% of households have inadequate sanitation (compared to 27% in Heidelberg), and only 4.9% are without water on site (compared to 73% of households in Cullinan). However, the fact that 53% of households have no electricity (compared to 56% in Heidelberg), means that Westonaria shifts from 21st to 15th most needy place when this need dimension is included.

There are also important shifts in the budget share of areas when relative need for electricity is introduced. Westonaria increases its budget by almost 70% (shifting from a 1% to a 4% share). Significantly the relative share of Heidelberg (which is worst-off on both indices) falls by about 3.5%. This reflects the fact that, even though Heidelberg has the lowest electrification rate, the distribution of the electrification rate is negatively skewed (–0.44). Thus the inclusion of this variable implies a lower degree of spatial selectivity in the allocation of funds.

In terms of absolute indicators of need, there is even less movement when a higher level of servicing is introduced. The rank-ordering of the worst eleven districts remains unchanged whether one includes or excludes electricity, and the percentage shifts in budget share are all less than 2%. This is because of the sheer scale of the absolute needs in Johannesburg relative to other areas.

5.3 Different Services Standards

Services can be provided at different standards. For example, one might regard any collectively provided sewerage disposal system as adequate (thus regarding bucket systems as acceptable), or one might only regard water-borne sewerage disposal as adequate. The choice of standards also implies a certain developmental orientation, which may be thought of as a breadth versus depth issue. For example, water may be provided on site or communally, depending on one's developmental assumptions. Using absolute and relative indicators, we compared the final development need ranking of the Gauteng magisterial districts in two scenarios:

- **High service standard:** – including housing units without electricity (25% weighting), shortage of houses (25% weighting), need for flush sanitation (25% weighting), and need for water on site (25% weighting).

- **Low service standard:** – including housing units without electricity (25% weighting), need for formal housing (a lower standard than housing shortage which imposes some space norm) (25% weighting), need for adequate sanitation (25% weighting), and need for safe drinking water (not necessarily on site) (25% weighting).

The relative positions of districts which resulted from comparing high and low service standards were small. In terms of relative need, Heidelberg and Bronkhorstspruit were the most needy at both high and low service standards, and in general shifts in the rank-ordering are very small. However, Heidelberg loses over 52% of its hypothetical budget allocation when one shifts from low to high (relative) service levels, reflecting the more skewed nature of the distribution of low level services.

Wonderboom magisterial district is the only district to shift significantly in the final rank-ordering (from 14th to 9th most needy place in a shift from low to higher service levels) of the relative index. This is because the district includes Mamelodi township, an area with most of the basic facilities at a low standard (only 3% of households have inadequate sanitation, but 46% do not have flush sanitation; only 22% have no access to potable water, but 46% have no water on site). Thus service needs at low standards are relatively small.

In the South African context this finding has particular relevance to debates about development assistance to established townships, and areas which have benefitted from Independent Development Trust capital subsidy funding.[14] A policy of giving these areas additional funding in order to raise existing service standards implies an acceptance of depth (as opposed to breadth) in the allocation of development resources. Currently unserviced informal areas would be relatively disadvantaged by such an approach.

In terms of absolute need, there are only small differences between the rank-ordering of low versus high standards. However, Pretoria magisterial district moves from 10th most needy to 21st most needy position in a shift from low to high service levels. The difference is driven by Pretoria's relatively low level of informal housing (12,829 units, as compared to 58,670 units in Johannesburg), and extremely low level of housing shortage (an estimated surplus of 17,480 units). However, this estimated surplus could be a reflection of the high number of small flats in central Pretoria, an observation which illustrates some of the inadequacies of the housing shortage indicator.

5.4 Weighting of Service Need Dimensions

The weight which one attaches to each dimension of need may also imply a particular development approach. For example, one may wish to weight electricity provision more highly than water supply because of a particular concern about an increase in the price of non-electrical fuel sources. In so doing, one is able to sophisticate the analysis of need by, for example, weighting elements which offer developmental potential more highly.

Using relative and absolute indicators, we compared the final development need ranking of the Gauteng magisterial districts in two scenarios:

- **Housing-need weighted index:** – including housing shortage (66% weighting), housing units without water on site (12% weighting), with inadequate sanitation (11% weighting), and without electricity (11% weighting).

- **General need weighted index:** – including housing units without water on site (22% weighting), without electricity (22% weighting), with inadequate sanitation (22% weighting) and housing shortage (34% weighting).

Clearly the differences between these two indices are small. However, on both absolute and relative indices, Westonaria was more needy when housing was given greater importance. This is because Westonaria has an indexed housing shortage of 134 units per 1000 of the population, which represents 24,711 units.

Furthermore, the housing weighted index represents a lower degree of spatial selectivity than the general need index. For example, for the absolute index, the shift from the general to the housing weighted index results in an almost 38% fall in the hypothetical budget of Johannesburg, which is the area of greatest need in both cases. This is because housing shortage is less skewed than all other indicators in this index.

6. CONCLUSION

The usage of sophisticated computer packages to manipulate data places a substantial responsibility on decision-makers and their advisors to be explicit about the underlying assumptions which are guiding their decisions. As has been shown in this paper, decisions about the allocation of development funding are not neutral, even where information technology is employed to assist in rational and objective decision-making.

The usefulness of the area-prioritisation which DIMS allows, is in first-order indicative planning and it should not be used as the basis for detailed planning without further in-depth investigation. However, perhaps the greatest weakness of a purely need-based approach is that it takes no account of the costs and benefits of development interventions. In our opinion, further work on the topic of indicator-based allocation of funds could benefit from the following two avenues.

Firstly, one may use a cost-effectiveness approach, where services would be provided first to those areas where the most people or households can be serviced for a given amount of money. The advantage of such an approach is that the maximum number of people could benefit from development actions, in a specific period of time and for a given fixed budget. The problem with such an approach is that it assumes that the benefits of supplying one particular area / group of people with services is the same as supplying any other group of people. This implies, inter alia, an underlying welfare assumption that denies a redistribution imperative. For example, it may be more cost-effective, but ethically ambiguous, to give those with water supply on site, a water-borne sewerage connection, than to give it to those without water at all.

This could hardly be regarded as an equitable policy decision. In other words, the cost-effectiveness approach does not take us much further than the simple needs-based approach to indexing need, since we still have to return to the underlying questions dealt with in this paper, namely the issues of dimensions of need, levels of services and weighting of need dimensions.

Secondly, one could argue, in a neo-classical economics sense, that services should be provided first to those areas where the net marginal costs of an additional unit of service provision are lowest. This would entail employing cost-benefit techniques to guide the allocation of development resources. For example, one might argue that the marginal costs of an electrical connection are so low (for example, because technology allows for complete cost-recovery through a pre-paid metering system), and that the marginal benefits are sufficiently large (because of small business opportunities thus created) to justify affording the provision of this service the highest priority.

There are at least three problems with this approach. Firstly, such an approach would require massive data inputs, including the measurement of certain near-to-unmeasurable development dimensions (such as assumptions on behaviour and value patterns in a given set of circumstances). It may even be argued that cost-benefit analysis has an inherent bias towards decisions that result in financially measurable outcomes; for example, the value of new business opportunities is always going to be more easily measured than the cost of deforestation, even though both are benefits of electrification. Secondly, a proper assessment of the costs and benefits of meeting service need should not simply compare different service-delivery options, but other policy choices as well. This can only further complicate the computational issues. Thirdly, the cost-benefit approach does not completely avoid the question of the underlying development assumptions highlighted above. If one accepts that there are problems with the current distribution of income, wealth and opportunity in society, then the cost-benefit approach has to address the trade-off between equity and efficiency. For example, it may be argued that the benefits of providing services to the poor may be greater than their willingness to pay for them.

The main conclusion thus of this paper is that development prioritisation is, and always will remain an essentially political decision-making process. We have shown that the identification of areas of need is subject to the developmental assumptions and index-construction method employed. This can have dramatic effects on the final rank-ordering of need, and thus on the allocation of development resources. However, this is not a total rejection of the use of indicators in the planning process. Rather, it is a call for the appropriate use of the tools that are available.

NOTES

[1]   Peter Gill was in the Division of Building Technology of the CSIR, and Peter Hall was in the Development Policy and Planning Unit of the Human Sciences Research Council when this research was conducted. The views expressed in this paper are those of the authors alone.

[2]   An example of an absolute indicator of need is the number of households without water-borne sewerage, while the relative indicator for the same dimension of need would be the percentage of households without water-borne sewerage. The indicators listed in this paper are marked by the letters "r" or "a" where "r" represents a relative indicator while "a" represents an absolute indicator.

[3]   The following indicators have been used in the paper and are coded to indicate service need category (e.g. water (W)), and whether a relative "r" or an absolute "a" indicator:

Housing backlog
H1(r): Informal housing units as a percentage of all housing units: An informal housing unit is defined as a structure which does not conform to building regulations. The informal unit does nevertheless, represent a form of shelter in that it is used on a permanent or temporary basis and affords it's occupants some protection from the natural elements.
H1(a): Informal housing units: Same as H1(r) but using absolute numbers.
H2(r): Housing shortage per 1000 of the population: Housing shortage is based on the assumption of "desired average household size." In this case the "desired average household size" is 4.5 persons per household. The population figure is divided by the "desired average household size" to derive the total "desired" number of dwellings within a given area. The number of formal housing units is subtracted from the number of desired dwellings to derive the calculated housing shortage. The housing shortage is expressed as a ratio per 1000 of the total population.

H2(a): Housing shortage: Same as H2(r) but using absolute numbers.

Access to Electricity Supply
E1(r): Percentage housing units without electricity: Given insufficient information around other forms of energy supply to households, the indicator is based on those with and without access to electricity.
E1(a): Housing units without electricity: Same as E1(r) but using absolute numbers.

Access to different standards of Water Supply
W1(r): Percentage housing units without reasonable access to potable water:
Potable water is defined in terms of those people who have access to water from a tap service point (on-site or communal). Non-potable water typically refers to rivers, boreholes, rain tanks, dams, or water having to be transported by water truck.
W1(a): Housing units without reasonable access to potable water: Same as W1(r) but using absolute numbers.
W2(r): Percentage housing units without access to potable water on site: This is based housing units which have access to tapped water service on site.
W2(a): Housing units without access to potable water on site: Same as W2(r) but using absolute numbers.

Access to different standards of Sanitation Supply
S1(r): Percentage housing units with inadequate sanitation: Inadequate sanitation is defined as those housing units that have access to no sanitation services (water-borne or otherwise) or the bucket system of sanitation.
S1(a): Housing units with inadequate sanitation: Same as S1(r) but using absolute numbers.
S2(r): Percentage housing units with non-flush sanitation: Non-flush sanitation is defined as those housing units that have access to no sanitation services, pit latrines (ventilated or not) and the bucket system of sanitation. Flush sanitation refers to waterborne sanitation systems or septic tanks.
S2(a):Housing units with non-flush sanitation: Same as S2(r) but using absolute numbers.

[4] The database used in this study was provided to Eskom and the National Electrification Forum (NELF) by the CSIR and Economic Analysis Systems (EAS). The CSIR conducted a postal survey of local authorities and administrative bodies throughout the then Republic of South Africa, TBVC (Transkei, Bophuthatswana, Venda, Ciskei) areas and the self-governing territories (SGT) of service levels in 1992. EAS provided the demographic and housing information by geographic area or suburb by adjusting the 1991 population census and the data for South Africa (including the SGT) and the former TBVC areas.
[5] The term homelands refers to the former six self-governing territories (KwaZulu, KwaNdebele, Kangwane, QwaQwa, Lebowa and Gazankulu) and the four so called independent states (Transkei, Bophuthatswana, Venda and Ciskei) established as part of the policy of segregation under the Apartheid government.
[6] The HDI is constructed out of a linear scale transformation (LST) of three variables, namely life expectancy, personal income and literacy. In the LST method, observations for each variable are scaled from 0 (the worst-off position) to 1 (the

best-off position). The index value for an area is given by the formula $1-((X_{max} - X)/(X_{max} - X_{min}))$, where X is the indicator value, and X_{max} and X_{min} are the maximum and minimum values in the range. Thus in DIMS, for example, if percentage electrification ranges from 50% to 100%, then a place with 50% electrification would receive an index score of 0, while a place with 75% electrification would receive an index score of 0.5, being half-way between the minimum and maximum observations. DIMS calculates the LST score for each indicator separately and then calculates a final composite index score by performing a LST on the sum of the individual LST scores. The individual scores may be weighted when calculating the final score.

[7] The test of transitivity is very similar to the 'voter paradox' (see DeSerpa, 1985) which posits that there is no consistent method for obtaining a transitive ranking of three or more options by three or more individuals.

[8] (1) Vanderbijlpark Magisterial District (MD) is a lies in the south of Gauteng, and contains the industrial white town of the same name, and the African townships of Sebokeng, Boipatong and Bophelong. Levels of poverty in this area are quite high in comparison to the rest of the province, and service levels are below average for all indicators of relative service need. The population in 1991 was around 434 000.

(2) Heidelberg MD forms the peri-urban south-east corner of the province. The small population(77 055 in 1991) is concentrated in Heidelberg town and Ratanda township. Recent establishment of informal settlements is reflected in below average service levels for all relative indicators of need.

(3) Johannesburg MD is the commercial and financial heart of the province and dominates with a 1991 population of over 1,5 million people. Although Johannesburg includes the township of Soweto, service levels are above average for all relative indicators of service need. This reflects the high service levels enjoyed in the non-township areas of Johannesburg, and the fact that Soweto is relatively well-serviced when compared to other townships. However, in terms of absolute need, Johannesburg is most needy for all services.

(4) Westonaria MD is situated to the west of Gauteng, in a mining zone. This results in a peculiar population profile where two-thirds of the 160 531 residents are male, reflecting the impact of the migrant labour system. A specific problem facing the area is that of housing shortage, concentrated in the township of Bekkersdal.

(5) Brakpan MD is situated in the industrial east of Gauteng. The 1991 population of around 130 000 enjoys slightly better than average levels of service.

(6) Cullinan MD is one of Gauteng's more rural areas, situated to the north-east of the province. The mining town of Cullinan and the township of Refilwe contain most of the 32 000 population. Low levels of water and sanitation supply are particular features of the area.

(7) Wonderboom MD is to the north of the province, and includes the large Pretoria township of Mamelodi. The 1991 population of over 260 000 is generally well-serviced at low levels, but not at higher levels.

(8) Pretoria MD contains the long-established areas of white Pretoria, Atteridgeville, Laudium and Eesterus. The 1991 population of close to 700 000 enjoys a high level of services. Various large townships which are functionally part of the city of Pretoria (Mamelodi, Soshanguve/Mabopane, Ga-Rankuwa) are not included in

the narrowly-defined magisterial district, although most of these areas now form part of the Greater Pretoria Metropolitan area.
[9] Base data and index value calculations for 23 Gauteng Magisterial Districts for Absolute (Table A1) and Relative (Table A2) Indices of Service Need:

Table A1: Absolute Service Need Rankings

Magisterial District	E1(a): Housing units without electricity	E1(a): Rank	H3(a): Housing shortage	H3(a): Rank	S2(a): Inadequate sanitation	S2(a): Rank	W3(a): Without water on site	W3(a): Rank	Composite Rank
JOHANNESBURG	85309	0	50737	0	18125	0	91664	0	0
VANDERBIJLPARK	48638	0.439	34785	0.234	10292	0.434	44598	0.513	0.424
ALBERTON	55102	0.362	26788	0.351	4210	0.771	35950	0.608	0.548
VEREENIGING	32920	0.627	33905	0.247	4430	0.759	33990	0.629	0.593
KEMPTON PARK	35153	0.601	24458	0.385	5525	0.698	28792	0.686	0.621
BENONI	27831	0.688	19161	0.463	3626	0.803	16887	0.816	0.726
HEIDELBERG	13830	0.856	16095	0.508	6749	0.630	16517	0.820	0.737
WONDERBOOM	19042	0.793	14757	0.527	1617	0.914	27018	0.705	0.770
OBERHOLZER	17026	0.818	27648	0.338	1706	0.909	9015	0.902	0.777
RANDBURG	19944	0.783	6281	0.652	3679	0.800	15846	0.827	0.802
SOSHANGUVE	13232	0.863	12283	0.564	2797	0.849	16152	0.824	0.812
WESTONARIA	17197	0.816	24711	0.382	1186	0.938	1602	0.983	0.817
KRUGERSDORP	16840	0.820	9785	0.600	977	0.950	11595	0.874	0.850
BRAKPAN	16299	0.826	7060	0.640	1000	0.948	8125	0.911	0.871
NIGEL	11434	0.885	8882	0.614	1023	0.947	7173	0.922	0.882
SPRINGS	6070	0.949	4661	0.675	1459	0.923	11843	0.871	0.895
RANDFONTEIN	7614	0.930	6971	0.642	1214	0.937	7047	0.923	0.899
BOKSBURG	4468	0.968	1740	0.718	2336	0.874	9768	0.893	0.905
ROODEPOORT	7369	0.933	825	0.732	2142	0.885	7120	0.922	0.910
PRETORIA	16351	0.826	−17480	1	2602	0.860	11231	0.878	0.933
BRONKHORSTSPRUIT	4358	0.969	4294	0.681	70	1	5520	0.940	0.940
CULLINAN	2517	0.991	3303	0.695	133	0.997	5014	0.945	0.951
GERMISTON	1789	1	−6762	0.843	533	0.974	4	1	1

Table A2: Relative Service Need Rankings

Magisterial District	E1(r): Housing units without electricity (%)	E1(r): Rank	H3(r): Housing shortage/ 1000	H3(r): Rank	S2(r): Inadequate sanitation (%)	S2(r): Rank	W3(r): Without water on site (%)	W3(r): Rank	Composite Rank
HEIDELBERG	56.07	0	148.39	0	27.36	0	66.96	0.084	0
VANDERBIJLPARK	51.15	0.094	78.29	0.374	10.82	0.623	46.90	0.358	0.35
BRONKHORSTSPRUIT	49.95	0.117	108.65	0.212	0.80	1	63.27	0.134	0.353
CULLINAN	36.69	0.369	102.67	0.244	1.94	0.957	73.08	0	0.381
SOSHANGUVE	42.61	0.256	83.95	0.344	9.01	0.691	52.01	0.288	0.383
OBERHOLZER	48.54	0.144	147.30	0.006	4.86	0.847	25.70	0.648	0.4
NIGEL	55.91	0.003	95.21	0.284	5.00	0.842	35.08	0.52	0.401
ALBERTON	54.81	0.024	68.39	0.427	4.19	0.873	35.76	0.511	0.448
WESTONARIA	53.02	0.058	133.78	0.078	3.66	0.893	4.94	0.933	0.481
VEREENIGING	33.29	0.434	96.35	0.278	4.48	0.862	34.38	0.53	0.517
BRAKPAN	50.48	0.106	51.03	0.520	3.10	0.914	25.17	0.656	0.541
BENONI	40.80	0.291	63.10	0.455	5.32	0.830	24.75	0.661	0.551

Table A2: Continued

Magisterial District	EI(r): Housing units without electricity (%)	Rank	H3(r): Housing shortage/ 1000	Rank	S2(r): Inadequate sanitation (%)	Rank	W3(r): Without water on site (%)	Rank	Composite Rank
WONDERBOOM	32.64	0.446	53.48	0.507	2.77	0.926	46.31	0.366	0.553
KEMPTON PARK	33.53	0.429	65.66	0.442	5.27	0.832	27.47	0.624	0.574
RANDFONTEIN	32.24	0.454	63.76	0.452	5.14	0.837	29.84	0.592	0.576
KRUGERSDORP	37.40	0.356	51.16	0.519	2.17	0.949	25.75	0.648	0.611
JOHANNESBURG	21.91	0.651	31.99	0.622	4.66	0.855	23.55	0.678	0.697
SPRINGS	16.26	0.759	29.34	0.636	3.91	0.883	31.73	0.566	0.706
RANDBURG	21.40	0.661	17.48	0.699	3.95	0.882	17.00	0.767	0.749
BOKSBURG	8.92	0.898	8.52	0.747	4.66	0.855	19.50	0.733	0.806
ROODEPOORT	12.40	0.832	3.62	0.773	3.61	0.894	11.99	0.836	0.832
PRETORIA	7.88	0.918	−25.31	0.927	1.25	0.983	5.41	0.926	0.94
GERMISTON	3.59	1	−38.90	1	1.07	0.99	0.01	1	1

[10] A Spearman's Rank-Correlation coefficient of 0,32 was obtained when the rank-ordering on the absolute and relative indices were compared. This is not statistically significant, indicating important differences between the final rank-orderings.

[11] It can be shown that Var. (I) = (Var. (X))/(X$_{max}$ − X$_{min}$)^2, where X is the indicator value, and I is the index value (I = 1−((X$_{max}$ − X)/(X$_{max}$ − X$_{min}$))). Thus the variance of index values is not directly related to the variance of the underlying indicator values.

[12] Formula for calculating the proportion of funding allocated to area I = (1− I$_i$)/$\Sigma(1-I_n)$, where I$_i$ is the index value for area I. Illustrative allocations are presented as a percentage of the total hypothetical budget.

[13]

Table A3: Percentage share in Budget under relative and absolute priority rankings

Magisterial District	Relative Priority Ranking	Absolute Priority Ranking	Percentage share of budget (relative)	Percentage share of budget (absolute)	Variance in share of budget*
JOHANNESBURG	0.448	0.548	5.44	8.47	−55.82
VANDERBIJLPARK	0.551	0.726	4.42	5.14	−16.33
ALBERTON	0.806	0.905	1.91	1.78	6.62
VEREENIGING	0.541	0.871	4.53	2.41	46.77
KEMPTON PARK	0.353	0.940	6.37	1.12	82.49
BENONI	0.381	0.951	6.10	0.93	84.81
HEIDELBERG	1	1	0.00	0.00	0.00
WONDERBOOM	0	0.737	9.85	4.93	49.99
OBERHOLZER	0.697	0	2.99	18.74	−527.03
RANDBURG	0.574	0.621	4.19	7.11	−69.44
SOSHANGUVE	0.611	0.850	3.83	2.82	26.47
WESTONARIA	0.401	0.882	5.90	2.21	62.58
KRUGERSDORP	0.400	0.777	5.91	4.17	29.45
BRAKPAN	0.940	0.933	0.59	1.25	−110.56
NIGEL	0.749	0.802	2.47	3.71	−49.87
SPRINGS	0.576	0.899	4.18	1.89	54.67
RANDFONTEIN	0.832	0.910	1.65	1.69	−2.54
BOKSBURG	0.383	0.812	6.08	3.52	42.04

Table A3: Continued

Magisterial District	Relative Priority Ranking	Absolute Priority Ranking	Percentage share of budget (relative)	Percentage share of budget (absolute)	Variance in share of budget*
ROODEPOORT	0.706	0.895	2.89	1.96	32.26
PRETORIA	0.350	0.424	6.41	10.78	−68.29
BRONKHORSTSPRUIT	0.517	0.593	4.76	7.64	−60.44
CULLINAN	0.481	0.817	5.12	3.43	32.90
GERMISTON	0.553	0.770	4.40	4.30	2.19

* Shift from budget based on absolute to relative priority rankings.

[14] The Independent Development Trust launched a capital subsidy programme in the early 1990's which was instrumental in developing an incremental approach to housing in South Africa. Through this programme, around 100 000 households around the country were given ownership of sites serviced at a basic level (McCarthy, Hindson and Oelofse, 1995).

REFERENCES

African National Congress: 1994, The Reconstruction and Development Programme (Umanyano Publications, Johannesburg).

Anand, S. and Sen, A.: 1994, Human Development Index: Methodology and Measurement. Human Development Report Office, Occasional Paper 12 (United Nations, New York).

DeSerpa, A. C.: 1985, Microeconomic Theory (Allyn and Bacon, Boston).

Green, A.E. and Champion, A.G.: 1988, 'Measuring local economic performance: methodology and applications of the Booming Towns approach', Built Environment 14, pp. 78–95.

Green, A.E. and Champion, A.G.: 1991, 'Research Policy and Review 35. The Booming Towns studies: methodological issues', Environment and Planning 23, pp. 1393–1408.

Hall, P., Saayman, G., Molatedi, D., and Kok, P.: 1993, A Profile of Poverty in the PWV (Southern African Labour and Development Research Unit, University of Cape Town, Cape Town).

Housing Indicators Programme: 1993, The Housing Indicator Programme, Joint Programme of the United Nations Centre for Human Settlement and the World Bank, Vol. 1–4, April.

Lipshitz, G. and Raveh, A.: 1994, 'Application of the co-plot method in the study of socio-economic differences between cities: a basis for a differential development policy', Urban Studies, Vol. 31, No. 1, pp. 123–135.

McCarthy, J., Hindson, D. and Oelofse, M.: 1995, Evaluation of Informal Settlement Upgrading and Consolidation Projects: report to the National Business Initiative (National Business Initiative, Johannesburg).

Møller, V., Schlemmer, L., and Du Toit, S.H.C.: 1987, Quality of life in South Africa: Measurement and Analysis. Pretoria: Human Science Research Council (Report S-167).

Morris, M.: 1995, 'Uplifting the urban poor: meeting basic needs in KwaZulu-Natal', Indicator SA, Vol. 12, No. 4, Spring 1995, pp. 85–88.
Rogerson, R.J., Findlay, A.M., Morris, A.S., Coombes, M.G.: 1989, 'Indicators of Quality of Life: some methodological issues', Environment and Planning A 21, pp. 1655–1666.
United Nations Development Programme. 1994. Human Development Report 1994 (Oxford University Press).

Peter Gill
Project Management Techniques (Pty) Ltd.
P.O. Box 739
Sunninghill, 2175
South Africa

Peter Hall
Urban Strategy Department
Durban Metropolitan Council
P.O. Box 5658
Durban, 4000
South Africa

MARI HARRIS

MONITORING OPTIMISM IN SOUTH AFRICA

ABSTRACT. The last two decades have been the most crucial and eventful ones in South Africa's history. During this time, the empirical research and knowledge provided by opinion polls yielded much-needed insight into the grass roots of a society in transition, providing an instrument with which to measure the political climate, to observe trends and developments, and to give input into the decision-making process of companies and political parties. Although the process of change and political transition still remains difficult to define properly, this article will provide some insight into the attitudes, perceptions and values of the South African public, by giving attention to trends that have transpired over the years. Special attention is devoted to perceptions on pertinent issues such as the mood in the country, optimism, economic well-being, social harmony and trust – all essential elements in an emerging democracy. Extensive use is made of data and findings of Markinor's bi-annual Socio-Political Trends surveys, the World Values Studies and the annual Gallup End-of-Year Poll.

"People live in the past far more than they realise. We interpret reality in terms of concepts and world views based on past experiences. This is inevitable – what we experience consists of millions of sensations, and we cannot focus on all of them. Making them coherent means abstracting a few simplified concepts that seem relevant to important goals."

(Prof. Ronald Inglehart, ISR, University of Michigan (USA))

Despite the many changes South Africa has undergone over the past years, the process of transformation is still very much in progress – in fact, our country still largely reveals the characteristics of a society in transition. Yet, however informed one is, it is still difficult to have an objective perspective of how attitudes and perceptions have changed – or did not change – over the years. This is especially true of South Africans themselves, who, in some cases, hold very diverse opinions about the process and also the perceived success of transition. Despite a plethora of conflicting opinions about the pace and magnitude of the sweeping social change, one consensual fact has emerged: that is, the issues of racism and inequality and their

Social Indicators Research **41**: 279–304, 1997.

destructive resonance which still reverberate throughout the entire South African society.

This undoubtedly has an influence on how optimistic South Africans are and how they view their quality of life. By monitoring various manifestations of optimism in the country regularly, researchers have a role to play in documenting the mindset change from past to future. Indeed, research findings can provide a vantage point from which attitude changes can be measured to chart the nuances of sentiment change as South Africans adjust their perspectives in line with the changes that have swept the country.

By presenting research findings in the form of trends that have transpired over the years, this chapter will share some of the attitudes, perceptions and values of South Africans. Special attention will be devoted to perceptions on pertinent issues such as the mood in the country, optimism, economic well-being, social harmony and trust, focusing on some findings of three tracking studies, namely the World Values Study, Markinor's Socio-Political Trends surveys and the annual Gallup End-of-Year poll. These surveys were conducted on a national basis and apart from the World Values Study, which was an ad hoc project, Markinor's National Syndicate was used as vehicle (see notes). In all three cases, results were projected to the universe and are representative of the universe, i.e. the adult South African population.

GENERAL MOOD IN THE COUNTRY

To establish the background against which to evaluate subsequent discussions, a view on how South Africans assess the direction in which the country is going, is essential (Figure 1). This issue was measured for the first time in June 1994 and respondents had to indicate whether they thought that the country was going in the right or the wrong direction.

As could be expected, the levels of agreement with the direction the country is taking were remarkably high during the euphoria following the first ever national election (26–29 April 1994). (This particular issue was measured for the first time in June 1994.)

There was quite a dip in agreement with the country's taken direction six months after the election – this phenomenon is shared by

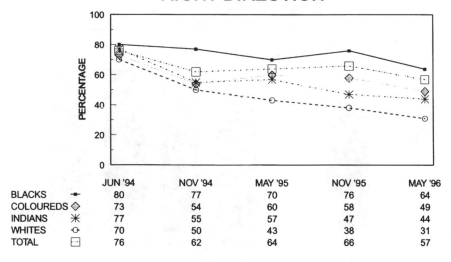

SOUTH AFRICA IS HEADING IN THE RIGHT DIRECTION

		JUN '94	NOV '94	MAY '95	NOV '95	MAY '96
BLACKS	■	80	77	70	76	64
COLOUREDS	◈	73	54	60	58	49
INDIANS	✳	77	55	57	47	44
WHITES	⊙	70	50	43	38	31
TOTAL	▭	76	62	64	66	57

Figure 1.

all population groups. It is also evident that whites are much more reserved in their praise of the direction the country is taking. In fact, they are becoming more critical and subsequently the percentage of whites who feel that the country is heading in the wrong direction, is increasing. These feelings amongst whites and, to a slightly lesser degree, amongst other population groups, can probably be attributed – as found in other surveys – to the despondency about the soaring crime rate and uncertainty concerning affirmative action. In addition, blacks have had to come to terms with the fact that the implementation of the RDP (Reconstruction and Development Programme) is a very slow process.

Are South Africans in general then in a negative frame of mind nowadays, with regard to their personal lives? (Figure 2). Not at all – as is evident from findings of the World Values Study (1995–1996).

As can be seen on this chart, more than seven in every ten South Africans responded positively to the question: "Taking all things together, would you say you are very happy, quite happy, not very happy or not at all happy?" This proportion is almost evenly split between those who have indicated that they feel "very happy" and those who feel "quite happy."

OVERALL DEGREE OF HAPPINESS

Very/Quite happy

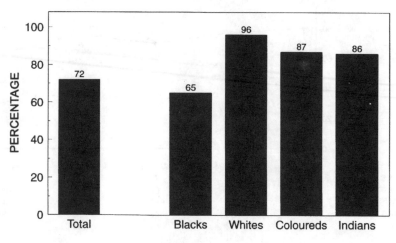

Figure 2.

A significant proportion of black people are happier now than in 1990–1991 (when the previous World Values Study was conducted, well before the national election in 1994). At that stage only just over half (54%) indicated that they were very or quite happy. The present finding undoubtedly reflects a higher level of acceptance of the current political, social and economic environment by this population group.

However, it must be borne in mind that still *only* two thirds of blacks regard themselves as happy, whereas around eight or nine in every ten whites, coloureds and Indians are happy with their lives at present. Between 50% and 60% of each of these population groups have indicated that they are "very happy."

The greatest unhappiness is found among those with low education and low income, indicating a strong correlation between happiness and financial status. (This issue will receive more attention later on.)

In addition to the issue of happiness, how satisfied are South Africans with their lives these days? On a scale of 1 to 10, where 1 means dissatisfied and 10 satisfied, the average indicated was 5.6. Blacks have again indicated that they are less satisfied than the other population groups (average 5). The very high levels of happiness expressed by whites, coloureds and Indians were all somewhat tempered when it came to the issue of "satisfaction".

However, overall, the mood in the country – both at the macro level (the country as a whole) and the micro level (an individual's personal life) – is still certainly more positive than negative.

SPECIFIC MEASUREMENTS OF OPTIMISM

These findings are mirrored by those of the Gallup End-of-Year Poll. This particular study is undertaken towards the end of every year to assess the strength of optimism about the year ahead. The question is posed whether the year ahead will be better, the same, or worse than the previous one.

As was the case with the issue of the direction the country is taking, local optimism has declined slightly in the last year, although almost six out of ten (58%) South Africans still felt that 1996 would be a better year than 1995, reflecting a feeling of hope and expectation amongst the majority of the population. However, twice as many blacks as whites believed 1996 will be better than 1995 – two thirds of blacks (67%) were looking forward to better fortune in 1996, while only 31% of whites shared this sentiment (in the beginning of 1995 these figures were 73% and 37% respectively). Optimism remained constant among coloureds (at 51%) while optimism among Indians has dropped (from 51% to 41%).

There were also differences amongst provinces and in the violence-plagued KwaZulu-Natal, less than half (46%) of residents were optimistic about the year ahead. The fact that local community elections in this province only took place in June 1996 – six months later than those held throughout most of the country and a month later than those held in some parts of the Western Cape – could also have an effect on the relative pessimism when compared to the rest of the country.

Conversely, optimism levels were the highest in the Northern Province where 73% were confident that 1996 will be better than 1995. (This province was one of the areas most severely hit by the droughts that prevailed in Southern Africa for the last years and interviewing was conducted a few days after it started raining!)

TABLE I

International optimism index: 20 most optimistic countries

		1994	1995	Position 1995	Change 1995–1996	1996
1.	Northern Ireland	123	160	1	–	160
2.	Israel	154	148	4	+12	160
3.	Gulf	173	124	16	+32	156
4.	New Zealand	147	145	6	+3	148
5.	Denmark	138	145	7	+3	148
6.	Georgia	–	103	33	+39	142
7.	**South Africa**	**131**	**144**	**8**	**–3**	**141**
8.	Norway	136	121	18	+18	139
9.	Korea	136	138	10	–1	137
10.	Australia	142	149	3	–14	135
11.	Ireland	118	140	9	–5	135
12.	Brazil	107	158	2	–25	133
13.	Finland	104	136	11	–3	133
14.	Iceland	128	147	5	–15	132
15.	UK (excluding N.I.)	–	–	–	–	132
16.	Turkey	70	72	42	+58	130
17.	India	120	128	14	+1	129
18.	Portugal	75	89	39	+39	128
19.	USA	144	–	–	–	127
20.	Germany	103	117	21	+8	125

The index on this chart is calculated by subtracting the percentage of people who said things will get worse from the percentage who said things will get better. This net figure is then added to or subtracted from 100.

But, how did we compare internationally?

In 1992/1993 South Africa was placed in 31st position on this index. However, things changed dramatically and South Africa was in the seventh position on the Annual Optimism Index for 1996. These results give a definite indication that South Africans, to a large degree, accepted the new developments in their country and, moreover, that the majority were fairly optimistic about the future, despite the reservations that were held. South Africa's position on the index is also the result of the relative success of the local elections (November 1995), improved economic prospects and greater international investment and interest from abroad at the stage when fieldwork was done.

PERSONAL ECONOMIC WELL-BEING

Feelings of optimism or pessimism can be linked closely with economic well-being. This is defined as being the perceived changes in one's economic prospects and is measured by improvements in terms of the availability of money.

To focus on this issue we can look firstly at the results of two questions forming part of the "Socio-Political Trends Surveys", namely:

- Thinking of the way your family lives, would you say your family is better off today in terms of money than a year ago, about the same, or worse off than a year ago?
- And how do you think it will be in a year's time? Do you think your family will be better off than today, in terms of money, about the same as today, or worse off than today?

From the findings collated over the years it is evident that these rather simple questions yield a lot more information than is suspected at first sight. It is actually quite a sensitive measurement of perceptions concerning optimism and quality of life that are prevalent in the country at a specific time, as important events in the country had a profound effect on the findings.

Figures 3 and 4 show the proportion of South Africans who felt that their families are either better or worse off economically compared with the past.

The effect of the unrest in black townships and the subsequent uncertainty is evident from the very high proportions of blacks who felt in 1977 and 1985/1986 that their families were worse off compared with the past (it must be borne in mind, however, that we were operating under a state of emergency during those years with very strict media curbs and therefore the general public might not have been well-informed on all aspects. This could have a bearing on the attitudes expressed).

The opinions of blacks were clearly affected by events in the country such as the release of Nelson Mandela from prison (February 1990), which made this population group more optimistic and

ARE FAMILIES BETTER OFF ECONOMICALLY COMPARED WITH THE PAST?

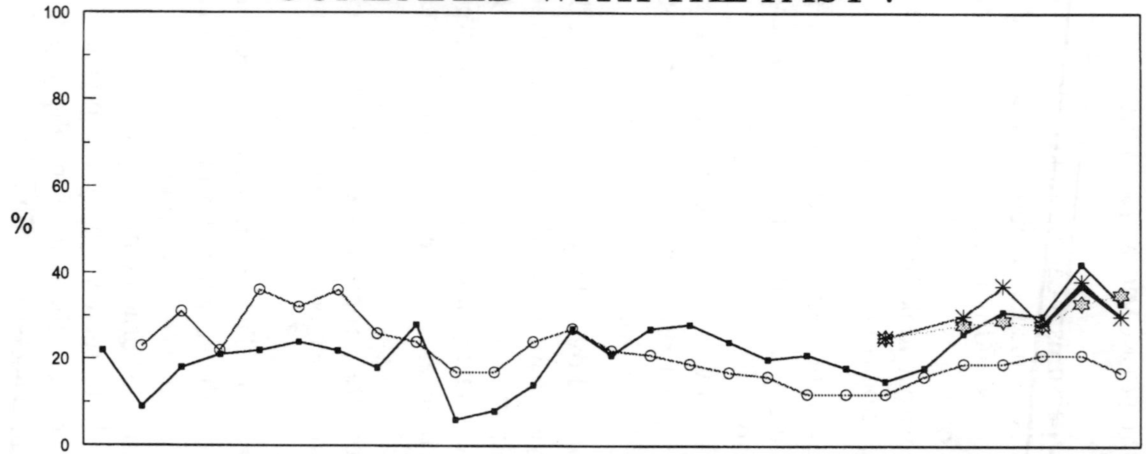

	76	77	78	79	80	81	82	83	84	85	86	87	88	89	May '90	Nov '90	May '91	Nov '91	May '92	Nov '92	May '93	Nov '93	Jun '94	Nov '94	May '95	Nov '95	May '96
BLACKS	22	9	18	21	22	24	22	18	28	6	8	14	27	21	27	28	24	20	21	18	15	18	28	31	30	42	33
COLOUREDS																					25		28	29	28	33	35
INDIANS		23	31	22	36	32	36	26	24	17	17	24	27	22	21	19	17	16	12	12	25	16	30	37	28	38	30
WHITES										17	17	24	27	22	21	19	16	17	12	12	12	16	19	19	21	21	17
TOTAL																							28		28	37	30

* ALL RESULTS FROM MAY '95 NATIONAL

Figure 3.

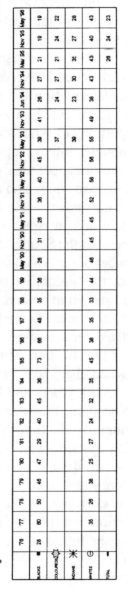

Figure 4.

positive about their financial situation, but then opinions started to follow a downward trend. Even the referendum in 1992, when more than two-thirds of the white electorate expressed their support for former President De Klerk's reform initiatives, brought about a temporary rise in the feeling amongst blacks that their families were better off economically than in the past.

The economic situation amongst whites deteriorated steadily, particularly since 1989. Very few experienced an improvement in their financial situation and particularly the period from May 1992 to May 1993 represented an all time low. During this same period record proportions of whites witnessed a further downward development. Although whites accepted the inevitability of reform, they were very unsure and apprehensive about the deterioration of their traditional power base and not so optimistic about the future.

In the meantime, the security situation in the country deteriorated rapidly and in April 1993, when Mr Chris Hani (then Secretary-General of the South African Communist Party and also a prominent member of the ANC) was assassinated, there was a lot of speculation about the possibility of a civil war. From November 1993 a new trend started to emerge: the election date was announced and South Africans started to view their situation in a more positive light.

This trend is even more evident since the 1994 election, and about two to three out of every ten South Africans felt that their lives had changed for the better (if the hard facts of very high levels of unemployment and low gross incomes in South Africa are taken into account, this was definitely not the case in reality). The local community elections also brought about a surge in optimism about their economic well-being amongst blacks, coloureds and Indians. However, the most recent findings indicate that all South Africans are starting to feel the economic pinch. This should be seen against the background of the greater feeling of pessimism regarding the direction in which the country is going and indicates apprehension about the future, especially amongst whites.

The findings of the other question regarding economic well-being of the family support this notion.

Figures 5 and 6 show the percentage who thought that their families would be better or worse off economically in another year's time. Again, it provides a sensitive measurement of the interpreta-

WILL FAMILIES BE ECONOMICALLY BETTER OFF IN A YEAR'S TIME ?

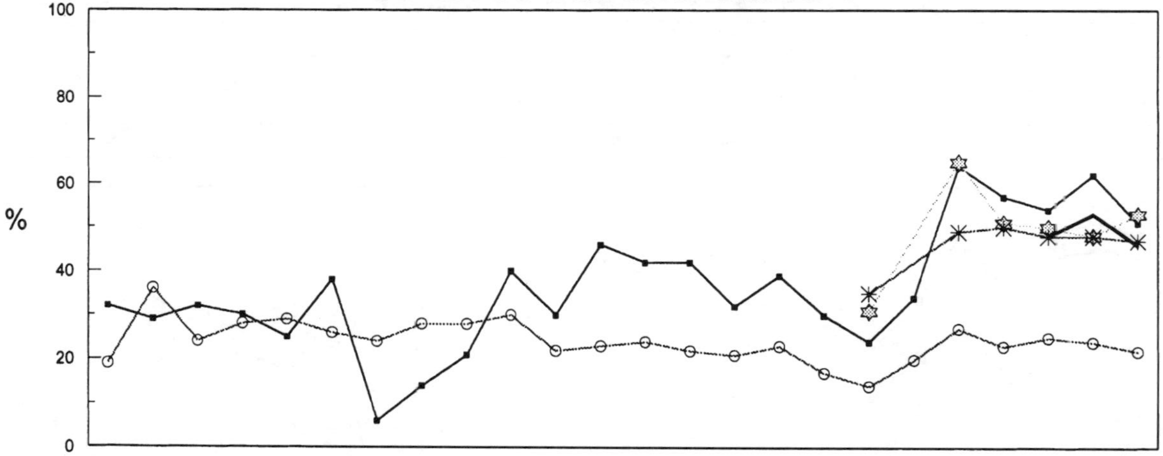

	79	'80	'81	'82	'83	'84	'85	'86	'87	'88	'89	May 90	Nov 90	May 91	Nov 91	May 92	Nov 92	May 93	Nov 93	Jun 94	Nov 94	May 95	Nov 95	May 96
BLACKS ●	32	29	32	30	25	38	6	14	21	40	30	46	42	42	32	39	30	24	34	64	67	54	62	51
COLOUREDS ☆																		31		65	51	50	48	53
INDIANS ✳																		35		49	50	48	48	47
WHITES ⊖	19	36	24	28	29	26	24	28	28	30	22	23	24	22	21	23	17	14	20	27	23	25	24	22
TOTAL ─																						48	53	46

Figure 5.

WILL FAMILIES BE ECONOMICALLY WORSE OFF IN A YEAR'S TIME ?

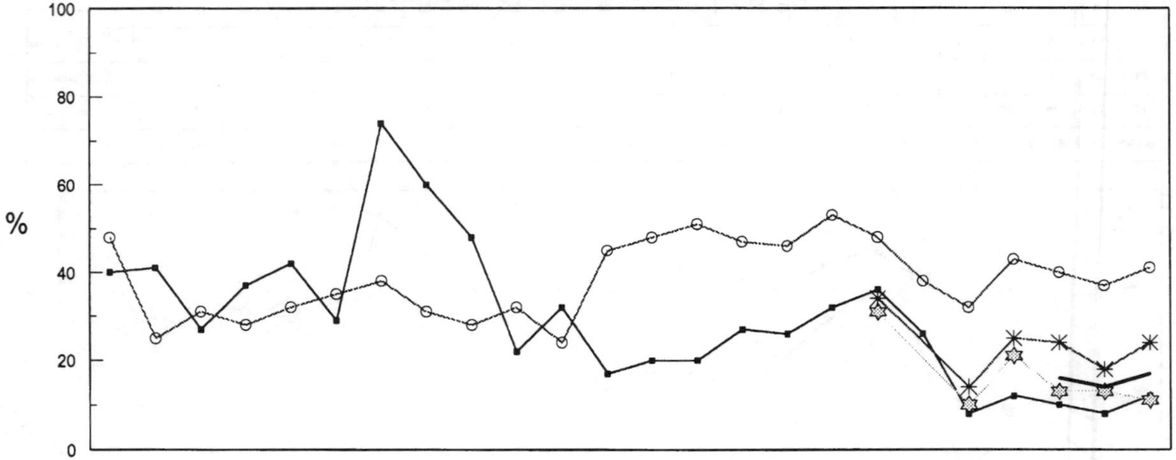

	'79	'80	'81	'82	'83	'84	'85	'86	'87	'88	'89	May '90	Nov '90	May '91	Nov '91	May '92	Nov '92	May '93	Nov '93	Jun '94	Nov '94	May '95	Nov '95	May '96
BLACKS	40	41	27	37	42	29	74	60	48	22	32	17	20	20	27	26	32	36	26	8	12	10	8	12
COLOUREDS																		31		10	21	13	13	11
INDIANS																		34		14	25	24	18	24
WHITES	48	25	31	28	32	35	38	31	28	32	24	45	48	51	47	46	53	48	38	32	43	40	37	41
TOTAL																						16	14	17

Figure 6.

tion of major events in the country as important events had an even more profound effect on the perceptions regarding the issue of the economic future of families.

The unrest in black townships and the turmoil the country went through in the seventies and eighties clearly had an effect on these results. (Blacks expressed the lowest level of optimism about their economic future in 1985, one of the most disruptive periods in the country over the last two decades.) Since the negotiations about the future of the country (the different Codesa talks and bilateral negotiations) started in the late eighties, the outlook for the future amongst blacks became fairly optimistic, but pessimism prevailed amongst whites. However, since the beginning of the nineties, fewer and fewer blacks and whites were expecting a brighter economic future.

We can also clearly see the effect of the deterioration of the security situation in the country, and just after April 1993, when Mr Chris Hani was assassinated, very low levels of optimism about the economic prospects for their families were expressed by both blacks and whites.

In November 1993 a slightly more optimistic picture emerged for the first time in two years. While it was true that the economic development over the previous twelve months had still been negative, the downward trend seemed to have bottomed out. Black and white South Africans believed that the worst was over and that 1994 would prove to be a turning point for the better, and after the election, blacks and coloureds were particularly euphoric – almost two-thirds were confident that they would be better off in a year's time. Even whites were swept up in this post-election feeling of optimism about the future.

In November 1994 the economic optimism, heralded by April's general election, continued to prevail, but to a lesser degree. This is an expected drop, given the tempering of the earlier post-election euphoria. Towards the end of 1995 only blacks felt more optimistic about the economic future of their families than they did six months prior to that date. The growing feeling of apprehension about the future amongst whites was commented on earlier, but it is also manifested very clearly in the trends emerging from the results of this question.

SATISFACTION WITH FINANCIAL SITUATION OF THE HOUSEHOLD

Average out of 10

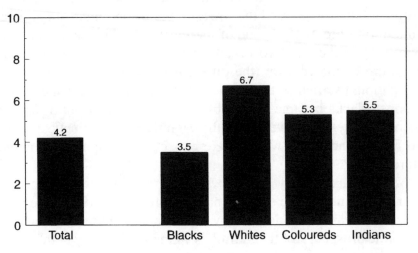

Figure 7.

In the last study (May 1996) South Africans as a whole indicated that their hopes for a golden economic future were slowly but surely declining. Nevertheless, expectations for a better future are still very high if seen in relation to the much lower percentages recorded in earlier years.

But are these trends reflected in the degree of satisfaction with the current financial situation of the household? These results are again from the latest World Values Study.

On a 10 point scale, 10 indicating "completely satisfied" and 1 signifying "completely dissatisfied", respondents had to indicate how they view the current financial situation of their households. The averages out of ten are depicted in Figure 7.

Not surprisingly, South Africans, as a whole, are not very happy with the financial situation of their households.

Contrary to the previous discussion where blacks were very optimistic about the future economic well-being of their families, they indicated that, of all population groups, they are the least satisfied with the current financial situation of their households. This pattern is similar to that observed in the previous World Values Studies (1981/1982 and 1990/1991). In addition, in the latest study, nearly six out of every ten blacks chose points 1, 2 or 3 out of 10 to describe their financial situation, i.e. indicating complete dissatisfaction. It must be borne in mind that blacks are still, on average, the lowest income earners in the country.

The dissatisfaction of South Africans when it comes to money matters can be explained by various factors. Although inflation has recently been curbed to below 10% and the country experienced a positive economic growth in 1995, the Rand is struggling against other currencies, saving levels are low, effective incomes are decreasing and retrenchments are still the order of the day. Moreover, the financial misery is aggravated by the high expectations (as demonstrated in previous discussions) following South Africa's first democratic election. As mentioned, the implementation of the RDP has turned out to be a very slow process and inequality will be a characteristic of the South African economy for quite some time to come. Overall, South Africans had to tighten their belts during the last few years.

SOCIAL HARMONY AND TRUST

Another dimension in assessing the process of democratisation in South Africa is the focus on *social harmony*. For the purpose of the article, "social harmony" is defined as being the unanimity and compatibility of race relations in a society. The concept was operationalised by measuring improvement in the relationships between the various population groups. Our country has been plagued by racial tensions for a very long time and this was bound to have a marked effect on attitudes and feelings of all South Africans.

Again, two questions from the six-monthly "Socio-Political Trends" will be discussed:

- Would you say the relationship between the various races is improving, remains the same, or is getting worse?
- How confident are you in a happy future for all races in South Africa?

The important events that had an influence on the way the electorate perceived their economic situation and prospects, had an even clearer effect on the relationship between different population groups.

After the unrest of 1976 and 1977 both whites and blacks felt that more understanding was developing between the two biggest population groups in the country. However, on the political front, progress was very slow and in 1985 relations were shattered again. The same happened in the first half of 1993. The disastrous effects of these events on perceptions about race relations are very clear from Figures 8 and 9.

Since 1986 the effect of reform measures on the perceptions regarding the relationship between population groups was evident: pass laws were abolished, the Mixed Marriages Act was scrapped, restrictions on blacks making use of recreation facilities (like cinemas) and open businesses were removed, job reservation was scrapped and some restrictions on informal trade removed. On the other hand, the country was governed by emergency regulations and the threat of sanctions became real. Violence was also on the increase. It is obviously not possible to isolate the effect of any one of these measures, positive or negative, but the net effect had a positive influence on the changing of opinions about the relationship between whites and blacks.

The announcement of the release of Nelson Mandela and other political prisoners and the unbanning of political organisations increased the uncertainty in the white community. However, they realised that change was not going to happen overnight and assessed the relationship between population groups more positively during the next measurement. The outcome of the referendum in March 1992 also affected black-white relationships positively and reversed the downward trend that had started to develop over the previous two years.

However, a number of factors caused and accelerated a new negative trend: the deterioration of the security situation, the killing of white farmers by APLA, the murder of Chris Hani and the violence and mass action that followed in the wake of his death led both whites and blacks again to become increasingly disenchanted with each other.

RELATIONS BETWEEN POPULATION GROUPS ARE IMPROVING

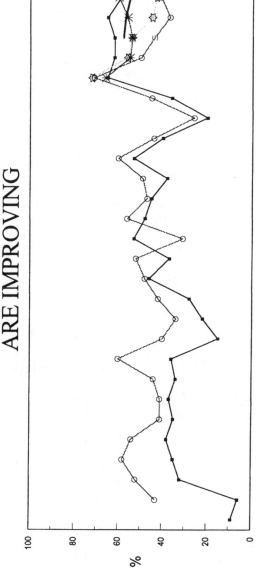

	'76	'77	'78	'79	'80	'81	'82	'83	'84	'85	'86	'87	'88	'89	May '90	Nov '90	May '91	Nov '91	May '92	Nov '92	May '93	Nov '93	Jun '94	Nov '94	May '95	Nov '95	May '96
BLACKS	9	6	32	35	38	35	37	34	36	15	22	28	45	37	53	48	45	38	53	40	20	36	65	62	82	65	59
COLOUREDS																							72	58	54	45	43
INDIANS																							66	55	54	58	60
WHITES		43	52	58	54	41	41	44	60	40	34	42	48	52	31	56	47	49	60	44	26	45	71	50	44	37	41
TOTAL																									58	57	55

Figure 8.

RELATIONS BETWEEN POPULATION GROUPS ARE DETERIORATING

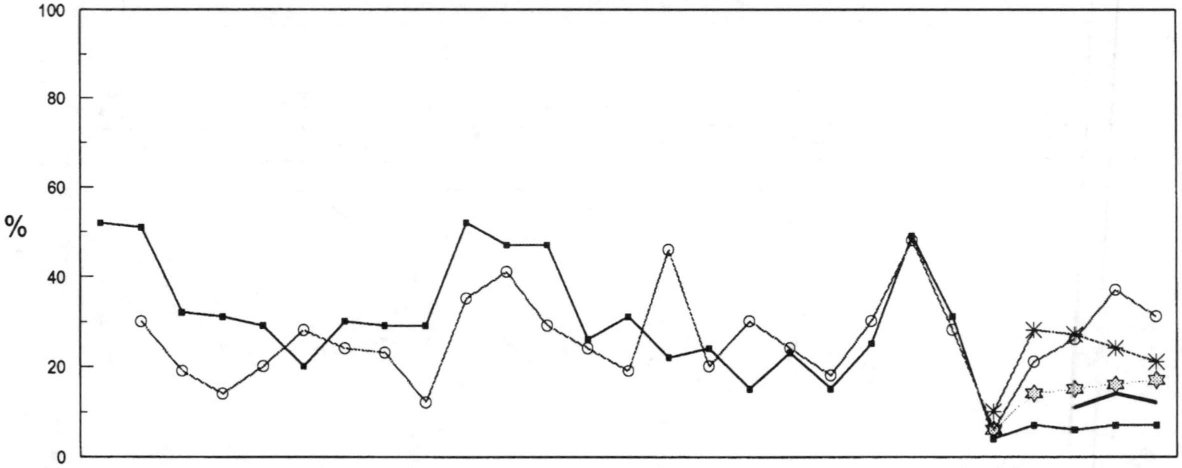

	'76	'77	'78	'79	'80	'81	'82	'83	'84	'85	'86	'87	'88	'89	May '90	Nov '90	May '91	Nov '91	May '92	Nov '92	May '93	Nov '93	Jun '94	Nov '94	May '95	Nov '95	May '96
BLACKS	52	51	32	31	29	20	30	29	29	52	47	47	26	31	22	24	15	23	15	25	49	31	4	7	6	7	7
COLOUREDS																							6	14	15	16	17
ASIANS																							10	28	27	24	21
WHITES	30	30	19	14	20	28	24	23	12	35	41	29	24	19	46	20	30	24	18	30	48	28	6	21	28	37	31
TOTAL																									11	14	12

Figure 9.

Subsequent events – the relatively peaceful election and the inauguration of a Government of National Unity on 11 May 1994 – impacted positively on the relationship between population groups.

As in other cases, this feeling has also been tempered a bit after the euphoria of the election, but a feeling of reconciliation and racial harmony still prevails to a great extent. This is definitely encouraging for prospects of nation building, promoting a common South Africanism and democratisation.

Going hand-in-hand with these findings is the strong belief of the vast majority of South Africans in the possibility of a happy future for all population groups in this country.

Figures 10 and 11, showing the percentages of people who are either very/fairly confident and not very/not at all confident that there will be a happy future in South Africa for people from all population groups, show the emergence of the same trends over the last two decades as those discussed so far. Violence, unrest and uncertainty also marred the perceptions about the future of the country.

The results of the last two years indicate quite a strong sense of hope for the future. In May 1996 three quarters of South Africans were confident that there will be a happy future for all South Africans. However, as was the case with other findings, a lower percentage are currently feeling confident about this issue than those who did two years ago. Whites, especially, are becoming quite despondent about the future and the percentage who feel very or fairly confident in a happy future is declining rapidly, from a high of 82% just after the 1994 election to only 50% in May 1996. Although whites have accepted the inevitability of reform, they feel very unsure and are apprehensive about the deterioration of their traditional power base.

The relative apprehension about the future of the country can be put into perspective when observed together with the opinion of South Africans regarding trust.

Despite the relatively widespread belief in a happy future for all races, the opinion of South Africans is a lot different when it comes to *trust*. Results of the latest World Values Study show that the vast majority of South Africans feel that one has to be very careful in dealing with other people (Figure 12).

This lack of trust in other people was also a prominent feature of the 1990/1991 survey. In fact, people are becoming more and more

A HAPPY FUTURE FOR ALL RACES ?
VERY/FAIRLY CONFIDENT

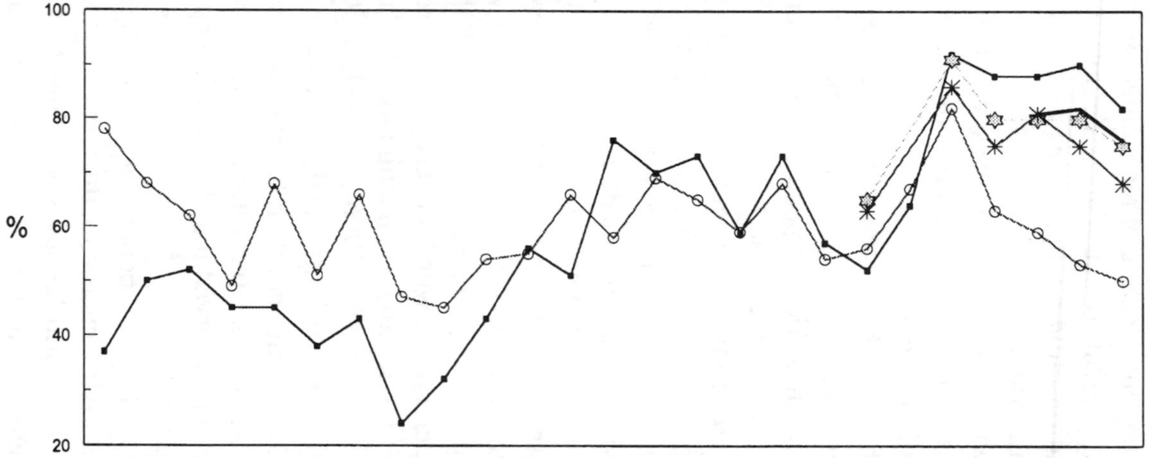

	'78	'79	'80	'81	'82	'83	'84	'85	'86	'87	'88	'89	May '90	Nov '90	May '91	Nov '91	May '92	Nov '92	May '93	Nov '93	Jun '94	Nov '94	May '95	Nov '95	May '96
BLACKS ●	37	50	52	45	45	38	43	24	32	43	56	51	76	70	73	59	73	57	52	64	92	88	88	90	82
COLOURED ☆																			65		91	80	80	80	75
INDIANS ✳																			63		86	75	81	75	68
WHITES ⊘	78	68	62	49	68	51	66	47	45	54	55	66	58	69	65	59	68	54	56	67	82	63	59	53	50
TOTAL ┤																							8*	82	76

* ALL RESULTS FROM MAY '95 NATIONAL

Figure 10.

A HAPPY FUTURE FOR ALL RACES ?

NOT VERY/NOT AT ALL CONFIDENT

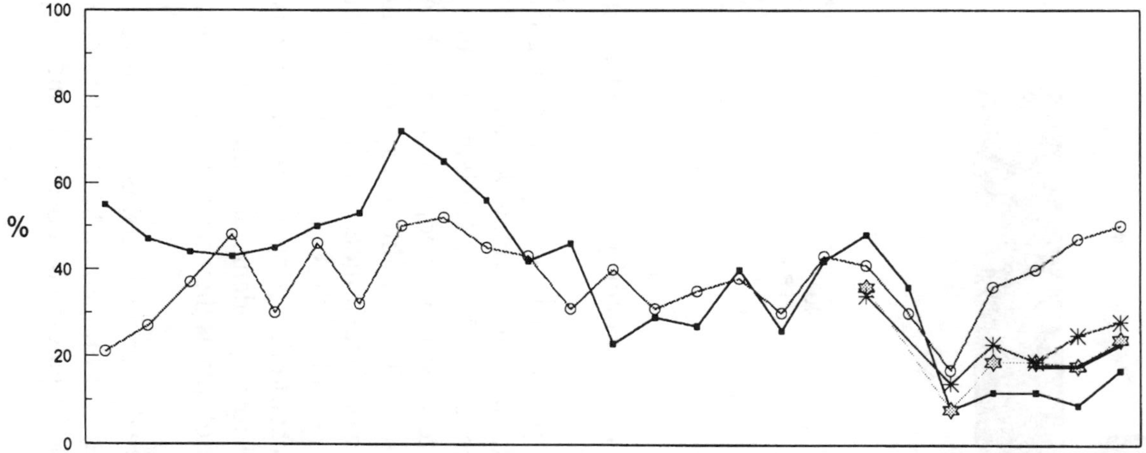

	'78	'79	'80	'81	'82	'83	'84	'85	'86	'87	'88	'89	May '90	Nov '90	May '91	Nov '91	May '92	Nov '92	May '93	Nov '93	Jun '94	Nov '94	May '95	Nov '95	May '96
BLACKS	55	47	44	43	45	50	53	72	65	56	42	46	23	29	27	40	26	42	48	36	8	12	12	9	17
COLOUREDS																			36		8	19	19	18	24
INDIANS																			34		14	23	19	25	28
WHITES	21	27	37	48	30	46	32	50	52	45	43	31	40	31	35	38	30	43	41	30	17	38	40	47	50
TOTAL																							18	18	23

* ALL RESULTS FROM MAY '95 NATIONAL

Figure 11.

CAN PEOPLE BE TRUSTED ?

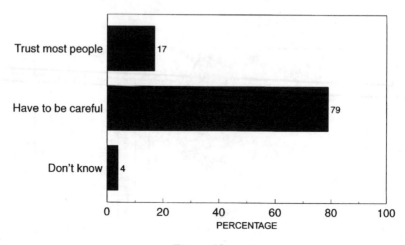

Figure 12.

distrustful and currently only a minority believe that most people can be trusted.

Trust also seems to be particularly lacking in certain provinces – Gauteng, North-West, Mpumalanga and the Western and Northern Cape. Conversely, the people in KwaZulu-Natal and the Eastern Cape are more inclined to trust other people than South Africans in the other seven provinces. This finding is especially surprising in KwaZulu-Natal. One would have thought that the violence and political strife would rather fuel the fires of distrust.

Still on the issue of trust of other people, a list of various groups of people was presented to respondents and they had to indicate those whom they would not like as their neighbours, i.e. not in their immediate environment.

As illustrated in Figure 13, drug addicts, people with a criminal record and heavy drinkers are the people least preferred as neighbours. Opinions are divided regarding homosexuals and people with AIDS.

However, it is important that racial differences do not really seem to be an issue when looking at the overall results. Confirming findings discussed earlier about the belief in a happy future for all South Africans, only about one in ten South Africans have indicated that

WHO SHOULD <u>NOT</u> BE MY NEIGHBOUR ?

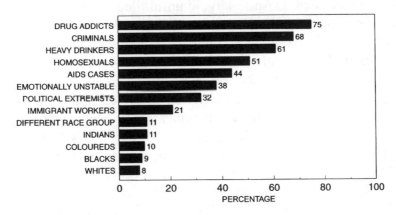

Figure 13.

they do not want to live next door to people of a particular population group, other than their own.

When looking at the results per population group, it shows that whites and coloureds are more inclined to indicate that they do not want a black as a neighbour, while blacks do not seem to have a problem in living next door to whites or coloureds.

CONCLUDING REMARKS

The last two decades were certainly the most eventful and significant in South Africa's history. It was a period of change, uncertainty and even sometimes anxiety for South Africans. On the other hand, it also witnessed the country's transformation from the pariah of the world to acceptance amongst other democratic nations in different political and economic forums.

The reform process, which started in early 1990, was met with mixed reactions among South Africans. Feelings of anxiety, if not fear of the future, competed with feelings of relief that apartheid would truly become history. Today, South Africans hold diverse opinions about the process itself, and also about the perceived success of transition. All South Africans, but especially whites and, to a lesser degree, coloureds and Indians, are still unsure about what the future holds for them in the "new" South Africa. As a result they are less enthusiastic about and even uneasy with some of the current political processes. Despite largely unfulfilled expectations, blacks are still extremely optimistic about the future.

It is also clear from the findings presented, that, in general, optimism about the economy has waned, and the post-election euphoria concerning improved race relations has abated. Differences in opinion are a common phenomenon in all societies, but the marked differences in South Africa are typical of a country undergoing fundamental changes in character and philosophy. Naturally these diverse views create the potential for renewed and increased conflict in South Africa, not only amongst different population groups, but especially amongst different political parties.

From the findings of the opinion polls it must be clear that the process of democratisation in South Africa is far from complete. It will definitely require a high degree of statesmanship and political insight to lead the country through its democratisation process. However, as was illustrated in this article, some of the most important building blocks and goodwill required in the process of nation-building and democratisation already exist in South Africa.

Opinion polls can definitely make a significant contribution to the process of nation-building, by providing insight into, and knowledge of, perceptions, feelings, attitudes and values of the South African population, the mood in the country, by tracking various trends in opinions and perceptions and by communicating the needs and aspirations of different segments of the society. Used in this context, political research is a valuable and almost indispensable tool for operational and strategic planning for any company or institution that wants to be involved in the future of the country, a compass whereby we sail the uncharted waters of transition to democracy.

NOTES

[1] Markinor has been tracking Socio-Political trends since 1976, the year of the first uprisings in Soweto. Since those days the same battery of questions was included every six months as part of a syndicate/omnibus study. The bulk of the costs of these surveys was carried by the company itself, although a nominal cost is paid by subscribers to the survey. Regular press releases are published.

The purpose of these surveys was to monitor the attitudes of South Africans towards key socio-political issues and developments, leadership, prominent politicians and organisations and expectations of the future.

Naturally the use of a syndicate/omnibus as vehicle for these surveys also had some inherent limitations. Syndicate/omnibus surveys were essentially developed worldwide to do product surveys, and therefore the coverage is usually limited to where the most lucrative markets are. For this reason, only black people in metropolitan areas were included initially in the trends surveys. It would have been far too expensive to conduct this survey countrywide regularly on its own. However, numerous other political surveys for clients were conducted with a national coverage, especially in the time leading up to the 1994 election. Whites have always been included countrywide. Coloureds and Indians have been included on a continuous basis since 1994 in the areas with big concentrations of these population groups.

The methodology and coverage were kept the same as far as possible throughout the years. Personal interviews were conducted with all respondents in metropolitan areas. Whites outside of metropolitan areas were interviewed over the telephone. (The telephone incidence amongst other population groups, especially blacks, is too limited to apply this method across the board.)

From 1995 the "Socio-Political Trends" was included in a new "National Syndicate." The mood of the *entire electorate* is thus gauged at present. The same vehicle was used for the Gallup End-of-Year Poll. A total of 3 500 interviews is conducted with a representative sample of adults in all nine provinces – there is an equal split between genders.

Samples are stratified as far as possible by region and community size. The interviewer is given a specific location (address in urban/metropolitan areas and place in rural areas) to go to. The specific household on a plot/stand is selected randomly, as well as the person to interview, by applying a random selection grid. Three efforts (different days and times) are made to talk to the chosen respondent. If the interviewer is still unable to secure the interview, the original is substituted in a prescribed way.

Official translations of all questionnaires are made into the relevant languages of the survey area. Only interviewers fluent in a particular language are allowed to work in the specific area.

[2] In the latest Gallup International End-of-Year Poll, over 58 000 people in 50 countries around the globe were interviewed about their thoughts on 1996. The survey was conducted by 44 member companies of the Gallup International Association and six non-member companies in November and December 1995. South Africa and Zimbabwe were the only two countries on the African continent that were included. Other countries covered in the survey ranged from New Zealand to Canada and featured 14 members of the European Union, three other western European countries, thirteen central and eastern European states, five countries on the American continents and fourteen other nations in the Middle and Far East (Markinor is affiliated with Gallup International).

[3] Universe and sample size of the World Values Study, 1995/1996:

- All adult South Africans, 16 years and older
- 2 935 interviews were conducted.

Sampling methodology: Probability sample, stratified by province, population group and community size. Within each stratum, sampling points were selected at random. From each sampling point, 10 interviews were determined according to a random selection and marked on maps which were given to the interviewers.

Within the qualifying households, all males/females 16 years and older were listed and the qualifying respondent selected according to a random system. If the thus selected person could not be interviewed, even after three calls, including evening calls, the person was substituted in a prescribed way. A minimum of 20% back-check was administered on each interviewer's work.

Weighting and projection: The sample was weighted and projected onto the universe and is representative of the universe from which it was drawn.

Interviewing procedure: All interviewers were briefed personally by their Field Manager or Field Supervisor.

Interviews were conducted on a personal, face-to-face basis.

The questionnaire was available in all the major languages and the interview was conducted in whichever language the respondent preferred.

REFERENCES

Gallup End-of-Year Polls. Data and press releases published by Markinor.
Inglehart, R.: 1990, Culture Shift in Advanced Industrial Society (Princeton University Press, Princeton).
Socio-Political Trend Surveys. Data and reports published by Markinor.
World Values Study: 1995–1996, Tabular results published by Markinor in April 1996.

Markinor
P.O. Box 56213
Pinegowrie 2123
South Africa
E-mail: marih@markinor.co.za

INDEX OF AUTHORS
VOLUME 41, 1997